BOLD ENTREPRENEUR
A Life of James B. Duke

BOLD ENTREPRENEUR
A Life of James B. Duke

Robert F. Durden

CAROLINA ACADEMIC PRESS
Durham, North Carolina

ISBN 0-89089-744-1
LCCN 2002116693

CAROLINA ACADEMIC PRESS
700 Kent Street
Durham, NC 27701
Telephone (919) 489-7486
Fax (919) 493-5668
www.cap-press.com

Printed in the United States of America

CONTENTS

PREFACE

James Buchanan Duke, I have somewhat belatedly decided, deserves a scholarly biography of his own. When a prominent Duke University faculty member and friend, who was on the board of the university's press, put that proposition to me more than thirty years ago, I demurred on several grounds. First, the thing that interested me most about the Dukes was their relationship with Duke University and its institutional predecessor, Trinity College. And I already knew that not James B. Duke, but his father Washington Duke and his older brother Ben Duke preceded him and long overshadowed him as far as involvement with Trinity College was concerned.

Secondly, I argued that the Dukes operated as a family and that it was in that context that their story should be told.

And finally, I knew that while we had a vast collection of Ben Duke Papers in the manuscript department of Duke's library, there was a dearth of J. B. Duke papers—and historians avidly crave access to such primary sources.

Consequently, I undertook a history of the family—especially Washington and his two sons Ben and "Buck" (as the family called him)—and published *The Dukes of Durham, 1865–1929* in 1975.

Now, however, I have become aware of holes in my argument. In the first place, James B. Duke was more important to Duke University than it was to him or his life. That is to say, his munificence in underwriting the establishment and permanent support of Duke University came towards the end of his life, after a long series of remarkable achievements in the business world. These achievements deserve at least equal billing with his great philanthropic action, which was taken less than a year before he died.

As for the Dukes operating as a family, that was true—but as I now realize, only up to a highly limited degree. Washington Duke did lead his family into tobacco manufacturing after the Civil War, and his sons became his partners in the family business. Precisely when the other family members realized that the youngest Duke was the shrewdest businessman among them is not known. But certainly by around 1880, when Buck turned twenty-four and when Washington Duke retired from an active role in the family business, J. B. Duke led the way. He did so in a quiet, tactful, consensual manner that, as far as the records reveal, aroused no resentment or jealousy.

Ben and Buck Duke were unusually devoted to each other throughout their lives, as they were equally close to their father. Their mother having died in 1858 when they were still toddlers, Ben and Buck demonstrated life-long sympathy for orphans and half-orphans, which they considered themselves to be. While Ben, born in 1855, was more than a year older than Buck, Ben was sickly and frail as a child and had intermittent health problems for much of his life, gradually becoming a semi-invalid during his final decade. Buck, on the other hand, was big and robust as a child and had no significant health problems until the illness that killed him in 1925.

I unfortunately missed an aspect of the brothers' relationship when I wrote *The Dukes of Durham*, but I now believe that Buck developed a loving, protective attitude and stance toward Ben from an early age. If the two brothers ever had a serious disagreement, surviving records do not reveal it. While Ben always kept a home in Durham and took more time for the family's charitable activities in Durham and North Carolina, he also played a role, albeit a secondary one, in the family's various business enterprises.

As for a paucity of J. B. Duke Papers, that turned out to be not as serious as I thought. After I had begun research for *The Dukes of Durham* a treasure trove of J. B. Duke Papers, especially for the late 1880s when he was pushing for the combination that became the American Tobacco Company in 1890, came to light.

An additional reason for a study focused solely on J. B. Duke is that in *The Dukes of Durham* I barely mentioned at least three important phases of J. B. Duke's life. Believing that extensive treatment of them was not appropriate for a history of the family—or would throw it out of balance—I deliberately skimped on them.

The first neglected topic was J. B. Duke's key role in the establishment and then management of the British-American Tobacco Company in and after 1901–1902. From the standpoint of business history alone, it was a pioneering and colorful venture that deserves fuller treatment than I gave it.

Secondly, J. B. Duke's venture into Canadian hydroelectricity needs to be dealt with in greater detail than I earlier provided. While it turned out to be a temporary diversion for him and his Carolina electricity business was the long-lasting commitment, Duke's Canadian foray was a a highly creative and bold move that dramatically revealed his entrepreneurial panache and genius.

Finally, when I wrote *The Dukes of Durham* I had never visited Duke's Farm (now Duke Farms) just outside Somerville, New Jersey. Even if I had, I again might have downplayed it to maintain "balance" in the earlier book. Now that I have visited it and also learned more about it, I realize that it was J. B. Duke's one, almost obsessive hobby, his principal diversion from the steady work that he enjoyed all his life. Starting in 1893 with a flat, 327-acre farm fronting on the Raritan River, he kept buying adjoining lands until he owned 2200 acres. Furthermore, he spent several million dollars transforming a large portion of the vast estate into a magnificently landscaped park. He did not just recontour his front lawn and add a few fountains, as I had mistakenly thought. Rather, he created a chain of seven sizable lakes, with water from the topmost one (pumped up from the Raritan) feeding into the next and so on until it returned to the river. With the excavated earth, he created small (200 feet high) mountains. Not just fountains, in large numbers, but waterfalls, cascades, and grottoes added visual interest, as did statuary of a wide variety especially ordered from Europe. An avid horticulturist (as were Washington and Ben Duke), he once informed a close colleague that he had a record of over 2,000,000 trees and shrubs that had been planted on the estate.

It was, in short, one of the late Gilded Age's most magnificent country estates, and it revealed an aesthetic and recreational aspect of J. B. Duke's character that I earlier glossed over and that deserves to be known.

In conclusion, a word about the two earlier biographies of J. B. Duke. They are both undocumented and unscholarly, but I now believe that each has a certain value that I did not fully appreciate a quarter century ago. Commissioned by George G. Allen and William R. Perkins (J. B. Duke's closest business associate and lawyer, respectively), John Wilber Jenkins, a newspaperman, wrote *James B. Duke: Master Builder* (1927) soon after Duke died. It is, as might be expected, too reverential in its treatment—and has neither footnotes nor an index -but because Jenkins had access to a number of people who had known and worked with Duke over many years, the book has a certain value, if used carefully.

In 1942 John J. Winkler, a professional writer of a whole series of "Robber Baron" biographies, published *Tobacco Tycoon: The Story of James Buchanan Duke*. Despite the semisensational, muckraking tone, the book also benefits from interviews that Winkler conducted with several people who had known J. B. Duke before he became famous. When these ring true, I have also used material from those interviews.

In the biography that follows, there is inevitable overlap with *The Dukes of Durham*. But I trust there is enough that is new to justify this treatment of a most creative entrepreneurial capitalist, one who, after a lifetime of big-time successes in business, finally turned his talent for thinking big in a visionary way toward a unique plan for perpetual philanthropy in the Carolinas. Unlike novelist Thomas Wolfe's legendary character who could not come home again, J. B. Duke was one Tar Heel who did come home to the Carolinas—and that homecoming had longlasting repercussions indeed.

After *The Dukes of Durham* appeared in 1975, a friend, congratulating me on the book, kindly noted that he had enjoyed reading it. But, he added, "I still don't understand Buck Duke." Laughing, I replied in a burst of candor, "Well, I don't either."

Now, more than a quarter-century later, I realize that I was so intent on explicating the Duke family's long involvement with Trinity College and on bringing forward less well-known members of the family (especially Ben Duke) that I simply either downplayed or virtually ignored important aspects of J. B. Duke's career and character.

Moreover, I hope I am not immodest in saying that I now believe I have grown to understand Buck Duke much better. Whether I have succeeded in reflecting that understanding in this biography is, of course, another matter—and one best left for the readers of it to decide.

While I did assert at one point in *The Dukes of Durham* that J. B. Duke was "the business genius of the family," I failed to elaborate and, perhaps, to advance sufficient evidence for the assertion. As for his character, I would now emphasize that, in addition to his keen intelligence and quick mind, he was an even tempered, soft-spoken person who passionately enjoyed his work. If he ever exploded in anger or indulged in a temper tantrum, I have found no evidence of that in a large body of records.

Deeply influenced by his father, Washington Duke, and by his father's beloved Methodist church, J. B. Duke developed a great knack for spotting talent and character in others. From an early stage in his career, he demonstrated that ability to identify men of talent and integrity and then, because he treated them generously and with respect, they remained with him throughout their careers. This pattern, appearing first in his work in the tobacco industry, was replicated in textiles, hydroelectricity, and finally in his long, careful planning for perpetual philanthropy to benefit the two Carolinas.

Raised a Republican (like his father) in a region then dominated by agrarian, racist Democrats, he early acquired a national outlook. Yet he retained a deep interest in and even love for his native region. While he payed close attention to detail in his role as a pioneering managerial capitalist, he always liked to "think big" and consider the long run, the future. This was finally and dramatically illustrated in his conception of The Duke Endowment, his perpetual philanthropy, and in his enthusiastic endorsement of President W. P. Few's audacious plan to organize a great national university around Trinity College.

Anne Oller Durden, my wife, has for the past half century assisted me in many ways in my research and writing. We have always shared the dubious joy of compiling the index, for example. For this biography, however, she has outdone herself, for she did all of the word-processing. I can never thank her enough.

Robert F. Durden
July, 2002

PROLOGUE

Anyone closely watching the neatly dressed young man as he walked the streets of lower Manhattan on a spring night in 1885 might well have been puzzled. He frequently stopped to scrutinize, maybe even count, discarded cigarette packets. (He would not have used the term, but he was quietly doing market research). And if he saw a straight pin pointed toward him on the sidewalk, he picked it up, for good luck, and stuck it on the underside of his coat lapel.

Twenty-eight-year-old James Buchanan Duke—"Buck" only to his family and friends of long-standing—had come to New York a year earlier to establish and then manage a branch factory of W. Duke Sons and Company, tobacco manufacturers based in Durham, North Carolina. Already richly experienced in the world of tobacco, the youngest of the Duke family also had established a reputation for bold, shrewd leadership in the family business.

Soft-spoken and even-tempered, he was clean-shaven, solidly but slimly built (at that age), a bachelor, and loved his work with a surprising passion. "I hated to close my desk at night," he later recalled, "and was eager to get back to it early next morning. I needed no vacation or time off.... There ain't a thrill in the world to compare with building a business and watching it grow before your eyes."[1]

Young Duke made it a practice to be in the factory in time to see the employees arrive, and then during the day he made frequent forays through the factory to examine the stock on the work tables. Some employees came to believe that he had an uncanny knack for spotting the only faulty pack of cigarettes in a lot containing hundreds of perfect ones. When he occasionally sent for an already-packed carton of goods, he would open it, examine each package, and if a label should be pasted on in a crooked fashion, he sent for the superintendent. In short, Duke kept the work force on its toes.[2]

After a twelve-hour day in the office, Duke grabbed a cheap meal in a nearby eatery and then began his market-oriented nocturnal operations. As he had earlier visited tobacco retailers across the South and West when he "drummed" the trade for W. Duke Sons and Company, so he now continued that practice in New York. A pioneer Manhattan tobacconist later remembered the first time Duke came into his cigar store: "He was tall, gawky, reddish (hair) with a southern accent as thick as butter." Duke wanted to sell some of his "newfangled machine-made cigarettes" on consignment, but the merchant insisted he would not handle cigarettes and that his customers did not want them. Duke seemed to take the rebuff in stride.[3]

A few months later, the tobacconist continued in his remembrance, a trade paper reported that Duke had opened a loft factory on Rivington Street in lower Manhattan. "Then the billboards began to flare out with Duke ads and the newspapers too," the merchant recalled. "I got circulars offering camp chairs and crayon drawings, if I'd order so many thousand Duke cigarettes. Customers started asking for the cigarettes by name." The climax seemed to come when Duke began putting into each package a small picture-card of a famous actress, an athlete, or the flags of different nations. "As I look back on it now," the merchant concluded, "I think this one stunt, more than any other, really put the cigarette over with the public."[4]

While the young Tar Heel was indeed hard-driving and ambitious, not even he could have realized that within five years W. Duke Sons and Company would be by far the largest cigarette producer in the nation. Not only that, but he would employ that commanding position in such a way as to take the lead in forming in 1890 the great combination—holding company actually—known as the American Tobacco Company. And having expanded the vast corporation's control over most of the nation's tobacco industry throughout the 1890s, he would in 1901 invade the British Isles and end up heading a pioneer multinational and globecircling enterprise known as the British-American Tobacco Company.

What prepared James B. Duke for this amazing achievement? He grew up in a South left poverty-stricken and desolated by the Civil War, yet by age thirty-three in 1890, he was well on his way to becoming vastly rich and the head of what would become one of the largest and most powerful American corporations.

More to the point, what strategies and skills did he use after 1890 that might help explain his achievement?

BOLD ENTREPRENEUR

A Life of James B. Duke

1

STARTING FROM SCRATCH

The single greatest shaping influence on James B. Duke was his father, Washington Duke. The patriarch of the family was in certain ways interestingly typical of the great majority class of antebellum white southerners. Those who derive their knowledge of the Old South from *Gone with the Wind* and other such romantic offerings will never know it, but great planters with large holdings of slaves were a quite tiny minority. The planters were vastly outnumbered by farmers who owned their land but possessed no slaves. They were, to use the Jeffersonian term, yeoman farmers, the great backbone of the South as they were also, in fact, of the pre-Civil War North. Such was Washington Duke.

Scantily educated, as was the case with most yeomen in that era, he was also typical in his Protestant evangelical religion, which was Methodist in his case. Dealt several cruel blows by life, Washington Duke clung steadfastly to his deep religious faith and raised his children accordingly. The church, in fact, more than any other institution or outlet, loomed largest in his life.

After the Civil War, Washinton Duke became atypical. For one thing, when most southerners, both white and black, resumed farming as the way of life they knew best, he soon led his small family into manufacturing. It was only small-scale at first but gradually grew in scope.

For another atypical development, when the Republican party, so hated and feared in the South before the war, actually came into North Carolina and other southern states around 1867–1868, Washington Duke possessed sufficiently independent judgment to join that party. He did so along with a minority of other southern whites — all

"Scalawags" to the white majority - -and also along with the over-whelming majority of the newly freed and enfranchised African Americans. Blaming the Southern Democrats for the tragedy of se-cession and war, he, and then later his sons, embraced a national out-look and scorned the bitter sectionalism and racial politics of the Southern Democrats, the "White Man's Party."

Washington Duke would also become atypical in that, while the great majority in the South long floundered in agricultural poverty, he and his family gradually grew prosperous from their involvement in manufacturing. Moreover, he early demonstrated by his own ex-ample the deep conviction that the proper and necessary concomi-tant to prosperity was systematic charity.

Born on December 20, 1820, to Taylor Duke and Dicey Jones Duke, Washington Duke was the eighth of ten children in the family. Taylor Duke was himself a yeoman farmer scratching out a living in what was then the northern part of Orange County. It was (and still is) beautiful, rolling country in the Piedmont region, and Taylor Duke was born there on the eve of the American Revolution. His fa-ther had been born in Virginia, where the family had come from Eng-land in the 1600s. Taylor Duke's wife, Dicey Jones, was of Welsh an-cestry.

Little is known about Taylor and Dicey Duke; but since he was a captain of the militia in his district and a constable, he was clearly a person of some substance and no doubt respected by his neighbors.

Washington Duke later recalled that he grew up in a section where there were no extremes of poverty or wealth. What he meant was that everyone had food, clothing, and shelter for beyond that, life was hard. For one thing, the lack of transportation facilities brought spe-cial hardships and problems for people in the Piedmont and moun-tain regions; there the rivers were not navigable and the railroads did not arrive until mid-century. Hillsborough, the nearest town and county seat, was some twelve miles away, and Raleigh, the state cap-ital, was about twice as far.

Given such isolated circumstances, Washington Duke had little choice but to spend his early years behind a plow. "I have made more furrows in God's earth," he later declared, "than any man forty years old in North Carolina."[1] Receiving only a few months of formal schooling (so that he could write his name, after a fashion), he spent most of his days toiling. For some years prior to his eighteenth birthday, he and one of his brothers lived with their older brother, William James Duke, who was born in 1803, but Washington Duke soon began to farm on his own.

Working diligently and living frugally, Washington Duke at first rented land. When he married Mary Caroline Clinton in 1842, however, her father gave land to the couple. Washington Duke managed to add to the holding, and by 1860 he owned some 300 acres, on the cultivated parts on which he grew corn, wheat, oats, and in the late 1850s, a small amount of tobacco. The couple had two sons, Sidney Taylor Duke born in 1844 and Brodie Lawrence Duke in 1846. When the latter was only a little more than a year old, his mother died.

Receiving assistance from relatives in the care of his young sons, Washington Duke soon found another wife when Artelia Roney from neighboring Alamance County agreed to marry him in 1852. For her he built a modest frame house of hand-dressed lumber, a typical yeoman farmer's residence which would later be known as the Duke Homestead.

In late 1853 Washington and Artelia Duke had a daughter whom they named Mary Elizabeth. Then on April 27, 1855 Benjamin Newton Duke was born, and on December 23, 1856, another son, James Buchanan Duke.

While Ben Duke was a slight, sickly child, his younger brother "Buck," as his family called him, was robust and healthy. Because of circumstances soon to be explained, the two young boys had more or less to depend on each other for mutual support. Moreover, while they were to maintain an unusually close and loving relationship throughout their entire lives, big, healthy Buck, at some unknown point, seems to have developed a protective attitude and stance towards his frail older brother Ben.

The precariousness of life in the nineteenth century was again brought home to Washington Duke when his oldest child, Sydney, died of typhoid fever in the late summer of 1858. Then ten days later the same disease killed Artelia Roney Duke. With a twelve-year-old son, Brodie; a five-year-old daughter, Mary; and two toddlers, Ben and Buck, Washington Duke needed help. He got it from two maiden sisters of his late wife, first Elizabeth Roney and then Ann Roney, and for a time from his own sister, Malinda Duke. The three youngest children may also have spent some time with their Roney grandparents in Alamance County.

Washington Duke also derived support and help from his beloved Methodism. It was still a relatively new variety of Protestantism during his youth, for the separate Methodist off-shoot of the Episcopal (or Anglican) church had been formally established in the United States only in the 1780s. It spread quickly, especially in the South. The impassioned evangelical movement that swept through American Protestantism in the early years of the nineteenth century—the Second Great Awakening—retained its full vigor in Piedmont North Carolina during Washington Duke's youth.

Converted at age ten during a revival or "protracted meeting" at Mount Bethel Church at a crossroads settlement known as Balltown (later Bahama), he developed a passion for his church. His oldest brother, William James ("Uncle Billy") Duke clearly exerted a large influence, for he was a Methodist exhorter or lay preacher. In the late 1830s he built a large arbor near his home where outdoor services and camp meetings could be held. Later he built a log church called Mount Hebron, which, after his death, became known as Duke's Chapel. It was "Uncle Billy" Duke who once sent up a memorable prayer, one that still resonates with farmers and gardeners: "Oh Lord, send us some rain. We need it. But don't let it be a gullywasher. Just give us a sizzle-sozzle."[2]

Washington Duke and his family frequently attended services at "Uncle Billy" Duke's Mount Hebron church. There was another Methodist chapel nearer their home, however, called Orange Grove. In 1860 this church moved to the hamlet of Durham where a few families had settled around a station on the new railroad. And it was this church, which eventually became Trinity Methodist, where Washington Duke long served as a church officer and where Ben and Buck had their own conversion experiences and joined the church in their early teenage years.

All of these Methodist churches with which the Dukes were involved were both small and poor in a monetary sense. That was why they could not afford to support a regular preacher who could hold weekly services on Sunday as well as midweek prayer meetings. They therefore shared a preacher who rode the circuit, preaching in one of the churches the first Sunday of the month, another the second, and so on. Especially devout lay Methodists such as Washington Duke often had to ride the circuit also if they wished their families to attend religious services more than once or at the most twice a month. In a hardworking farming community where diversions were scarce, these churches played an important social as well as spiritual role. Dinner-on-the-grounds and week-long revival meetings were important events that helped relieve the monotony of a hardscrabble existence.

Thus it was that, come Sunday, Washington Duke loaded his family into a wagon and, bouncing over rough dirt roads, travelled to hear the often-fiery preaching of the circuit riders and to enjoy the lusty singing of such favorite hymns as "Amazing Grace" and "The Old Ship of Zion." "My old daddy always said," J. B. Duke often told his close associates later, "that if he amounted to anything in life it was due to the Methodist circuit riders who frequently visited his home and whose preaching and counsel brought out the best that was in him. If I amount to anything in this world I owe it to my daddy and the Methodist church."[3] Growing up knowing well the vibrant but struggling country churches of North Carolina Methodism, J. B. Duke would later choose to include them as an important beneficiary of his philanthropy.

If the church loomed large in the lives of Washinton Duke and his family, politics did not, probably because he simply had no spare time for it. Though the matter became cloudy after the Civil War, when the Dukes became such loyal Republicans, the scattered evidence suggests that he and other adult male members of the family were Jacksonian Democrats. In 1840, when Washington Duke was still too young to be actively involved in politics, both Taylor Duke and William J. Duke served on a "committee of vigilance" for the Democratic party and the presidential candidacy of Andrew Jackson's successor, Martin Van Buren.[4] More to the point is the fact that only a few weeks after a Pennsylvanian Democrat, James Buchanan, won the presidential election in 1856, Washington Duke chose that name for his youngest son.

However little Washington Duke may have involved himself in the bitterly sectional politics of the 1850s, he, like the great majority of North Carolina voters, opposed immediate secession when the new, all-northern Republican party won the presidental election in 1860. Nevertheless, the Confederate firing on Fort Sumter in April, 1861, and President Abraham Lincoln's ensuing call upon all states for troops to be used against "rebels" seemed to leave North Carolinians no alternative but to throw in their lot with their fellow Southerners.

Though unhappy about a war that he, like so many others, had not wanted, Washington Duke made preparations late in 1863 to join the Confederate service when the government moved to draft men up to forty-five years of age. A widowed father with a teenage son, Brodie, and three young children to care for, he no doubt resented the necessity that confronted him but he had no choice.

Auctioning off all his livestock, tools, wagon, and other supplies, he sent young Mary, Ben, and Buck to live with their Roney grandparents in Alamance County. Deprived of their mother five years earlier, the three youngest childen now faced the prospect of losing, at least temporarily, their father. Brodie Duke, at age seventeen, wished to enlist but since he weighed only ninety-six pounds he was forced instead to do guard duty at a Confederate prison in Salisbury, North Carolina.

Washington Duke entered the Confederate military service in April, 1864. He ended up as an artillery gunner in the trenches surrounding besieged Richmond. Then in the confusion surrounding General Robert E. Lee's evacuation of Richmond, he was captured by Union troops in early April, 1865 and imprisoned in Richmond a week before Lee's surrender. Paroled some weeks later, he was sent by ship to New Bern, and from there had to walk 130 miles to reach home. Soon reunited with Brodie, Mary, Ben, and Buck, he faced the same challenge as did so many other thousands of ex-Confederates: starting over from scratch while penniless.

A big man in his prime, nearly six feet tall and with a muscular frame, Washington Duke was a person of few words, dignified, and with a dry, laconic sense of humor. (His youngest child was much like him in many ways.) Although he never became a professional "Wearer of the Gray" and took no part in romanticizing the late war, he lived to a venerable old age (85) and became widely respected in his community and state, known to many as "Wash" Duke or "the Old Gentleman." But at forty-five years of age, he had a new life to start.

In beginning anew, three things were in the Dukes' favor. In the first place, they labored under no psychological burden produced by a sense of a "golden age before the war" that had passed forever. Residing in a state sometimes known jokingly as the "valley of humility between two mountains of conceit," North Carolinians actually did not carry the burden of past glories—some real and some fanciful—that oppressed many Virginians and South Carolinians.

Secondly, the coming of the railroad, no less than the destruction of the old slave-holding society made a new era possible. By 1854 the North Carolina Railroad, moving westward from Goldsboro through Raleigh, reached the land that Dr. Bartlett Durham gave for a station. Consisting of fewer than a hundred people at the end of the war, the hamlet of Durham lay some three miles to the south of Washington Duke's farm.

Finally, and in addition to the coming of the railroad, the development of a new variety of tobacco, bright leaf, had a great deal to do with the rise of Durham and the postwar careers of Washington Duke and his sons. Pioneered from the late 1830s by, among others, the four Slade brothers of Caswell county in central North Carolina along the Virginia border, the new variety of tobacco flourished in relatively poor soil which contained silica. The best curing process, established only after much experimentation, proved to be a system of flues conveying heat from a wood fire throughout a simply built tobacco barn in which the tobacco leaves, tied into small bundles or "hands" and attached to a stick, were hung for curing. By 1860 or so, the lemon-yellow and mildly fragrant tobacco that resulted from the combination of the siliceous soil and careful curing was finding an ever-widening market. It was first used as a wrapper for plug or chewing tobacco; then it became especially popular for pipe-smoking. With bright-leaf tobacco and the railroad, pushy little Durham had both a product for the outside world and a means for getting it there.[5]

Late in his life, Washington Duke recalled that he had begun to think about somehow escaping from the poor-paying drudgery of farming about the time the Civil War began. That was why, he explained, he had sold off everything he owned before entering the Confederate service. Getting a start in manufacturing and selling smoking tobacco were not, however, easy things to do. Consequently he and his sons initially put most of their time after his return home into farming, including the growing of tobacco. A much more demanding and labor-intensive crop than corn or wheat, tobacco was tricky—and this was when young Buck Duke got his first lessons in the production of the crop.

Since Washington Duke, desperate for even a little cash, had hauled flour and fodder in a wagon to peddle in Raleigh before the war, this method of marketing was nothing new for him. Accordingly, he and his sons used as their first "factory" a log shed near their house. In it on rainy days they used sticks to flail the dried tobacco leaves, put the resulting semi-pulverized tobacco through a sieve, and then packed the final package in small cloth bags labelled "Pro Bono Publico." (No one knows who thought up the Latin label.) Loading the smoking tobacco and two barrels of flour in his wagon, which was also equipped with a "victuals box" for simple cooking along the roadside, Washington Duke headed into the eastern part of the state and proceeded to peddle and barter.[6]

Pleased with the results of his venture, Washington Duke continued both to grow tobacco and to buy it from his neighbors for the production of "Pro Bono Publico." While the male members of the family put in long hours in the fields and in the "factory," Mary Duke attended to many housekeeping chores. A traveller making a trip by buggy in cold, rainy weather in 1871 stopped by the Duke home to thaw out and later provided this glimpse of Mary Duke at age eighteen:

> It was a simple house, two frame buildings of two stories each, joined by an open covered way (known as a "dog-trot" porch). We were hospitably taken into a room with a large open fireplace.... A young woman, I think Mr. Duke's daughter, sat at a table where, by the light of a lamp, she was filling little cotton bags from a pile of finely-shredded tobacco before her. These little bags, stuffed to bursting, were drawn up with a sturdy string run through the top and tied with a bow knot. From time to time she took a pen and wrote in "Pro Bono Publico" on an oblong label which she pasted on the filled bag of tobacco. The lamplight on this table and her quiet deftness and complete absorption...held our fascinated attention.[7]

Although every member of the family worked hard, Washington Duke saw to it that the younger children received more education than he had been given. A Roney aunt probably taught them to read, and later, in slack periods during the agricultural cycle, Ben and Buck Duke attended sessions at an academy in Durham. In 1871 Washington Duke enrolled Mary and Ben Duke in the New Garden School (which later became Guilford College), which was run by the Quakers and located near Greensboro, North Carolina. While they enjoyed their year at New Garden, when it was Buck's turn to go there the next year, he found that he was not enchanted with literary study, missed the farm and factory, and returned home before the term was half completed. Since he had earlier proved to be quick in his school work, especially in arithmatic, he persuaded his father to let him attend a session at the Eastman Business College in Poughkeepsie, New York. A far cry from graduate business schools in a later era, the Eastman Business College taught the hard-driving young Tar Heel, then about seventeen, basic bookkeeping and rudimentary accounting. Both would prove helpful to him, but he obviously learned most and fastest from his deep involvement in the family business—in farming and in helping to produce and sell "Pro Bono Publico."

The first member of the family to go out on his own and move into Durham was not Buck Duke, however, but his older half-brother, Brodie. In 1869, at age twenty-three, he purchased a small frame building on Durham's Main Street and, while living most frugally in the upstairs room, began to manufacture on the ground floor his own brands of smoking tobacco, including the later famous "Duke of Durham." Brodie Duke, who at some point along the way acquired what would become for him a disastrous taste for whiskey, was later described in this beginning phase of his life in Durham as a teetotaler, "his only beverage... the pure unadulterated ale of father Adam— branch water."[8]

Lured by the better opportunities for business offered by bustling little Durham and probably inspired by Brodie Duke's earlier move, Washington Duke sold his farm and moved his family into town in 1874. The town's population of 256 in 1870 jumped to 2,041 by 1880 — and it would continue to climb in succeeding decades. With unpaved streets and all manner of livestock enclosures and vegetable gardens interspersed with homes, Durham was still on the raw side but splendidly vibrant, soon billing itself proudly as the "Chicago of the South."

The Dukes built their frame factory on the south side of Main Street, approximately where a large plant of the Liggett and Myers company would stand in the next century. At first a partition separated that portion of the building to which Brodie Duke removed his business from the half where Washington Duke and his two younger sons established themselves. That arrangement was later replaced by two separate, adjacent buildings, but Washington Duke sold goods for Brodie and vice versa.[9]

By the time of the move to Durham, Washington Duke had progressed from wagon-borne peddler to a rail-riding travelling salesman or "drummer" who covered much of the continent pushing the family's various brands of tobacco. A ledger for the 1870s lists the names and addresses of dozens of tobacconists from Maine to California with whom the Dukes did business.[10]

While Washington Duke travelled, Buck Duke found plenty to keep him occupied at home. Durham acquired its first tobacco-auction warehouse in 1871. A big success from the start, others soon followed, for little Durham was on its way to replacing Richmond as the hub of the southern tobacco industry. Buck Duke, temporarily escaping from his labors on the farm and in the family's "factory," liked to attend the colorful auction sales with their spell-binding chants by the auctioneers and the dramatic tension between buyers and sellers. Young Duke soon developed a reputation as one of the best judges of leaf and shrewdest buyers in the town. As his first biographer put the matter, "the youthful trader reveled in the daily battles of wit and trade, and held his own with the best of them."[11]

As the family business grew in later years and gradually became a key component of the American Tobacco Company in and after 1890, J. B. Duke continued this practice of buying tobacco leaf directly from the warehouse sales. This meant, of course, that he was bypassing the huge numbers of speculative middlemen, and their great anger at being thus bypassed and displaced would be one of the major sources of bitter public attacks against Duke and the American Tobacco Company in later years. But J. B. Duke believed, correctly, that his method of acquiring leaf was both more efficient and more economical. In fact, while he would hardly have understood the term, he was achieving what economic historians later hailed as vertical integration of his business.

Buck Duke also began to "drum the trade" across the South and West, possibly when he was nineteen in 1875. The earliest of his letters known to survive, however, and one of the longest of his few extant handwritten, personal letters, was written when he was not quite twenty-four and on the road as a salesman in 1880. "I have been very much discouraged ever since I left home," Buck declared to brother Ben, "knowing that I was not paying expenses, but there is one consolation[:] I have done my duty whether it was successful or not, & shall put in some very hard work from now until I reach home & if I do not succede better this shall be my last Trip. I will stay at home & work."

Despite his temporary discouragement on the road, Buck Duke kept thinking about ways to help advance the family business. He explained that he had thought up a process that would make the "finest smoke out." He would put tobacco in a dry room and completely dry it so that there would be no moisture left in it. Then he would dip it in boiling flavored rum that would "give it a pleasant flavor and make it smoke sweet & uniform."

Much of Buck Duke's long letter dealt with the fine time he had enjoyed visiting the family of his uncle, John Taylor Duke, in Milan, Tennessee. Among other things, Buck Duke said he had met the "liveliest girl I think God ever put breath in." There were also two young girl cousins about his own age, and the hilarity ranged from water fights to much teasing. "We walked about 2 miles in the country one night to Church, a camp meeting & had a big time," he reported. "Cousin Lockie gave us plenty of wine & I got a gallon besides so we kept the crowd jolly all the time & it was a regular tare for 3 days & nights."

Since Buck Duke, despite occasional worry about "not paying expenses" on his drumming trip, was clearly much enjoying himself, he urged his brother Ben to embark on an even more extensive tour and to take his young wife. Both had been unwell, and Buck believed such a trip would help them regain health. "It does really appear that you have very bad luck [with] so much sickness," Buck wrote, "& I think I cant be thankful enough to my maker for giving me such good health."

Buck argued that he was spared so much expense because of his good health that he felt it was his "duty to offer you part of your expenses on your pleasure trip & if you will accept same I can assure you it is cheerfully given...." Trying to cheer up his ailing brother, Buck continued: "You must not let yourself become discouraged. I know it requires a great deal of nerve to stand up to it & we can't always do it but must make the best of it we can...."[12]

Whether Ben and his wife took the trip as Buck Duke encouraged them to do is not known, but the Dukes gained additional strength in 1878 when the family business was organized on a partnership basis as W. Duke, Sons and Company. Buying into the firm as a partner at that time for the sum of $14,000 (capital welcomed by the Dukes) was twenty-seven year old George W. Watts from Baltimore, Maryland. He would remain closely associated with the Dukes for the remainder of his life, and he and later his son-in-law, John Sprunt Hill, would play important roles as capitalists in Durham and North Carolina.

By that time (1878), the family consensus had clearly become that, despite Buck Duke's youth, he obviously had the sharpest mind for business. Accordingly, he attended to manufacturing and marketing while Ben Duke and George Watts handled the correspondence and ran the front office. Washington Duke at age sixty in 1880 had wearied of the "drummer's" life and believed that the time had come for him to stay at home and enjoy the Methodist church and involvement in Republican politics. Therefore, he sold his interest in the business for $23,000.

The purchaser was Richard Harvey Wright, a young man who had come from a family farm in nearby Franklin county to seek his fortune in Durham. Born in 1851—and thus about the age of George Watts and a few years older than Ben and Buck Duke, Wright was hard working, ambitious and single-minded in his attention to business. He was also quick to litigate and would eventually come to an angry break with the Dukes. But for two years or so he headed a branch office in Chicago and covered much of the West for W. Duke,

Sons, and Company. Then in June, 1882, the firm sent Wright on a globe-circling tour lasting over a year and a half to introduce Duke tobacco products in Europe, South Africa, the East Indies, Australia, and New Zealand.[13]

Although W. Duke, Sons and Company was clearly doing a modestly successful business by 1880 or so, it was only one of about a dozen tobacco manufacturers in Durham, and the firm that loomed far above all the others was W. T. Blackwell and Company, with its already globally-famous "Bull Durham" smoking tobacco. Although the antecedents of the company reached back to the eve of the Civil War, by 1869 William T. Blackwell became a partner, soon purchased the entire business, and took as his partner twenty-five-year old Julian Shakespeare Carr. Blackwell and Carr pioneered in the techniques of advertising their "Genuine Bull Durham" smoking tobacco, spending large sums of money for that era on advertisements in weekly newspapers as well as in larger daily ones and on prizes or premiums, ranging from razors to mantle clocks. Most spectacular of all, huge printed signs of the Durham Bull appeared all over the United States, in Europe, and even at one point on the pyramids of Egypt.

The Bull Durham plant ultimately became, at least for a time, the largest smoking tobacco factory in the world. Then the Blackwell company built a new brick factory equipped not only with the increasingly expensive machinery that tobacco manufacture had begun to require but also with a large steam whistle designed to imitate the bellow of a bull.[14]

The Bull's whistle could be heard for miles around Durham, but one may be sure that the Dukes and their partners took no pleasure in the sound. Having to compete with the Blackwell company in the smoking tobacco business was, in fact, one the main reasons why Buck Duke persuaded his partners that they should go into the cigarette business. "My company is up against a stone wall," Duke is reported to have said. "It cannot compete with the Bull. Something has to be done and that quick...."[15]

Popular in the Spanish-speaking parts of the world earlier, cigarettes did not appear widely in England until the 1850s. Immigrants and rich Americans who could afford to travel in Europe helped introduce the new fad into the United States, and by 1864 the manufacture of cigarettes had begun in New York City. There the practice of smoking them caught on first, and there American cigarette production was centered until 1875, when John F. Allen and Lewis Ginter began their manufacturing business in Richmond, Virginia.[16]

The new bright-leaf tobacco of North Carolina and Virginia proved ideal for use in the cigarette and soon outdistanced Turkish and other types of tobacco, even in Europe. The fragant golden leaf could be obtained more easily and cheaply, in fact, than cigarettes could be produced. That was because they had to be made by hand, and initially the skilled hand-rollers had to be brought over from Europe to train American workers.

When the Duke company began cigarette production in 1881, J. B. Duke arranged for skilled cigarette makers from New York, most of them Jewish immigrants from eastern Europe, to be brought to Durham. Eventually more than a hundred such hand-rollers worked, temporarily as it turned out, in the Duke factory.[17]

The hand labor involved in cigarette manufacture was obviously expensive, but factories in the state of New York in 1880 produced over 384,000,000 cigarettes, about three-quarters of the total in the country. The Duke company only produced 9,800,000 cigarettes in its first year of making them.[18] W. Duke, Sons and Company, however, was only beginning to be heard from in the tobacco world.

J. B. Duke's shrewd instinct for business, aggressive salesmanship, and close attention to a quality product laid the basis in the late 1870s for the rise of the Duke firm. The 1880s, a time of vast expansion and prosperity for much of industrial America, brought the company a new preeminence. With their "Duke of Durham," "Pin Head," and "Cross-Cut" brands of cigaretts, among others, the Dukes and their partners, Watts and Wright, moved ahead vigorously.

Letters from the company to one of its best salesmen, Edward Featherston Small, afford a glimpse of the inside operation of the business at this crucial stage. Since the tobacco industry was ruthlessly competitive, intense secrecy surrounded much of its operation, so the letters to Small present a relatively rare insight. In the spring of 1884, as Small worked Atlanta, the home office informed him that he was being sent a sample of a new cigarette, "Pin Head," which had been produced especially to run against a rival brand. The claim was that

"Pin Head" was "finer & lower-price[d] than the rival, while 'Old Rip' [another rival] ain't worth within 50c to 75c per M[thousand] as 'Pin Head.'"

On the back of this letter, J. B. Duke scrawled a revealing message, for, just as he strove to by-pass the middlemen in buying leaf, he was eager to by-pass the old-time commission merchants and wholesalers in getting his cigarettes to consumers. Therefore, he wanted Small to report about the reaction of retailers and consumers to the company's brands. "I want to know," Duke demanded, "how the sales of retailers compare on our Duke [of Durham] with other brands, both with the prominent retailers and the smaller ones."[19]

The home office soon boasted to Small, "Our cig[arette] business was never so good, orders ranging from 200M to 400M daily while the Bull has purchased stamps this month for only 250M altogether; if you mention this, do so in confidence or you might get our Collector [of Internal Revenue] in trouble." Small would soon receive circulars for each retailer in Atlanta and the company was "also preparing some other physic for the Bull which we will administer from time to time."[20]

As Small proceeded to Savannah, the home office notified him that a case containing 20,000 pieces of advertising matter and 99 packs of playing cards, among other things, was on the way. That, in addition to the cards and posters sent earlier, ought to give Small a "pretty good send off in Savannah." The office prodded too: "We want the city and surrounding country worked for all it is worth. We sincerely hope you will create a big boom in Savannah & we don't want you to leave there until you make every possible effort to create such."[21]

Creating a "big boom" was something Small proved himself adept at, for he hit on a sensational ploy in Atlanta. A well known French actress of the day, a Madame Rhea, was playing in the Georgia capital, and the city was covered with advertisements about her, including life-size lithographs. Small inquired of Madame Rhea if she would consent to have the life-size lithograph of herself reproduced with a package of Duke cigarettes in her hand and the caption "Atlanta's Favorite" printed beneath. When the actress quickly agreed and the ad appeared in the most popular tobacco store in the city and then in a large advertisement in the Atlanta *Constitution*, Small had achieved a salesman's dream of gaining the public's attention. With sales soaring in Atlanta and its environs, the home office applauded: "We think you made a happy hit with Rhea. Give the Bull's tail another twist."[22]

The combination in advertising of beautiful women and cigarettes proved to be a long-lived development despite the shock it initially caused to much of the public. The sexual slant was clearly designed to appeal to the male market. "Loose women" and certain sophisticated society women in New York might privately use cigarettes, as novels of Edith Wharton reveal, but the day of any widespread public acceptance of cigarette smoking by women was several decades in the future.

Meanwhile, Small had the further inspiration of employing an attractive widow in St. Louis as a pioneer saleswoman for Duke cigarettes. Not only did this attract much free publicity, as was the case with Madame Rhea, but the home office, after receiving a photograph of the widow, reported to Small that she had "made a mash" on Washington Duke and another man in the plant. Small "need not be surprised any day to have one or both of these gentlemen reach St. Louis to succeed" him.[23]

Although Small clearly had a flair for capitalizing on the feminine angle, he did not slip into a stale pattern. Roller-skating on indoor rinks became a widely popular fad in the mid-1880s, so Small secured the services of a "polo club" on skates. He then out-fitted them handsomely as the "Cross Cut Polo Club of Durham, N.C." and arranged for them to play widely publicized matches in Ohio and Michigan. In Cincinnati where the "Cross Cuts" played in a leading rink, the match took on a sectional aspect, with the South once more "battling against the North for the honors of the hour." Headlines in newspapers and on handbills played up the "desperate battle between the North and South" while also advancing the interests of W. Duke, Sons and Company. One newspaper reported that the "Cross Cut club have won many hands [of applause] by their gentlemanly acting, and the only thing to be avoided tonight is the possibility of both clubs doing the slugging act. It was bordering on it last night." Presumably the "slugging act" was avoided, and as the spectators left the rink each man was given a five-cent package of ten Duke "Cross-Cut" cigarettes and each woman a set of five small photographs.[24] Rolling-skating "polo

clubs," photographs of presidents and monarchs and just about everything else imaginable, a chair to every dealer who gave an order for a
certain number of cigarettes—all these and more were the schemes
used by the Dukes as well as by their competitors.[25]

Part of the struggle also involved price-cutting, which was always
a welcome development by consumers. One of the Duke company's
bolder moves in the area of pricing came in 1888, when the federal
excise tax on cigarettes was cut to less than a third of what it had been,
from $1.75 to 50 cents per thousand. Immediately upon passage of
the new tax law and before it could be put into effect, J. B. Duke persuaded his partners to reduce the price for their cigarette by the full
amount of the tax cut. Advertising then stressed that "the Dukes are
ambitious for a very large cigarette business, and to obtain such are
dividing their profits with the dealers and consumers."[26]

The dramatic price-cutting move helped the Duke firm to increase
market share, and the company continued to respond quickly whenever the market seemed to demand it. When W. S. Kimball and Company of Rochester, New York, came out with a "cheap cigarette" called
"Old Gold," the Duke home office complained that some few jobbers
and retailers wanted low priced cigarettes regardless of quality or the
opinion of the smokers, and concluded that the only thing to do was
"to accomodate all such parties and meet competition, and…we will
at once put the price of Pin Head down…."[27]

Though J. B. Duke believed in advertising as much as anyone,
when the office sent Small the 10,000 "cabinet photographs" that he
had requested, Duke cautioned that the photographic cards cost half
as much as a package of ten cigarettes and "must be used very judi-
ciously." As for himself, Duke added that he was introducing the company's "Cameo" brand cigarettes in New York City and that they were
"catching on very nicely without any effort on our own part so far,"
but "I am going to push them hard from now on."[28]

W. Duke, Sons and Company, with its sharp young president,
began by 1884 to pull up alongside Blackwell's Bull Durham Company, which also produced cigarettes but continued to emphasize
smoking tobacco. "The cig[arette] business with us continues splendid," the Duke home office reported to Small. "We are getting repeated orders from every section of the country when [our cigarettes]

are once tried, [and we] expect to ship more this month than ever before & keep on increasing until we make it 500 M per day." Soon afterwards, management proudly announced, "Our orders on the glorious 4th [of July, 1884] were 1,905,000 cigtts."[29]

The very success of the Duke products brought new problems. The home office congratulated Small on his sales and advertising feats but confessed that production was three weeks behind orders, so "at present it is useless for us to endeavor to enlarge the territory." Relief was in sight, however: "We are now [October 1884] opening a factory in New York from which to supply our Northern trade and as soon as we get that to running all right, we hope to supply all our Southern trade promptly from here [Durham], so that factory [in New York] will relieve us of 3 to 400 M per day."[30]

Despite all the firm's success, margins could still be painfully close. "Only $200 in mail today & with nothing in Bank I don't know how I am to pay what has to be paid this week[,] say $12,000...," moaned Ben Duke. He requested Richard Wright in New York to try and arrange for the renewal there of the company's note for $5,000, and then he, Ben Duke, would see what could be done about a short-term loan from the bank of Durham. "Money is awful tight here," he explained, "& it will require several days notice or they cannot aid us." Intended as a more cheerful note, no doubt, was the information that there were orders on hand for 340,000 cigarettes.[31]

The new factory in New York, which J. B. Duke was establishing and where he would make his permanent headquarters, was only part of the company's response to its success—and to the problems associated with that success. Much more important for the future was the move that J. B. Duke was urging on his partners: the production of machine-made cigarettes. At a time when the users of cigarettes gave every indication of liking the hand-rolled variety—as did most of the established manufacturers, such as Allen and Ginter in Richmond—a switch to a machine-made product could involve great risk. Moreover, a completely satisfactory machine to make cigarettes had not yet appeared, although the race to make such a machine had been on for several years.

Nevertheless, by 1885 J. B. Duke had persuaded his partners to take a large gamble and give the cigarette-making machine invented by James A. Bonsack of Virginia more than a casual try. W. Duke, Sons and Company would be the first cigarette manufacturers in America to take such a step—and it would pay off handsomely, even if no one could know that for certain in 1885.

2

J. B. DUKE AND
THE ORIGINS OF THE
AMERICAN TOBACCO COMPANY

Developments in the years between 1885, when W. Duke, Sons and Company decided to bet heavily on the Bonsack cigarette machine, and 1890, when the American Tobacco Company was established, long remained obscure. The dealings of the American Tobacco Company after 1890 were extensively revealed early in the twentieth century , first by the federal government's Bureau of Corporations and then by the Department of Justice in its successful antitrust action against the company. Letterbooks of J. B. Duke that came to light in the 1970s, however, afford a close, inside view of the most dynamic sector of the American tobacco industry during the late 1880s; they also underscore the key role of the Bonsack machine, not only in the rise to preeminence of W. Duke, Sons and Company but also in the organization of the American Tobacco Company. The phenomenal growth of the firm headed by J. B. Duke, who turned thirty late in 1886, and the actual negotiations that he led and that resulted in the formation of the great combination in 1890 may now be much more clearly understood from these letterbooks.[1]

J. B. Duke arranged for the installation of a Bonsack machine in the Durham factory in the spring of 1884. The machine had first been tested in the Richmond factory of Allen and Ginter, then the largest cigarette producers in the country, and was theoretically capable of producing in a day about as many cigarettes as forty-eight skilled hand rollers could make. The Bonsack Machine Company, the joint-stock company which had been organized to produce and handle the invention, leased the machines on a royalty basis of approximately two-thirds of the cost of producing cigarettes by hand. In other words, the Bonsack company charged thirty cents per thousand cigarettes for "plain work" and thirty-three cents per thousand for "printed work," with the Bonsack company installing the machine and furnishing an operator for it.[2]

There were two major obstacles blocking wide acceptance of the Bonsack machine: first, it worked only sporadically and imperfectly; and second, most cigarette manufacturers clung to the belief that consumers preferred the hand-rolled cigarette that had become popular in the nation since the Civil War. Overcoming the machine's imperfections was, in part, a triumph for the persistence and ingenuity of J. B. Duke; but even more was it his great good luck when the Bonsack company sent him William T. O'Brien, an Irish-American mechanic from Lynchburg, Virginia. Working patiently and tirelessly, O'Brien made no fundamental changes in the complicated machine; but more importantly, he gradually made it work effectively. J. B. Duke announced unreservedly to the president of the Bonsack Machine Company, D. B. Strouse of Salem, Virginia, that O'Brien was able to run the complex machine better than "any other man you now have or may have hereafter."[3]

J. B. Duke's shrewd assessment of O'Brien's talents and the way in which he (J. B. Duke) treated him may be used as an early example of one of the most important keys, or secrets, to Duke's remarkable career: he was an extremely keen judge of men and of their character and ability. Moreover, when he spotted someone whose talent he respected and whom he judged to be reliable and trustworthy, he treated him fairly, respectfully, and generously. This would be demonstrated repeatedly—in Duke's selection of the crucially important coterie of middle-managers for the eventually vast American Tobacco Company; in the selection of W. A. Erwin to oversee the Dukes' move into textile manufacturing; and in the engagement of a promising young engineer named William States Lee for the development of hydroelectricity in the Carolinas. The list could continue much longer, but the point is that J. B. Duke's success in enterprises owed a great deal to highly talented people who worked with and for him, and who generally remained loyally with him throughout their careers. Duke would have been the first to admit that, for he was essentially a modest, albeit extremely hardworking person.

In O'Brien's case, J. B. Duke's life-long policy of giving his key coworkers a stake in success was exemplified when Duke employed O'Brien directly and gave him three cents per thousand, and then four cents per thousand, for all cigarettes made on the machine. O'Brien himself eventually surrendered this commission as excessive, and he was made superintendent of the Durham factory in 1897.[4]

Perhaps it was O'Brien's unusual skill with the Bonsack machine that helped convince J. B. Duke that his firm should gamble on being able to overcome the alleged consumer resistance to machine-made cigarettes. Starting late in 1884 and continuing into 1885, Duke was in hot pursuit of a special deal with the Bonsack company. Responding to one of his overtures, D. B. Strouse assured him that, "You are our largest patron and we feel disposed to forward your interests in every possible way." Strouse explained that he expected to visit Durham soon to see what could be worked out to their mutual advantage and, in the meantime, congratulated Duke "upon the wonderful success of your firm."[5]

Serious negotiations between J. B. Duke and Strouse began in April, 1885, and culminated in New York in May, 1885. Eager for a wide market for the Bonsack machine as well as for its use in the production of the better, more expensive brands of cigarettes, Strouse had good reason to woo J. B. Duke and to fear certain companies that scorned the Bonsack machine while continuing to advertise the alleged superiority of hand-rolled cigarettes. J. B. Duke well understood what his firm could do for the Bonsack company and was determined that Strouse should pay accordingly.

The verbal agreement that the two men negotiated would be put into writing in two later stages, and it was one of the pivotal secrets of the cigarette industry in the late 1880s. It called for W. Duke, Sons and Company to utilize at once two of the Bonsack machines on their best brands and gradually to increase the number of machines as fast as practicable in light of the popular prejudice against machine-made cigarettes and the necessity of phasing out the hand-rollers and trying to avoid labor trouble. Strouse, for his part, agreed that the rate of royalty on machines at the Duke factory should at once be reduced from thirty-three cents per thousand for printed cigarettes and thirty for unprinted ones to twenty-four cents per thousand on all cigarettes; furthermore, when and if all cigarettes produced by the Duke firm were made by machines, the rate would be reduced to twenty cents per thousand; and finally, if the Bonsack rate of royalty to any other manufacturers should ever be reduced below the standard rate of thirty-three and thirty cents respectively, W. Duke, Sons and Company should have its rate proportionately reduced so that it would always be charged 25 percent less than any other manufacturer.[6]

Just as J. B. Duke wrestled with the task of securing favorable treatment from the Bonsack company, a serious internal problem cropped up for W. Duke, Sons and Company. Organized as a five-man partnership in 1878, the company found in Richard H. Wright, who had contracted for Washington Duke's share in 1880, an unhappy partner who threatened drastic action. The immediate cause of his discontent sprang from the call from the other partners, led by J. B. Duke, for more capital to plow into the rapidly expanding enterprise. A deeper cause arose from Wright's dislike of playing second fiddle to Buck Duke, who was almost five years younger. Every bit as hardworking and ambitious as Duke, Wright was a proud, strong-willed man who ended up in litigation involving a large number of those with whom he became associated in business. At any rate, the Duke brothers and George Watts were soon given a painful lesson in the hazards of the partnership form of business organization and the advantages of the joint-stock company or corporation.

Wright's attorney advised him early in 1885 that when a partnership continued after the expiration of the term prescribed for its duration—as was the case of W. Duke, Sons and Company after January 1, 1885—it did so at the will and pleasure of the partners and was dissolvable by any one of them. "If your partners will not give you a *full* price for your interests," the attorney continued, "you can make it to their interest to come to terms. You have the game *very much* in your hands."[7]

Given this assurance by his attorney, Wright proceeded coolly to play the "game." J. B. Duke sought to increase the company's capital from $100,000 to $150,000, but Wright demurred. He had not yet paid Washington Duke for the share in the company that Wright had purchased in 1880, and the head of the Duke family was finally forced to foreclose the mortgage on real estate in Durham which Wright had given as security for his note to Washington Duke.[8]

Prior to that public sale of a portion of Wright's real-estate holdings, however, he and his partners had begun negotiating cautiously, and abortively. The Dukes and George Watts tried various ways to keep Wright in the firm while also increasing the capital, but Wright declined to go along. Wright, in fact, began, as he put it, "to look outside for capital to buy my interest or to join me & buy them all out on a give or take proposition...."[9] In other words, Wright made overtures to some of the major tobacco companies in the country, including a couple of the largest cigarette manufacturers, about their possible interest in buying into or buying out W. Duke, Sons and Company.[10]

Within twenty-four hours of J. B. Duke's final understanding with D. B. Strouse about the Bonsack machine, J. B. Duke informed Wright of the agreement. Wright, in a characteristic putdown, minimized Duke's achievement by suggesting, "Hell, he [Strouse] ought to have given you the twenty-cent rate at once." Wright argued that the Duke firm should decline to accept the proposition, not install any more Bonsack machines for a while, and therefore bring Strouse to offer even better terms.[11]

With Wright subsequently refusing to confer with his partners, they too retained counsel; and finally they issued a public notice on July 2, 1885, that the old five-man partnership, "having expired by effluxion of the time limited for its duration," was from thenceforth dissolved. "The business of manufacturing Smoking Tobacco and Cigarettes will be continued at the old stand by" Brodie L. Duke, Benjamin N. Duke, James B. Duke, and George W. Watts.[12] Securing the services of disinterested parties to inventory the firm's "physical, tangible, perishable assets," the Dukes and George Watts invited Wright or his representatives to be "present to see that everything is properly and correctly listed."[13]

Although Wright ignored the invitation, he allegedly told J. B. Duke in July, 1885, that he, Wright, would sell his share of the firm "to a rival who would buy, to wreck the business and get the Dukes out of the way."[14] Wright's attorney advised that "a suit in the U. S. Court, asking for a dissolution [of the firm] & settlement, and in the meantime a re-

ceiver," would quickly bring the Dukes and George Watts to terms. The attorney argued that some of the federal courts were "very liberal in the appointment of receivers" and that such a course would not only to "very distasteful to your partners" but "calculated to cause much alarm." Even if the court refused to appoint a receiver, the lawyer continued, it would unhesitatingly order a "speedy settlement," and that "would necessitate a sale of everything, and the third parties, to whom you referred, could become competitors for the brands, trade marks etc etc." The attorney believed that "the *firm name* is one of the most valuable" assets of W. Duke, Sons and Company, and the "good will includes the *firm name.*"[15]

Sure enough, Wright filed his bill in equity in Federal District Court in Greensboro, North Carolina, in mid-July, 1885, and only the elusiveness of J. B. Duke, who somehow managed to avoid being served a subpoena, slowed Wright's legal maneuvers aimed at the appointment of a receiver and the forced sale of the firm. A settlement out of court, one closer to the price demanded by Wright, was probably what he wanted all along. Both sides proceeded warily as they edged toward a settlement. After much maneuvering, when Wright finally offered to sell his interest "in the good will, trade marks, effects, assets and property, real and personal, of the firm for $39,750," the Dukes and Watts promptly accepted the offer.[16]

While the Dukes and George Watts had by no means heard the last from Richard Wright, they escaped from a painful and dangerous dilemma in 1885. Moreover the firm, now reorganized as a joint-stock company, proceeded to forge to the top of the cigarette industry. Characterized by one economic historian as "the leading innovator in the American cigarette business during the 1880s," J. B. Duke vigorously led his company in making "entrepreneurial contributions in marketing, in purchasing, and in production which were the driving force for change."[17]

One further "change" which J. B. Duke now pursued was to bring about a combination of the leading cigarette producers, and the Bonsack cigarette machine played a key role in his strategy. The Duke firm first demonstrated that the Bonsack machine was preeminently successful. Among the larger cigarette manufacturers, both Allen and Ginter Company of Richmond and F. S. Kinney Company of New

York were tardy in switching from hand-rolled cigarettes, to which their advertisements attributed great superiority. By 1887, however, they too were forced to turn to the Bonsack machine. Two other large manufacturers, Goodwin and Company of New York and W. S. Kimball and Company of Rochester, used machines that were rivals of Bonsack's invention, Goodwin employing the Emery machine and Kimball the Allison.[18]

J. B. Duke, wishing to keep down the number of producers in the fiercely competitive industry, began pushing D. B. Strouse as early as 1885 to restrict the use of the Bonsack machine to the major manufacturers. "Please let me know as soon as possible," Duke wrote, "what proposition you will be able to make, looking to a concentration of the business, and I will do what I can to bring about such a move." Duke thought it would be wise for the Bonsack company to "make just as close a figure as possible [on rates], so as to induce those who are using other machines which you claim are infringements, to drop them rather than go into litigation over the matter."[19]

The "concentration of the business" that Duke referred to would be the American Tobacco Company and would take more years and effort than perhaps he initially realized. But in the meantime, the Duke firm clamored for more Bonsack machines than Strouse could supply. Too, there was a constant, nagging worry about fire. "We think it very important, for your sake, as well as ours," George Watts admonished Strouse, "that you should always keep duplicate machines to those that we use, for in case of fire here [in the Durham factory] and the destruction of your machines we would be in a bad way, unless we could immediately secure the same number of other machines from you. A few months' inability to supply our cigarettes might destroy our trade upon them, as the smokers would not wait upon us, but try other goods...."[20]

While the threat of loss from fire increased with the switch to the Bonsack machine, the problem of maintaining a contented labor force also escalated. The Jewish emigrant hand-rollers, who had been brought down from New York, greeted the first machine in 1884 (and W. T. O'Brien also) with threats and open hostility. Since the first machine worked so imperfectly, however, and the demand for cigarettes kept the hand-rollers occupied, the initial friction with the workers passed. By late 1885 and 1886, however, the machine had clearly triumphed, and the leaders among the rollers, as Washington Duke later recalled, gave the company "no end of trouble." Well might the hand-rollers protest, for they were early victims of the technological revolution that would eventually eliminate the jobs of carriage-makers, blacksmiths, and countless other groups. "We have today notified our hands of a reduction in the price of making [cigarettes] and many of them may leave," the Duke firm informed Strouse in early 1886, "in which event we would need at least one more machine at once."[21]

The Duke partners kept a sharp eye and steady pressure on the Bonsack company. When the Duke firm had unfilled orders for four additional machines at the very moment when one arrived at the old rival and neighboring Blackwell plant, George Watts protested: "We do most emphatically object to your giving anyone preference over us, as you have admitted to us that we were the most profitable factory that was using your machines."[22]

J. B. Duke may have been the leading tormentor of Strouse. The Bonsack company gave the exclusive agency to sell its machine in Africa (especially South Africa and Egypt) and Asia to none other than Richard Wright. He was to operate at his own expense and pay the company one half of the gross receipts after deducting the cost of the machines laid down in the foreign country.[23] When J. B. Duke learned of this arrangement, he roared in anger to Strouse: "The world is now our market for our product, and we do not propose sitting idly down and allowing you or any one else to cut off any of the channels of our trade by establishing factories where there have been none and tying up your machinery with them, and afterwards you could say to us, 'You must manufacture your goods in the United States; this country and that country is taken.'" If such really was to be the Bonsack company's policy, Duke announced that he and his associates would have to encourage some inventor "to get up a better machine" which would be "controlled solely by W. Duke, Sons & Co."[24]

In Cuba, where an entirely different kind of tobacco from the famed North Carolina-Virginia bright leaf was used, Duke had no objection to the introduction of the Bonsack machine. "But where mild cigarettes are sold or wanted," he insisted, "the U. S. leads the world in their manufacture, and Strouse could not "in good faith to us and your other patrons carry out your intentions to open up competition for us."[25]

Despite all of the protests of J. B. Duke, Strouse stuck by his contract for Africa and Asia with Richard Wright. And for all of Duke's complaints to Strouse, the Bonsack company's president continued to play a key role in the realization of Duke's long-standing hope for the "concentration" of the nation's cigarette manufacture. As the Duke firm moved toward the installation of Bonsack machines in its New York factory, Strouse in the summer of 1887 sent Duke a "Personal & Private" message from Rochester, New York: "Kimball is in favor of a combination which will restrict the machines to the large factories — so is Ginter. I can easily arrange matter all around here. Can you see as to Kinney and Emery[?]"[26]

Expressing to Strouse his satisfaction that the other major cigarette producers thought "favorably of the arrangements which I have advocated to you for quite a while," Duke felt more confident than ever that concentration would be best for the Bonsack company as well as for the cigarette manufactures. He had suggested the idea to F. S. Kinney early in the year, and since nothing more had been done by Kinney, Duke thought the matter should be left quietly to ripen. The rising young tobacco magnate indulged in a rare burst of near-philosophizing: "It requires time to get competitors to see things in the same light, but it requires hard work to smother out a good idea, and if you [Strouse] are prepared to be patient (since you already have a good thing with Kimball, Ginter and Duke to rest upon), you can rest assured that time will bring the others in. We were the first to give you substantial support, and I told you at the time, that our doing so would bring the others in, and you see that my predictions are coming true to the extent of two large manufacturers, and you now have more than three-fifths of the business on account of making it an inducement to us to handle your machines."

With five large cigarette manufacturers who had most of the business, J. B. Duke saw no chance for any new firm to compete "unless they are willing to sacrifice $1,000,000 on chances of being successful." Despite the "sharpest competition" in 1887 that he had ever seen in the business, Duke noted that his company had "made the largest increase" in its history. "Our aggregate orders now are 2,000,000 [cigarettes] per day," he asserted, "and if we keep on at the present rate of increase, it will not be long before they greatly exceed this amount." Ordering five Bonsack machines for the New York branch, with five more to follow upon the installation of the first batch, Duke could not resist a boast: "I claim that our house is the leader in the business, and it certainly is in enterprise, and the others must follow us or find that they will gradually be left. These are the facts, but I would not make use of them, unless I believed that you would keep them *STRICTLY CONFIDENTIAL*." Reiterating his constant message to Strouse, Duke insisted that the "fewer number of hands you have the machines in, the more you will make."[27]

Apart from the larger matter of the much-sought combination, J. B. Duke's meticulous attention to details is well illustrated in his letter to Strouse (August 23, 1887), where Duke ordered five printing dies each of the Cameo and Cross-Cut brands so that all five of the first machines in the New York factory could produce either brand, depending on the calls of the trade that varied from day to day. He also outlined plans for the switching of full production, including operators, between the Durham and New York factories in case of fire at either plant.

While never forgetting to be careful about small matters that, in case of accident or the unforeseen, could easily come to loom large, J. B. Duke persevered in pursuit of his larger goal. After a conference of J. B. Duke, Lewis Ginter, and D. B. Strouse in Richmond in early February, 1888, Duke learned that a Bonsack machine was being shipped to the Hess Company of Rochester, New York. "You ought to countermand such orders as far as possible at once," he urged Strouse. "You have a good arrangement with Ginter and ourselves and you will be proud of it in a very short while but you must keep off the mosquito[e]s."[28]

Responding to Duke's demands, Strouse, after conferring with the other officers and directors of his company, wrote identical letters, which he termed the official "agreement between us," to the Duke firm and to Allen and Ginter. The Bonsack company pledged to supply the two firms with as many machines as they desired, "you paying the same royalties you now pay." The Bonsack company also agreed "not to place any of our machines in any house in the United States in which we have no machines now, and not to place any more machines in any house in which they are now in the United States, unless in our judgment we are legally or honorably bound to do so, and that as the opportunities may occur to remove the machines from the other factories in the United States, in which they now are, we will remove them, so that such removal shall not be in violation of good faith and fair dealing with such houses, not obligating ourselves, however, to purchase the right to make such removals." The Bonsack company's condition for the preceding arrangement was that "at least one half of the cigarettes made in the United States during 1888 and each year thereafter, be made on our machines, and whenever we shall find that such is not the case, we shall have the right at our option to cancel this agreement."[29]

Although J. B. Duke had finally gained a large part of what he wanted from Strouse and the Bonsack company, there was a fly in the ointment having to do with Strouse's phrase about the Duke firm's, as well as Allen and Ginter's, "paying the same royalties you now pay." Duke's original contract of 1885 called not only for a reduction in the royalty rate from twenty-four to twenty-cents per thousand cigarettes when machines were engaged exclusively in the Duke factories, toward which condition Duke was moving after 1887, but there was also the final clause, added to the written contract early in 1886, concerning the 25 percent lower rate for the Duke firm than charged to any other manufacturer. Strouse clearly had hoped to escape from that original contract, but James B. Duke seems to have grown up reading fine print—as well as between the lines. He promptly replied to Strouse: "We don't want this [new] contract to, in any manner [,] interfere with the one which we have with you regarding use of machines, royalties etc. We don't know that it does as we are not lawyers and have not consulted any." Duke also suggested that Strouse's phrase about the Duke firm's and Allen and Ginter's being allowed the "continuous use" of the Bonsack machine be changed to the "'exclusive use' of it."[30]

"The restriction to the royalties as *now paid*," Strouse then confessed, "was an item that induced us to make the agreement." Strouse pointed out that Allen and Ginter had agreed to it (as well they might, since the Duke firm's special rates were highly secret). Assuring Duke that the Bonsack company would remove the machines from the other, smaller houses as soon as possible consistent "with what we shall regard as fair dealing," Strouse pressed for early acceptance of the terms he had offered.[31]

Duke finally responded in a strong and lengthy letter: "I have been taught by experience that in settling difficulties the surest mode of success was to use perfect candor and fair dealing. In that spirit I am determined to treat you on this occasion and shall be disappointed if it does not bring you to treat us justly, and give us what we feel we are so clearly entitled to by reason of the risk and hazard we took upon ourselves in testing and proving the merits of your machines, by which you were so much benefit[t]ed." Duke then repeated the circumstances surrounding his firm's original gamble on the Bonsack machine and the gradual triumph of the machine-made cigarette which followed. The reduction of the force of hand-rollers had necessarily proceeded slowly, Duke pointed out, "to avoid all possible danger of doing injustice to our employees and all risk of collision with labor organization," and Strouse had been "humane enough and considerate enough to recognize the truth that we were moving as fast as good judgment and sound policy dictated for us."

Now that the time approached when the firm could do all of its work on the machine "without doing injustice to any of our dependents," Duke insisted upon a "faithful performance of that contract [of 1885] on your part, by promptly giving us such a drawback as will reduce our royalty to 20 cents per M cig[arettes]." Dropping the lofty tone, Duke termed the new contract about rates which Strouse had proposed as "absolutely childish" and a matter that had not been discussed at all in conferences at Richmond and elsewhere. "When you are prepared to offer a contract carrying out the understanding as it was made," Duke concluded, "then we are ready to entertain it; otherwise we have no further time to waste with something entirely foreign to our understanding."[32]

Duke stuck by his guns, and matters hung fire as Strouse engaged in legal battles to protect the Bonsack company's patents and Duke coped with labor problems in New York. Finally Strouse sent Duke a revised contract to sign and declared: "With this contract I don't care who knows what you pay, for you will see that I have set out the true grounds ample to sustain it. You will stand just as you do now and I will be free from any embarrassment." A contract for the Kinney Company had been prepared, and Strouse had successfully resisted Kinney's efforts to include a clause stipulating that he should have all the advantages that anyone using the Bonsack machines had.[33] Duke apparently signed the revised contract, for he subsequently reminded Strouse that the Bonsack company had pledged that the Bonsack-controlled machines, which eventually included not only the original Bonsack invention but also the Emery and Allison rival machines, were not to be placed in the United States outside of the five major cigarette firms, that is, Duke, Allen and Ginter, Kinney, Goodwin, and Kimball.[34]

Even larger developments loomed in the cigarette industry as the pace quickened in 1889 toward the combination which J. B. Duke had sought for nearly five years. Strouse informed him that some of the manufacturers had suggested a meeting to be held in New York "with a view to the organization of a consolidated cigarette company." Duke, however, replied warily: "I am perfectly willing to meet the manufacturers at any time to discuss any matter for our common good, but if you mean by consolidated cigarette company that there is to be another factory started or a trust formed, and want us to take stock in them, I am opposed to anything of the kind, as we want the full control of our business, which we could not have with a trust. If there is any other proposition to discuss I will meet if called."[35]

In light of J. B. Duke's later reputation, his disdain for "anything" like a trust was ironic. He meant, of course, that he intended to remain in control of his own business—regardless. Strouse, after conferring with Kinney and explaining to him why Duke wanted no part of any absolute consolidation of the various firms, informed Duke that Kinney was most eager to get out of the advertising madhouse in which the cigarette industry had come to operate and to end what Kinney termed "this damned picture business." Strouse agreed that the business was undoubtedly "being greatly degraded" by all the advertising stunts and suggested that eventually an agreement might be worked out among the big five "on a basis of the number of cigarettes [produced] or gross sales."[36]

Duke soon replied that he had seen Ginter, who agreed to meet with the other four major manufacturers, and that a meeting had accordingly been called at the Fifth Avenue Hotel in New York on April 23, 1889. Beginning then, therefore, and in a series of meetings continuing intermittently throughout the remainder of the year, J. B. Duke and his former leading rivals hammered out the organization of the American Tobacco Company, which one economic historian described as "one of the first giant holding companies in American industry."[37]

The "tobacco trust," as the American Tobacco Company soon came to be popularly known, was not, in fact, a trust in the sense that John D. Rockefeller's original model of that form of business organization, the Standard Oil Company, had been. That is, W. Duke, Sons and Company and the other four firms did not turn over the stock in their companies to trustees in exchange for trust certificates. Rather, the five formerly competing businesses were sold outright to the American Tobacco Company in exchange for its stock. As might be expected, the thorniest problem faced by J. B. Duke and his new associates concerned the apportionment of that stock among the owners of the five old firms.

J. B. Duke, though regarded as something of a Tar Heel upstart by Major Lewis Ginter of Virginia, was not a person, even at age thirty-three, to take a back seat to any one. Basing his claim on the assets of his firm and on past as well as prospective earning records, Duke held out for parity with Allen and Ginter, and in the end, got it, along with the presidency of the new company. Chartered under New Jersey's accommodating new incorporation law in 1890, the American Tobacco Company was capitalized at $25,000,000 — $10,000,000 in preferred stock and $15,000,000 in common. W. Duke, Sons and Company and Allen and Ginter each received $7,500,000 in stock — $3,000,000 in preferred and $4,500,000 in common. The share of the Kinney Company of New York City was $2,000,000 in preferred stock and $3,000,000 in common; and the Kimball Company of Rochester and the Goodwin Company of New York City each got $1,000,000 in preferred and $1,500,000 in common.[38]

Boasting privately late in 1889 that the five combining firms controlled "between 90 and 95% of the entire paper cigarette business in the U. S.," J. B. Duke thus spotlighted the economically powerful base from which the American Tobacco Company launched its operations.[39] While it would soon grow into one of the most successful and powerful industrial corporations in the nation, J. B. Duke himself was destined to become "king of the mountain" in the whole tobacco industry by the late 1890s.

3

BUILDING AN INDUSTRIAL EMPIRE

J. B. Duke and the American Tobacco Company,
1890–1904

When James B. Duke climbed to preeminence in the American tobacco industry in the 1890s, he took his place alongside John D.
Rockefeller, Andrew Carnegie, and numerous other pioneering industrial capitalists in the late nineteenth century. Bitterly attacked by
the "muckraking" journalists and publicists of the Progressive Era,
these business magnates acquired their most familiar label as "robber
barons" when Matthew Josephson published his famous book with
that title in 1934, at the height of the Great Depression.

A well-written, lively, and highly colorful group portrait of the nation's most prominent and successful leaders of Big Business in the
late nineteenth century, Josephson's *The Robber Barons* portrayed
them as ruthless and greedy exploiters of labor who unscrupulously
clawed their way to the top in their various fields of endeavor while
doing little or nothing of any permanent value to the nation. In short,
Josephson produced a profoundly anti-capitalist book, which was ex-
actly what he set out to do. In 1932 when he was still in the preliminary stages of tackling his project, he wrote his publisher that he
wanted "to place the brand of obloquy squarely upon the masters of
capital in 1870–1890...."[1]

As a member of an intellectual and literary Northeastern elite that
moved steadily leftward in the early 1930s, Josephson, in his biographer's words, "was not alone in his infatuation with the Commu-
nists...." While he never joined the Communist Party, as many did,

he "rushed enthusiastically into his role as a fellow traveler." He gathered the bulk of his material for *The Robber Barons* from secondary sources, most of which "could be classified under the general heading of 'anticapitalist.'" In short, Josephson saw his book as more than a simple history—"it was also a polemic against the capitalist order in the United States, past and present."[2]

Given the intellectual and social climate of the mid-1930s, it is not surprising that the book appeared on best-seller lists soon after its publication and became a Book- of-the-Month Club selection. For the long run,what was more important was that teachers of American history enthusiastically embraced the book, making it the longstanding "classic" study of its subject. College students for several decades would derive whatever understanding they possessed of the nation's pioneer entrepreneurs from Josephson's volume. C. Vann Woodward, then in the early stages of his career but destined to become one of the most widely read and influential American historians in the last half of the twentieth century, hailed Josephson's work. When Josephson turned to the Gilded Age's political leaders and gave them in *The Politicos* the same sort of scathing treatment that he had given the business leaders, young Woodward wrote him in 1938 that the book was "masterly, and quite up to the *Robber Barons*."[3] A survey of history textbooks in the 1970s revealed that Josephson's portrait of the period still dominated the general studies.

After World War II there did begin to appear individual biographies of certain pioneering industrial capitalists that challenged Josephson's interpretation. Historian Allan Nevins portrayed John D. Rockefeller, for example, not as a robber baron but as an industrial statesman who did much that was constructive and helped build the greatest industrial economy in the world. Numerous other entrepreneurs received similar rehabilitation in biographical studies. These historians, however, focused on individuals rather than the economic institutions they created.

Wearied of the argument as to whether the "founding fathers" of the nation's modern economy were robber barons or industrial statesmen— "that is bad fellows or good fellows"—business historian Alfred D. Chander, Jr., published a breakthrough study in 1977. He wryly noted that, even into the 1970s, "most historians, as distrustful as the economists about the enterprises these men built, agreed that they were bad."[4]

Since Chandler uses J. B. Duke and the American Tobacco Company, along with many other examples, to make his argument, a careful look at the book's thesis may be helpful. "The theme propounded here," Chandler states in his introduction, "is that modern business enterprise took the place of market mechanisms in coordinating the activities of the economy and allocating its resources." In numerous sectors of the economy "the visible hand of management replaced what Adam Smith referred to as the invisible hand of market forces." While the market continued to be the generator of demand for goods and services, "modern business enterprise took over the functions of coordinating flows of goods through existing processes of production and distribution, and of allocating funds and personnel for future production and distribution." Chandler then concluded: "As modern business enterprise acquired functions hitherto carried out by the market, it became the most powerful institution in the American economy and its managers the most influential group of economic decision makers. The rise of modern business enterprise in the United States, therefore, brought with it managerial capitalism."[5]

Turning specifically to J. B. Duke, Chandler asserts that of "the innovating entrepreneurs who created modern integrated industrial enterprise few were more successful" than the Tar Heel tobacco magnate. Since Duke leased his cigarette-producing machine and hired the services of advertising agencies, his swift rise to power, according to Chandler, was due neither to his technological skills nor his advertising talents. Rather, "his success resulted from his realization that the marketing of the output of the Bonsack cigarette machine required a global selling and distributing organization." Duke emerged as the most powerful entrepreneur in the cigarette industry "because he was first to build an integrated enterprise."[6]

Many of the policies and practices that had earlier helped W. Duke, Sons and Company achieve its rapid rise were now extended to the larger, national scope of the American Tobacco Company. For example, Duke immediately inaugurated a strict system of cost accounting throughout the company. William R. Harris, whom Duke had earlier hired from the Pullman Palace Car Company, headed the auditing department; its accounts were in such detail that "each brand showed cost per unit, running into five decimal points, of every item entering into its manufacture—tobacco, wrapping of package, casing or sweetening material, shipping cases, down to the straps and nails." Likewise, labor in processing tobacco, operating the machinery, putting goods in cases and handling them was recorded carefully, "carried out to the last decimal...."[7] Comparisons between costs of different factories and within the same factory for different time periods allowed Duke and his plant managers to decide where different brands and products could be produced most cheaply.[8] Eliminating many of the less profitable brands of cigarettes and smoking tobacco, as well as closing some of the less efficient factories, Duke was able to reduce costs per unit sold, lower prices, and still increase profits.

For a couple of years after the American Tobacco Company was organized, the constituent companies kept their own separate administrative organizations. By 1895, however, the administrations of the other four companies had been merged into the structure that J. B. Duke had created in the 1880s. First there was a single purchasing department; then sales departments were unified. The sales department of the American Tobacco Company, according to a 1909 report of the Bureau of Corporation, was "so organized as to secure a high degree of efficiency." The company had sales agents throughout the nation, with each in charge of a particular class of product. The branch offices were comparable to those that J. B. Duke had established in the 1880s, but larger and more numerous.

As business expanded Duke moved his headquarters in 1898 from 45 Broadway to a more spacious building at 111 Fifth Avenue. The sales department and what was called the leaf (buying) department took up much of the space in the new building. The heads of the functional departments at 111 Fifth Avenue, the crucial middle managers, were men whom J. B. Duke carefully selected. John B. Cobb, for example, was the vice president in charge of the leaf department and had worked as a tobacco buyer for a considerable time before joining American Tobacco in 1890.

After the 1890 merger, cigarette-producing plants in New York City were consolidated, and those in Rochester, Virginia, and North Carolina were enlarged. By 1898 production reached 3.78 billion cigarettes from the company's six factories. Two of the six—the one in Durham and the one in Rochester—concentrated exclusively on making the 1.22 billion cigarettes sold in foreign markets, accounting for about 100 percent of all cigarettes exported from the United States. J. B. Duke later testified that his company preferred to manufacture in the United States for foreign markets. If protective tariffs or great distance affected the final price, however, he was quite willing to buy or build factories abroad. Thus in 1894, the American Tobacco Company established factories in Australia; and in 1898 it purchased a leading Japanese firm and sent a richly experienced tobacconist from Durham, Captain E. J. Parrish, to head the profitable enterprise.[9]

Control of the flow of 3 to 5 billion cigarettes from factory to retailer via the jobber remained at 111 Fifth Avenue. Such control not only kept factories operating at a steady pace, but it also protected the quality of the product. That was so because in the days before cellophane wrapping, cigarettes could quickly become dry and taste bitter. Therefore all orders received by a branch office were telegraphed to New York, and managers there selected a factory to process the order, usually sending it to the factory nearest the customer. Factories had attached to them assembling and distribution depots where their products were gathered for shipment. Thus the New York headquarters, with its daily reports from factories and depots and its daily statements of "sales by brands by towns," kept a continuous check on the flow of cigarettes and other tobacco products throughout the country and the world. The report on "sales by brands by towns" was one that J. B. Duke liked especially to study regularly.[10]

One of the most frequently heard charges against such giant corporations as the American Tobacco Company grew to be was that they sought to gouge consumers by raising prices. The fact was, however, that the price of cigarettes declined during the 1890s, while profits remained high. The Bureau of Corporations reported that wholesale prices fell from an average of $3.20 a thousand in 1893 to $2.01 in 1899. In the same period costs fell from $1.74 per thousand to $.89. According to the Bureau, the "proportion of the profits to the net price less tax from 1893 to 1900 ranged from 42.4 percent to 55.7 percent." These profits, according to Chandler, were made possible, at least in part, "by the high, steady throughput and stock-turn," and Duke expected the profits to provide the financial resources he needed to expand the company's activities in the United States as well as abroad.[11] From all across the nation and growing portions of the rest of the world, the profits of the American Tobacco Company poured into the home office in New York. After paying 8 percent on the preferred stock and 12 on the common in 1891, the company retained a surplus of nearly $1,300,000; the following years proved even more lucrative despite the panic of 1893 and the grim economic depression which continued until late in the decade.

While J. B. Duke wanted to use the surplus to expand the scope of the American Tobacco Company, other directors of the company, such as Lewis Ginter and W. H. Butler (formerly a major owner of the Kinney company), disagreed with Duke's preferred strategy of growth and wanted instead to increase and enjoy current dividends. Duke won the fight with his board, and the company embarked on an expansionist strategy that eventually led to control of about four-fifths of the entire tobacco industry, except for cigars. It was this very expansion, however, that eventually led to the federal government's successful antitrust action and the eventual dissolution of the original American Tobacco Company.

One reason for Duke's determination to expand the company was that cigarettes, as profitable as their production proved to be, comprised only a small fraction of the total tobacco industry. As late as 1904 only five cents out of every sales dollar received by the nation's tobacco industry were derived from cigarettes; snuff, which brought in only two cents of the sales dollar, was even less important than cigarettes, but chewing and smoking tobacco accounted for thirty-three cents, while sixty cents was derived from cigar sales.[12] To gain a larger share of the nation's tobacco sales dollar, J. B. Duke led his company in the early 1890s into the expansion of its business in chewing and smoking tobacco by purchasing various firms in Baltimore, Louisville, and other cities.

When asked in the antitrust proceedings of 1908 why the company had embarked so promptly on its program of expansion, J. B. Duke explained: "We wanted to have a full variety...of the different styles of tobacco...." Pointing to the changeable nature of the public's taste,

Duke argued that if "one style [of tobacco product] went out of fashion we would have another style ready for the public to take up...."
Too, certain religious groups and others began to crusade against the 'evil of the cigarette" in the mid-1890s, and, Duke noted, for a year or two sales of the bright-leaf cigarette declined. "Well, I was the one that promoted the idea that we should go into the plug business," Duke declared, "and some of [the other officers and directors] didn't seem to favor it much....."[13]

Not until late in the 1890s did the climax come in the so-called "plug war" between the American Tobacco Company and the older, established manufacturers of chewing tobacco. As early as Christmas, 1892, however, J. B. Duke was already so caught up in the early stages of the competitive battle that he was unable to return to Durham— and the usual visit with his beloved father— during the holidays. He explained why in a handwritten note to his brother Ben: "1st Because ½ dozen plug salesmen from the west will be here next week & I must see them. We are making Rome howl on Plug & are making preparation to do great work the 1st of the year[.] We will make the Plug Mfgrs hustle like we once did Cigarette Mfgrs....I will invest the 30 M [thousand] you sent me for Pa next week. Wishing you all a merry Christmas & happy new year, I am your devoted Bro."[14]

J. B. Duke made "Rome howl on plug" in a variety of ways, some of which were later to figure prominently in the antitrust action. To encourage jobbers, that is wholesale merchants, to handle only the products of American Tobacco, the company resorted to rebates. When this aroused widespread protests as well as various legal actions against the company, the rebates were temporarily dropped despite the opposition of J. B. Duke. Then the system was revived in another form until mounting difficulties led the company to abandon it.[15]

By the mid-1890s the "plug war" raged in earnest, with the Liggett and Myers Company and the Drummond Company, both of St. Louis, teaming up with the Pierre Lorillard Company of Jersey City to fight back against the moves of the American Tobacco Company. With "Battle Ax" as the fighting brand of chewing tobacco, Duke sold it below manufacturing cost, spent large sums on advertising, and absorbed the losses on profits made on cigarettes. John B. Cobb, old friend of the Dukes and head of American Tobacco's leaf department, reported to Ben Duke in 1895 that "indications now are that there will be a considerable quantity of cheap cigarettes put out in the next year or so." To explain why, Cobb continued: "The big Western [i.e., St. Louis] Plug factories are certainly going into the business and it's going to be a lively fight." Cobb believed that American Tobacco had "a good advantage and if the 'Conservatives' don't bother Mr. J. B. D. we will whip the life out of them." Business was "good in nearly every line," Cobb noted, and "Mr. J. B. D." was working harder then ever, like the "war-horse that scents the battle...I really believe he enjoys the prospect of the fight."[16]

Soon after the above optimistic report, Cobb conveyed the news that J. B. Duke had just returned from the company's large plug-producing branch in Louisville, Kentucky, and that the branch would shortly be able "to turn out full 100,000 lbs of Plug per day." Orders were running about 125,000 pounds a day, Cobb added, and the company was about a million pounds behind in orders. "You never saw people appear so glad that they have a business as the A[merican] T[obacco] people are of the Plug business today," he declared. "You know the Plug Factory has been regarded by some of our Co. as a sort of cancer and now we would be almost 'one-legged' without it. Well its just still another proof of Mr. J. B. D's farseeing wisdom. I never saw a more confident man than Mr. J. B. and he has got everybody around here in the same mood.... There can't be but one result, we will down them sure."[17]

Just as Cobb predicted, the St. Louis manufacturers did begin to produce cigarettes to compete with those from the American Tobacco Company. The Drummond company distributed coupons redeemable for cigarettes with packages of its chewing tobacco; and Liggett and Myers, the largest of all the plug producers, also pushed its new brand of cigarettes. It was able to do so because not only had rivals to the Bonsack machine been developed, but as a result of adverse judicial decisions the Bonsack company in 1895 lost certain important patent rights. The American Tobacco Company, consequently, ceased to have exclusive use of the Bonsack machine. As a result of these developments and of the fierce competition between the American Tobacco Company and its rivals in St. Louis, that city led the country in cigarette production in the latter half of 1897.[18]

As the "plug war" raged, consumers of tobacco products no doubt enjoyed their cheaper and cheaper cigarettes and "chews." No consumer relished the struggle more, however, than did J. B. Duke. He explained to one of his allies in St. Louis that Ohio was being worked "on the Knife Scheme by giving a card to consumer to attach 12 tags to," along with a sample of "Battle Ax" and a spiel on its merits. Then sixty-tag cards were distributed "to hold the fellows that have gotten a knife with 12 tags." Duke declared that "all reports are of the most encouraging nature, and I believe that we have hit upon the best scheme ever tried to make chewers." He conceded that the plan was "slow and expensive at the start" but insisted that it would be cheap in the long run. Once Ohio was captured, the campaign would be shifted to other states. As for the lowering of the price of "Battle Ax," which had once sold for fifty cents a pound, to fifteen cents a pound in combination with the purchase by jobbers of the products of the company, Duke argued that it was "a great benefit to other brands, and we are killing two birds with one stone."[19]

By 1898 J. B. Duke and his allies were close to victory in the "plug war." In 1894 the American Tobacco Company had sold only nine million pounds of chewing tobacco; by 1897, however, sales had reached thirty-eight million pounds and were still climbing, In other words, from 5.6 percent of the total plug-tobacco production in 1894, the American Tobacco Company had jumped to nearly 12 percent. The company's losses on plug tobacco alone totalled more than $1,000,000, but profits from cigarettes and other products made that tolerable. Consequently, "it was but natural," the Bureau of Corporations later noted somewhat laconically, that "competitors should become disposed to make peace by combining with the American Tobacco Company interests."[20]

The trend toward the formation of "combinations," small ones as well as vast ones, reached epidemic proportions in the United States around 1900. Before the new combination in the plug-tobacco industry could be achieved, however, J. B. Duke met and largely overcame a new kind of challenge to his leadership of the American Tobacco Company. In order to effect many of the combinations of previously competing companies, enormous amounts of capital were required, and that need opened the way to control of a number of key industries by investment bankers. In steel, farm machinery, and shipbuilding, for example, control shifted from manufacturers to financiers. But in the case of the American Tobacco Company, as one historian has noted, "the financiers apparently shared the goals of James Duke, for he remained president of the firm."[21]

One of the keys to Duke's ultimate success lay in the understanding which he reached with Oliver H. Payne, a multimillionaire who had grown rich in Standard Oil. Working through James R. Keene, then one of the shrewdest operators on Wall Street, Payne and his associates quietly purchased large blocks of stock in the American Tobacco Company and got ready for a showdown at the annual meeting of the company's board of directors. Having learned of what was afoot, J. B. Duke arranged for an interview with Payne, made clear his determination to manage the business in his own manner—or to get out and launch a new, rival business—and ended up by gaining additional and important support from Payne and his friends. A prominent New York banker apprised Ben Duke about the situation: "I spent last night with Colonel Payne on his yacht, and it gave me great pleasure to hear him express his opinion of the President of the [American] Tobacco Co. He thoroughly recognizes his great ability and regards him in all respects with the highest esteem. He had made up his mind that he [J. B. Duke] is the kind of man that he is willing to be harnessed up with."[22]

Payne did indeed become "harnessed up with" J. B. Duke, and before 1898 ended the new plug-tobacco combination, known as the Continental Tobacco Company, was formed. The American Tobacco Company had purchased two of the independent plug businesses in St. Louis in the early fall of 1898; then it sold its four plug-tobacco plants to the Continental company in exchange for stock in the latter company. Six other independent producers, including the Lorillard company, which was allowed to continue its separate organization, also sold out to the Continental Tobacco Company. Although the American Tobacco Company did not own a majority of the stock in Continental, J. B. Duke was elected as its president. He later explained that he had neither planned nor desired to head the new plug combination, which also produced considerable smoking tobacco as well as some snuff, but that "quite a contest" developed between Pierre Lorillard, Harry Drummond, and one or two others who were candidates for the presidency. Payne and one of his associates then came and urged Duke to accept the post. "At first I declined," Duke explained, "and they then said that we had a large interest in the concern and they they did not believe that these [other] fellows would ever be able to organize and run that thing and that…we would lose a lot [of money] unless I did." Duke added that many of his friends urged him not to undertake the additional new task, "but I did it."[23]

Liggett and Meyers alone of the manufacturers of plug tobacco remained out of the new combination—but not for long. In 1898 a group of powerful financiers, including Thomas Fortune Ryan, P. A. B. Widener, William A. Whitney, Anthony N. Brady, and others, organized the Union Tobacco Company. Buying up Blackwell's Tobacco Company in Durham and the National Cigarette Company of New York, which was one of the last independent manufacturers of any importance in that line, the Union Tobacco Company also secured an option on the controlling portion of the Liggett and Myers stock. Aside from the firms that the Union Tobacco Company had rounded up, the financial resources represented by the men involved—all immensely wealthy and experienced tycoons of New York and Philadelphia—made the new organization one to be watched closely.[24]

Despite a flurry of excitement in the tobacco world and on Wall Street, J. B. Duke soon came to terms with the powerful challengers. In New York for these exciting developments, Ben Duke wrote back to Durham: "Tell Pa the business of both the Continental & A[merican] T[obacco] Co is fine. The stocks have been sold down by Union Tob[acc]o people & those who are alarmed at the competition they fear." A few days later, Ben Duke had additional good news: "Confidentially Union Co will be ours. Tob[acc]o was never in so strong a position. I expect to see it sell at $200 soon, [and] it was up to 178 today."[25]

The American Tobacco Company paid heavily to acquire the Union Tobacco Company—$12,500,000 in the former's common stock. J. B. Duke argued, however, that it was "largely a trade to get people, financiers and moneyed people[,] into our concern, and they had of course also bought the Blackwell's Durham concern which was a very old established [firm] and one of the best brands in the country...." Duke always regarded the purchase of the Union Tobacco Company as a special case, as he later admitted somewhat defensively: "I never bought any business with the idea of eliminating competition; it was always [with] the idea of an investment except probably in that one case of the Union Tobacco Co[mpany] and in that case we had an idea...of getting in with ourselves a lot of rich financial people to help finance our properties."[26]

The "rich financial people" to whom J. B. Duke referred—Ryan, Widener, Brady, and others—became directors of the American Tobacco Company as well as of the Continental Tobacco Company in the spring of 1899. Lewis Ginter, Francis Kinney, and the others who helped put together the American Tobacco Company in 1890 had already ceased to be directors, and some had disposed of their stock in the company. Only J. B. Duke, together with his brother Ben and their partner George Watts, remained of the original group of tobacco men, and it was, of course, the president of the two great combinations who continued to be the pivotal figure in the ever-expanding tobacco empire.

That empire reached even grander dimensions with the American Tobacco Company's acquisition of Liggett and Myers. To purchase it, J. B. Duke, O. H. Payne, and H. D. Terrell joined Thomas F. Ryan's group of financiers in forming a syndicate. For the assets of Liggett and Myers and $5,000,000 in cash, the Continental Tobacco Company exchanged $17,500,000 of its common stock and the same amount of its preferred. The total capitalization of the plug combination, the Continental Tobacco Company, thus became and remained $97,690,700. The American Tobacco Company, which had initially been capitalized at $25,000,000 in 1890, paid to holders of its common stock in 1899 a stock dividend of 100 percent, or $21,000,000, from the company's accumulated surplus and the profits from the sale of its plug business to Continental. The stock dividend, together with the $12,500,000 in common stock paid for the Union Tobacco Company, added $33,500,000 to the American's capital stock. From 1899 down to 1904, therefore, the American Tobacco Company was capitalized at $54,500,000 in common stock and $14,000,000 in preferred.[27]

The purchase of Liggett and Myers' was vital for the Continental Tobacco Company's control of "western" chewing tobacco, which was made of the burley tobacco grown in Kentucky and nearby states. But for the "eastern" or "southern" variety of flat plug, less sweet than the western variety and made from bright-leaf tobacco, the acquisition of R. J. Reynolds Tobacco Company of Winston-Salem, North Carolina, was equally important. Although the Continental Tobacco Company acquired about two-thirds of the outstanding capital stock of the Reynolds company in 1899, the Winston-Salem subsidiary enjoyed a high degree of autonomy. Through the acquisition of a number of smaller plug factories, the Reynolds company, according to the Bureau of Corporations, "accomplished a consolidation of the manufacture of plug tobacco in the South somewhat similar to that brought about by the Continental Tobacco Company in the West."[28]

According to J. B. Duke, R. J. Reynolds came up with the proposal to sell his business to Continental. "I personally told Reynolds," Duke explained, "that the Continental Tobacco Company had no organization to manufacture, or that knew how to manufacture[,] his style of goods and I would not favor buying it unless he should stay and run it...." Duke added that in discussing the business he had always told Reynolds, "You run it any way you like." Reynolds accepted Duke's terms and proceeded to build an increasingly important business.[29]

Thus in chewing and smoking tobacco, as earlier in cigarettes, J. B. Duke and his associates had achieved dominance by 1899. Snuff was the next to be conquered, and after a price war between the Atlantic Snuff Company, a combination of four companies formed in 1898, and the Duke-led producers, the American Snuff Company was organized in March, 1900, with a capital of $23,000,000. Less than half of that went to the American Tobacco Company and Continental for their snuff interests, and J. B. Duke, for a change, served as a mere director of the new company rather than as its president. Controlling about 80 percent of the nation's snuff production when formed, the American Snuff Company raised that figure to over 96 percent in a decade.[30]

Compared with the cigar business, however, snuff was small potatoes indeed. A mentioned earlier, sixty cents of each sales dollar received by the nation's tobacco industry in 1904 was derived from cigars. In an effort to gain a larger share of that lucrative business, Duke and his allies organized the American Cigar Company in 1901. Despite intensive efforts, it never gained dominance in the cigar industry, because there were so many small and scattered producers who continued to depend largely on hand-rollers. The American Cigar Company's share of the national output never rose above about 16 percent. As one economic historian has noted, the "persistence of industrial decentralization in cigars indicates the importance of the Bonsack machine in making possible the heavy concentration of the cigarette industry."[31]

Even without control of the cigar industry, Duke and his associates enjoyed ever-increasing profits. The combination bought up subsidiary companies that produced licorice paste, tin foil, cotton bags, wooden boxes and tobacco machinery. It also acquired control of the 392 retail outlets of the United Cigar Stores Company which was organized in 1901.[32]

As if all the expansion—forward, backward, and even sideways— were not enough, J. B. Duke and the inner group that controlled the combination pulled a complicated maneuver in 1901 that was to be short-lived. But it also played a part in bringing down on the combination the antitrust club of the federal government. That maneuver was the formation of the Consolidated Tobacco Company.

Much of the vast expansion of both the American Tobacco Company and the Continental Tobacco Company had been accomplished through the exchange of blocks of stock in the two companies for the various properties being acquired. Ownership was, therefore, scattered. Furthermore, with dominance achieved after about 1900 in much of the tobacco industry, save for cigars, every prospect was for increased earnings by the combination. There was also an immediate need for additional capital for expansion, both in the cigar industry and in foreign countries. Accordingly, J. B. Duke and the financiers who had joined him in the late 1890s organized the Consolidated Tobacco Company in June, 1901, with a capital stock of $30,000,000, paid for in cash. The sixteen directors of the new company—including its president, J. B. Duke, Ben Duke, and George Watts as well as a New York financial firm that had worked closely with the combination for a number of years, Moore and Schley—held 94 percent of the Consolidated stock.[33]

Consolidated offered to exchange its 4 percent bonds for equal par value of the Continental company's common stock and at the rate of $200 per $100 of the American Tobacco Company's common stock. Since Continental had not paid a dividend and had been selling on the stock market for $20 to $30 a share, the holders of Continental common were naturally happy to make the exchange and have the guaranteed 4 percent from the Consolidated bond. The American Tobacco Company had paid 6 percent dividends on its common stock after the 100 percent stock dividend in 1899, and the Consolidated bond promised 8 percent. Consolidated's offer was quickly accepted by almost all of the stock holders in the other two companies.

The men who owned Consolidated thereby acquired effective control of both the American and Continental companies. They also became entitled to all the profits of both companies in excess of the fixed amounts that would be required for the dividends on preferred stock and for the interest on Consolidated's bonds. That profits would increase substantially was a strong bet. The costly expenditures of the battles in plug and snuff were now a thing of the past, and the excise taxes on tobacco products, which had been raised in 1898 at the time of the Spanish-American War, were scheduled for reduction. In fact, Congress passed the act reducing the taxes before Consolidated was organized. Since the prices of the combination's products were not correspondingly reduced, much of the increase in earnings of the tobacco companies went to the men who owned the Consolidated company. It lasted only a little over three years, but during that time the earnings of the American and Continental companies were sufficient to pay dividends on preferred stock, interest on the Consolidated bonds, and to leave a profit of around $30,000,000 to the Consolidated Tobacco Company on its investment. Put another way, Consolidated paid $6,000,000 in dividends, accumulated a surplus of $17,000,000, and, in the words of the Bureau of Corporations, "substantially became entitled" to the increase in the surpluses of the American and Continental companies, which amounted to over $7,000,000.[34]

While the formation of the Consolidated Tobacco Company enriched those who owned it, the new capital furnished by Consolidated played a vital role in the foreign expansion of the American Tobacco

Company, as will be shown. J. B. Duke's satisfaction about the profits in the expansion was tempered, however, by developments in the United States having to do with President Theodore Roosevelt and his trust-busting proclivities.

In 1904 in a trail-blazing case, the Supreme Court of the United States upheld the federal government's contention that the Northern Securities Company, a vast holding company involving J. P. Morgan and other powerful magnates, was an illegal device for restraining trade and therefore in violation of the Sherman Anti-Trust Act of 1890. The Consolidated Tobacco Company, also a great holding company, was not unlike the Northern Securities Company—and J. B. Duke and his associates moved quickly in an attempt to avoid trouble from Roosevelt and the Department of Justice.

Needless to say, Theodore Roosevelt was not beloved by the J. P. Morgans and J. B. Dukes of America. Duke's all-time favorite president was, in fact, none other than the late William McKinley. Duke went to great trouble to commission in Italy a ten-foot-high bronze statue of McKinley and have it prominently installed on the estate near Somerville, New Jersey, known as Duke's Farm. Moreover, when Senator Mark Hanna, McKinley's close friend and ally, died early in 1904, Duke conveyed his deepest sympathy to the family "because I feel the loss of a personal friend to whom I had been attached, and feel also that the country has lost its most useful citizen."[35]

The "good old days" of McKinley and Hanna were gone, however, and the Consolidated Tobacco Company was an embarrassment in view of the Northern Securities case. Moreover, investors on Wall Street and elsewhere had been confused all along by the complex relationship between the American, Continental, and Consolidated companies. In October, 1904, therefore, the three companies were all merged into one company called the American Tobacco Company. All intercompany holdings of securities were canceled, and the securities of the reorganized American Tobacco Company were exchanged for the remaining securities of the old companies. The preferred stock of the old companies was exchanged for 6 percent bonds of the new company, and the Consolidated bonds were exchanged, half for 6 percent preferred stock and half for 4 percent bonds of the new company. Common stock in the new American Tobacco Company was swapped for Consolidated common stock, and, as one historian notes, "the previous concentration of control was perpetuated and strengthened in the new arrangement."[36]

The abandonment of the old holding-company arrangement in the Consolidated Tobacco Company did not suffice, of course, to remove the vast tobacco empire headed by J. B. Duke from the scrutiny of the aroused Justice department. One may be sure that as Theodore Roosevelt began his own, full term as president in March, 1905, Duke and his associates kept a sharp eye on the president. Well they might, for the American Tobacco Company was headed for trouble with the federal government.

4

J. B. DUKE OFF DUTY

As hardworking as J. B. Duke truly was, he also enjoyed what might be called off-duty moments. Before the 1890s, when he became increasingly prominent in the tobacco industry, little is known about his private life. As much as he believed in advertising his business, he strongly shunned personal publicity and kept as low a personal profile as possible. Moreover, when J. B. and Ben Duke began to possess surplus capital in the early 1890s, the first use they put it to was the establishment of a large textile mill in Durham, which will be discussed subsequently. In other words, conspicuous consumption, which was rampant among the rich in the 1890s, did not interest the Dukes at that time.

Concerning the colorful and paradoxical decade of the 1890s in the United States, one historian has declared that, among rich people, "conspicuous waste and conspicuous leisure were more obvious than at any other time in American history," and "extravagance was tasteless, blatant, and unremitting."[1] Two social historians of the era note that "'conspicuous living' reached absurd heights in the United States during the 'gay nineties'—a decade marked...by five years of depression and widespread unemployment."[2]

While New York and other large cities were divided as never before between a relatively small class of high-living haves and a mass of economically deprived have-nots, the farmers of the South and West floundered miserably in the serious economic depression sparked off by the "panic of 1893."

Seeking an explanation for their grim economic plight, farmers, first in the Farmers' Alliance and then in the People's (Populist) party,

57

blamed, among other things, the "trusts." Tobacco farmers in the South particularly blamed J. B. Duke and the "tobacco trust" for the painfully low prices they received for their crops. Finding some person or some thing to blame for one's economic misery is, of course, a completely human and perhaps inevitable reaction. The tobacco farmers were, however, not correct in their analysis.

In the first place, the last thirty or so years of the nineteenth century brought a "broad, fairly steady decline in prices;" and the wholesale costs of every major category of goods, including farm products along with most other things, "fell considerably during the years which produced big business."[3] In other words, not only did the price of leaf tobacco hit new lows in the 1890s but so also did the price of cotton, wheat, corn, and most other commodities.

In the second place, the American Tobacco Company, as powerful as it grew to be, was never the sole buyer of tobacco produced in the United States, and the company was never in a position to set or control the price of leaf tobacco. Both bright leaf and burley tobacco had buyers from Britain as well as from continental and Asian nations. (In fact, J. B. Duke helped to create much of that foreign market.) The leading British tobacco manufacturer became worried in 1894 about the increasing power in the leaf market of the American Tobacco Company; after a careful investigation, however, he concluded that "the American Tobacco Company was not in a position to dictate prices on its purchases of leaf."[4]

These economic facts about prices, and especially leaf tobacco prices, were either unknown or ignored in the 1890s (and after) by those who specialized in verbal assaults on J. B. Duke and the "tobacco trust." The fact that Duke, like his father and brother, made no secret of strong support for the Republican party added to his attractiveness as a target for such Democratic newspapers as Josephus Daniels' Raleigh *News and Observer*. Washington Duke, living in North Carolina, probably worried more about the bitter attacks on the "tobacco trust" and its president than did J. B. Duke himself.

Eschewing a yacht or even an impressive residence, J. B. Duke continued to live in rented rooms in the early 1890s. He was, in fact, remarkably restrained for the 1890s, the flamboyant era of Lillian Russell and 'Diamond Jim' Brady. Like many persons in the pre-automotive age, however, J. B. Duke did take pride in his horses. On a visit to New York in 1892 George Watts reported back to Durham: "Buck is enjoying his horses, [and] his mate to Maud is a fine one so he has a dashing team now. He spends the evenings talking & planning his new stable...."[5]

Sure enough, the first thing Duke arranged to have built in New York was an impressive multi-story stone stable uptown. For his driver he pulled a light-skinned African American from the factory's shipping room. The driver, as one of Duke's biographers relates, "took to his promotion with vast aplomb, sporting a rakish cockade in his glazed coachman's hat and in his scarf a moonstone pin large as a silver dollar."[6]

Two things happened in 1893 that were to loom large in Duke's off-duty life: he met Mrs. Lillian McRedy, and he bought a farm on the Raritan river just outside Somerville, New Jersey. Just how or where he met Mrs. McRedy is not known, but since her first husband had encouraged her to become an accomplished equestrienne, a mutual interest in horses may have brought Duke and her together. Another story has it that they met in a hotel lobby. At any rate, she quickly became an important part of J. B.Duke's life. Born in Camden, New Jersey, she was musically talented and received vocal training from a prominent teacher in Philadelphia before moving to New York in pursuit of a concert career. There, however, she met and married a well-to-do coffee broker and sportsman named W. E. McRedy.

Not so much beautiful as handsome, Lillian McRedy was full-figured in the hour-glass style of the era, and she dressed with great flair. Blonde, blue-eyed, and flirtatious, she began to quarrel with her husband; when she sued for separation, however, he countered with a suit for divorce, naming three men as corespondents and introducing incriminating letters. W. E. McRedy won an outright divorce. Soon after that Lillian McRedy met J. B. Duke.[7]

The thirty-five-year-old bachelor may never have met such an enchantress before. In addition to her musical interests and talent, she read French novels in French, so Duke, who was never known to read anything beyond business reports, had encountered a phenomenon new and strange to him. Within some months after their meeting, she had become his mistress, and Duke purchased for her a commodious graystone house on West 68th Street, just off Central Park. While his nominal residence had become the Hoffman House Hotel, he actually spent much off-duty time at the house on West 68th.

The family came to know Lillian McRedy as "Uncle Buck's sweetheart." Ben Duke's young daughter Mary was so taken by her that, for a number of years, she added "Lillian" as her middle name. Washington Duke, whom his sons deeply venerated, for a long time knew nothing about his youngest son's private life. When the "Old Gentleman," as many in Durham referred to the family patriarch, did learn certain facts about his son's relationship with Lillian McRedy, the president of the American Tobacco Company received a preemptory parental summons to Durham, and a dire chain of events was set off. But that would come early in the twentieth century.

In the 1890s Washington Duke had only to worry about some of the advertising material used by the American Tobacco Company—specifically, the small pictures of actresses clad in acrobatic tights and other such costumes that were distributed with packs of cigarettes and avidly collected by millions of Americans. "My dear Son," Washington Duke began his letter to Buck, "I have received the enclosed letter from the Rev. John C. Hocutt and am very much impressed with the wisdom of the argument against circulating lascivious photographs with cigarettes…." The senior Duke noted that he had "always looked upon distribution of this character of advertisement as wrong in its pernicious effects upon young man[-] and woman-hood, and therefore [it] has not jingled with my religious impulses." Insisting that "we owe Christianity all the assistance we can lend it in any form, which is paramount to any other consideration," Washington Duke went on to note that "this mode of advertising" would be used against cigarettes and strengthen the arguments against them "in the legislative halls of the states." Concluding with the statement that he would be much pleased to learn of a change in advertising policy, Washington Duke remained "Affectionally, your father."[8]

Although J. B. Duke could hardly end the time-hallowed use of pictures of curvaceous women in cigarette advertising, he no doubt sent some sort of conciliatory message to his father. After 1890, J. B. Duke wrote fewer and fewer business letters and rarely took the time for a personal letter. When Ben Duke, for example, wondered if he should go up to New York for what promised to be an important meeting of the directors of the American Tobacco Company, he wrote W. W. Fuller, legal counsel for the company: "I wish you would do me the kindness to ask Buck if he does not think I should come. I would write him myself but know he does not answer letters and I do not care to trouble him with one."[9]

Happily preoccupied with his work during the day—and with Lillian McRedy in the evenings, J. B. Duke stumbled on to his one lasting recreational passion in 1893. At a time when many rich New Yorkers were acquiring elaborate country estates in the Adirondack mountains, in the new Tuxedo Park development, or on Long Island, Duke displayed his independent streak by buying a 327-acre farm on the Raritan river just outside Somerville, New Jersey. While fronting on an attractive bend in the Raritan and convenient because of a rail connection with New York, the land itself was flat and uninteresting and the soil poor. That did not faze Duke, however, for he soon set about transforming his purchase.

Almost immediately he began buying adjacent farms and eventually ended up with a 2200-acre estate known as Duke's Farm. (After his death, his daughter Doris Duke added 500 acres to what had then become known as Duke Farms.) Duke's plans for his rural retreat evolved over the years. Initially interested in thoroughbred race horses, he hired an architect to design two stables, one in New York and one on the farm. He also had a half-mile race track constructed on the farm. When a New York journalist visited the farm in 1895, however, he reported that Duke was switching from horses to cows and that the "grand" stable was being converted to a dairy barn for a collection of 250 registered Guernsey cows, for which feed was produced on the farm. There was also a large poultry operation that included prize-winning species from England.[10]

Perhaps because Washington Duke and his sons all began as farmers, they had a special fondness for growing things and for flowers and ornamental trees and plants. Although the scale of operations would increase dramatically around the turn of the century, J. B. Duke's landscaping on his farm began modestly in 1895 when he brought up from Durham an old friend of the family's who was a horticulturalist and former Methodist minister, Reuben Hibberd. After his work got underway, Hibberd reported back to Durham that J. B. Duke seemed "very pleased" so far. With a "big force of hands and teams," Hibberd expected "to make a very pretty job." Yet he had certain reservations about the undertaking: "I shall be very glad to get back into Christian civilization again. All the hands I work 'Cuss.' The Newspaper man 'Cussed.' The fountain man in New York Cussed and I think the whole crew cuss from the boys on the street to the city Mayor. The Methodist Preacher did not cuss perhaps he *couldn't*[;] neither could he preach.... New York for money, Durham for Christianity & Brotherly Love.'"[11]

Hibberd soon returned to his more comfortable environment in Durham, but J. B. Duke had barely begun his estate-improving activities. Toward the end of the century he engaged a well-known architectural firm in Boston to begin an extensive building program on the estate. In addition to numerous and spacious cottages for key personnel, Duke had the architects design and build a vast coach house that was (and still is) perhaps the most interesting building on the estate. Commanding its site by its great length, it contained housing for coaches, landaus, and such in its central cross axis; stables for thoroughbred horses were at one end and offices for Duke and his estate manager at the other. Above these offices, on the second floor, was a spacious apartment, perhaps for the coachman or, later, chauffeur. Asymmetrically placed to the side of the main entrance was a five-story Norman clock tower with faces on all four sides and a pointed spire topped by a weather vane. Contemporary newspapers described the building as "palatial."

In contrast, Duke merely added rooms to the original farmhouse, which he made his residence and referred to in his bachelor days as "The Clubhouse." Eventually it consisted of about fifty rooms, but it never quite matched in style or distinction the magnificent landscaping of the estate.

A vast but graceful glass conservatory contained a palm house as well as many exotic plants. In 1909 a second conservatory was designed by a leading architectural firm of the era, Horace Trumbauer of Philadelphia, and used for the growing of fruits as well as exotic plants. The original greenhouse then began to be reserved for the growing of orchids. (The 1909 conservatory would later become a part of Doris Duke's "Gardens of the Nations" display.)

While the greenhouses no doubt gave Duke much pleasure, what he especially liked and focused on was the landscaping of the grounds. He personally planned an internal network of roads to ramble informally from one vista to another, with trees and shrubs planted along their edges. Deciding to use large rocks - - boulders - - Duke brought them on to the estate in massive quantities and finally purchased a quarry in a nearby county to obtain an unlimited supply. He had rustic bridges, large and small, laid up in boulders, constructed numerous well-houses and pavilions, and built miles of walls constructed of them.

Perhaps recalling the gently rolling hills of his childhood home in the Carolina Piedmont, Duke had enough earth moved on his estate to totally transform the topography. Hillocks and knolls, all densely planted in conifers and hardwoods, replaced the originally flat fields, and two small (200 feet high) "mountains" became prominent features.

Duke had a passion for water, especially dramatically moving water. As a result, he ended up with a chain of nine lakes covering a total of about seventy-five acres. (Earth excavated to create the lakes was used to make the knolls and hills.) The highest lake was a reservoir into which water was pumped from the Raritan and from which water then flowed downward from one lake to another until it returned to the Raritan. To enjoy water in action, Duke had it "flowing over boulder-made rapids, and small dams, tumbling over craggy cliffs, and rising skyward in jet streams, falling in multiple arrangements, overflowing bowls and basins."[12]

Although all of this reflected his vision and choice, Duke did not, of course, accomplish it without expert help. In 1903 he hired Horatio N. Buckenham as his chief landscape architect and engineer. A native of England with offices in Boston, Buckenham's work became known to Duke when he visited the estates where Buckenham had worked, such as William A. Vanderbilt's Biltmore in Asheville, North Carolina, and estates of Whitelaw Reid and William Whitney in the New York area. Since Frederick Law Olmsted, the nation's foremost designer of parks and landscapes, had worked at Biltmore over a number of years (1888-1895), Buckenham had enjoyed direct exposure to the handiwork of the nation's chief exponent of the naturalistic park.

Buckenham's colleague, Louis L. Miller, was also a landscape architect and an engineer who specialized in water projects. Both Buckenham and Miller took up residence in Sommerville, where Miller remained. Working with this team, then, Duke largely completed his landscaping project by around 1911.[13]

While on a tour of Europe following his first marriage in 1904, Duke summoned Buckenham to join him in studying estates that Duke particularly liked. Buckenham also helped purchase plants, including thousands of rhododendrons. In addition to many thousands of evergreens — 60,000 in just one order from Europe and 20,000 blue spruce in another order — Buckenham planted many native hardwoods, including some outstanding specimens purchased in the Somerville area. When a friend once asked Duke just how many trees and shrubs he had planted at Duke's Farm, he replied over 2,000,000 — and that he had a written record of all purchases.

How much all of this cost, no one really knows, though various estimates have been made. A reporter from the *New York Times* visited Duke's Farm in 1905 and noted that J. B. Duke had, over the previous five or so years, "already [probably] expended upward of $2,000,000" above the cost of the land.[14] Since many of the most expensive improvements came in the five or so years after the reporter's visit, a conservative estimate of the final total cost might be around $6,000,000. Regardless, Duke is reported to have said, "Hang the expense but give me my money's worth."[15]

For many years, Duke welcomed the public to visit the estate. The local newspaper reported in 1900 that people enjoyed picnicking in "Duke's Grove" and that on Sundays they gathered wildflowers as they enjoyed seeing "the many improvements this popular man is making on his property...."[16] Duke enjoyed friendly relations with his neighbors in Somerville. Not only did he occasionally attend services in the local Methodist church and contribute generously to it, but he also joined the Chamber of Commerce and a local country club. Allowing the grounds of Duke's Farm to be used for various public events, he did considerable business in Somerville and employed a great number of its residents in all categories from laborers to professionals.[17]

When some visitors to the grounds at Duke's Farm began to abuse the privilege by trashing up the place and otherwise acting thoughtlessly, Duke hired off-duty policemen to patrol the grounds on horseback. Then after Duke's daughter, Doris, was born in 1912 and with continuing problems from careless or thoughtless visitors, he finally closed the estate to the public in 1915.

Among the many items of interest at Duke's Farm, the fountains ranked high. There were about three dozen, many with adjustable sprays that Duke preferred. They were described by *American Home and Gardens* in 1914 as ranking with "the most beautiful in the world."[18] Complementing the fountains, Duke selected or had made dozens of statues which he placed strategically around the estate. By 1903 he had forty and during his visit to Europe in the winter of 1904, he purchased a number of additional ones. A bronze figure of the "Durham Bull" was one of his early and favorite pieces; the ten-foot-high statue of President McKinley was mentioned earlier. On a visit to Duke's Farm, Bishop John C. Kilgo so much admired one of Duke's statues, the "Dresden Farmer," that Duke had it shipped to Durham to be placed on the campus of Trinity College. There it remains to this day (2001), is now known as "The Sower," and has become an important icon or symbol for Duke University. "The beautification of the estate with outdoor statuary of marble and bronze was more than a rich man's display of wealth," declared the compiler of the estate's nomination for the National Register of Historic Places. "His choices were very personal, many pieces being made especially for him." More significant perhaps than the acknowledged works of art were the pieces that reflected his roots and personal history, such as the Durham Bull, President McKinley, the Dresden Farmer, and several others.[19]

Ironically, J. B.Duke never built a residence at Duke's Farm to match the splendor of the grounds. In 1904, he talked of having an appropriate mansion built, but his first marriage proved to be so disastrous and short-lived that nothing came of those plans. In 1909, after his second marriage, he commissioned the Trumbauer firm to design two mansions, one on Fifth Avenue at 78th street, which was actually built, as will be discussed, and one at Duke's Farm.

For the New Jersey mansion, Duke reversed the usual procedure and had elaborate landscaping done around the proposed site for the mansion before any construction was begun. Abandoning the rustic boulder style that had hitherto predominated on the estate, Duke chose a more formal style of stone and cement bridges and balustrades, such as he had come to admire on numerous British country estates. Duke and his landscape architects spent a year laying out vistas from the elevated site that had been chosen for the mansion and even built a temporary tower to check out the views.

The Trumbauer office, probably utilizing the great talent of Julian Abel, the pioneer African-American architect who would later design the buildings at Duke University, came up with the plans for an elegant mansion inspired by historic French chateaux and somewhat resembling William Vanderbilt's Biltmore. In 1911 construction proceeded as far as the building of a two-level underground basement, a service court, and a tunnel. Construction was abruptly halted at that point, and it was never to be resumed. This was probably because the United States Supreme Court on May 29, 1911, rendered its decision in the federal government's anti-trust action against the American Tobacco Company and ordered the dissolution of that company. To say that J. B. Duke was shocked and angered by the decision would be an understatement: he would soon be contemplating the purchase of a great mansion in London and was clearly no longer interested in building one at Duke's Farm.

Apparently indifferent to music and literature, J. B. Duke expressed his aesthetic side in his deep love for landscaping and horticulture, for various types of water displays, and for statuary. All of those interests found their fullest expression at Duke's Farm from 1893 until his death in 1925. Workaholic he may have been, but he also relished and knew how to enjoy his off-duty time.

5

J. B. DUKE INVADES BRITAIN—AND THE BRITISH-AMERICAN OUTCOME

Speaking not so much boastfully as ambitiously, J. B. Duke had declared in 1889, concerning W. Duke Sons and Company, "The world is now our market for our product...."[1] By 1900, Duke's American Tobacco Company had gone a long way toward achieving that global goal. By 1900 the foreign market accounted for around one-third of sales of cigarettes produced by the American Tobacco Company in its United States factories. Conspicuous areas of "unconquered" territory remained, however, especially on the European continent and in Great Britain.

State monopolies kept the door shut in some European countries, but for access to the German market, Duke arranged for the American Tobacco Company in 1901 to acquire a controlling stake in the Jasmatzi firm of Dresden, one of Germany's largest cigarette manufactures. Equally if not more tempting, however, was the British market, for tobacco played an increasingly important role in the nation's and the British Empire's economic life since the days of King James I in the early 1600s. The American Tobacco Company maintained an important depot in London and by 1897 employed in Britain four "travelers," as the British called drummers or sales agents.[2] Facing vigorous competition from British firms, the American Tobacco Company suffered declining sales for several years in the last 1890s and then actually lost money in its important London depot by 1900. One reason was that, in response to the cost of the Boer War in South Africa, the British government raised import duties on a number of things, including manufactured tobacco products.

J. B. Duke, armed with plenty of capital made available through the formation of the Consolidated Tobacco Company, determined to do something about the American Tobacco Company's situation in Britain. Accordingly, in the fall of 1901 he made what seems to have been his first trip abroad. Accompanied by two of his associates, he soon thoroughly shook up the British tobacco industry by paying a bit more than $5,347,000 for Ogden's Limited, one of the major tobacco firms in Britain.[3]

An "American invasion" led by J.B. Duke had for some years been anticipated with a mixture of fear and disdain by many in the British tobacco industry. The rapid growth of the American Tobacco Company, both within the United States and in the global market, had been closely watched. At one point in the mid-1890s there were fears in Britain that the American Tobacco Company might become powerful enough to control the leaf market in the United States. (In 1902 over 90 percent of unmanufactured tobacco entering Britain came from the United States.) Careful investigation revealed, however, that, contrary to the loud oft-repeated allegations of American farmers and demagogic politicians, Duke's "trust" could not dictate prices on its own leaf purchases, much less cut off the supply of leaf to foreign buyers.[4]

The largest and most influential tobacco manufacturer in Britain, the W. D. and H. O. Wills firm of Bristol, England, naturally took the lead in scrutinizing the moves of J. B. Duke on the global front. Tracing its origins back to 1786, the Wills company gained additional strength and superiority over its British rivals when it bet on the Bonsack cigarette machine even before young Buck persuaded his partners in W. Duke, Sons and Company to to the same thing. Henry (Harry) Wills, an engineer himself, travelled to Paris to see the Bonsack machine on exhibition there; then he persuaded his partners to invite James Bonsack to set up a machine for a trial in England, and the Wills firm ended up gaining the exclusive right to use Bonsack's invention in Britain. By 1888 Wills had eleven Bonsack machines in use at Bristol, and, as concerned cigarette production, Wills was way ahead of its British rivals.[5]

Nevertheless, the large, rich Wills family had, as one British historian states, "long trembled when the name of Duke raised in conversation.[6] As early as 1895, the Wills' board discussed amalgamation with other British tobacco firms as a protective measure against Duke's possible predatory moves. Alternatively, the board considered amalgamation with the American Tobacco Company itself as a possibility.[7] Nothing was decided about the matter at that time.

Despite earlier dilly-dallying, when J. B. Duke not only materialized in London but also quickly purchased Ogden's, the Wills family took the lead in organizing a bold defensive action. Although some nervous directors of Wills favored selling out to the American Tobacco Company for a stiff price, Sir William H. Wills, a senior member of the family who exercised great influence as chairman of the board, held out strongly for amalgamation with the leading tobacco manufacturers in Britain.

On October 1, 1901, London's *Tobacco Trade Review* correctly reported, with suitable patriotic overtones, the rumors that were flying around:

> We are authoritatively informed that in view of the 'American invasion' a defensive organisation of British manufacturers has been formed, and that it will be a strong body of a most influential and representative character, including in its ranks already the leading British firms. Its object will naturally be to protect British industry, British trade, British methods, and British capital, as opposed to American methods and American dollars.[8]

Within a few days of the above report, the formation of the Imperial Tobacco Company was announced. Led by Wills, thirteen British tobacco manufacturers had come together in a sort of federation to do battle against the "American invasion." At a time when amalgamations of varying types were generally unpopular in Britain, the press sympathized with the tobacco manufacturers. In this case, the thinking was, foreign invasion could only be met by a counter-amalgamation, and "a British combination was infinitely preferable to a foreign one."[9]

J. B. Duke, perhaps unknowingly, had chosen an interesting time to "invade" Britain.Queen Victoria died early in 1901 and was succeeded by her oldest son, who became King Edward VII. Duke, therefore, arrived as the colorful Edwardian Era was getting underway. Although thoughtful Britons were painfully surprised by how few foreign nations felt any sympathy at all for Britain in the Boer War, the public at large allowed it patriotism to slide easily into jingoistic chauvinism. The general mood in 1901 was probably not too different from what it had been when Queen Victoria in 1897 celebrated her Diamond Jubilee with unparalleled pageantry and imperial splendor. The great historian Arnold Toynbee later remembered watching, as a young boy, the vast procession of representatives from all parts of Britain's far-flung empire as they paraded through the streets of London. "I remember the atmosphere," he wrote. "It was: Well, here we [Britons] are on top of the world, and we have arrived at this peak to stay there—forever! There is, of course, a thing called history, but history is something unpleasant that happens to other people. We are comfortably outside of all that...."[10]

Be that as it may, J. B. Duke was not impressed. His views would gradually change— but in 1901 his initial reaction to Britain, so long widely recognized as the world's greatest military and industrial power, was distinctly on the negative side. The shock of being abroad must have influenced Duke, for he did an uncharacteristic thing: he sent a hand-written letter to his aging father. Sounding like a typical American chauvinist himself, he declared that he was "not much impressed with this country" and considered the people to be "back numbers" who were "narrow minded & slow." After pointing to the United States' favorable balance of trade and England's excess of imports over exports, Duke turned to the purpose of his trip: "We have bought one of the best concerns in England [Ogden's] & it has raised a great howl[;] they call us the American invaders & are appealing to the public to repel us. I don't know how much public prejudice will affect our business but fear it is going to make it hard for us." Duke added that he had "worked very hard" since arriving in London but hoped to get off shortly to Paris and "from there to Italy for a couple of weeks to see if I can get some ideas to further develop the Farm."

After mentioning that his eczema had "been worse then usual" for ten days or so but that otherwise his health was splendid, the youngest son closed on an affectionate note: "I regret exceedingly that business is such that I can't be more with you & when I get back I want you to try & come up & pay me a long visit at the farm. I know that it must be very lonely for you since Ben is away from home so much. I hope to be able to see more of you when I return, & that your health may continue good. With much love to your dear self & all the family. I am your devoted Son."[11]

J. B. Duke's fear that attacks on the "American invaders" would complicate his British plans proved entirely correct. Urging smokers to "Buy British," the new Imperial Tobacco Company demonstrated a mastery of many of the techniques that American manufacturers, and especially J. B. Duke, had long used. One of the patriotic advertisements used by Imperial declared:

> Rule Britannia! Britannia rules the waves!
> Britons to Yankee Trusts will ne'er be slaves!
> We'll not encourage Yankee Bluff
> We'll support John Bull with every puff![12]

While Imperial appealed to British patriotism, Duke had Ogden's (which was really the American Tobacco Company) go for the pocket nerve. That is, Ogden's slashed prices on all its leading brands. In attempting to counter this, Imperial decided not to lower its prices but to use a bonus scheme for retailers, a scheme that was pushed by Harry Wills. The bonus was available, however, only for those jobbers and tobacco retailers who pledged not to display or sell any American-made or Ogden's-produced goods for a term of years. (This would probably have been illegal in the United States.)

Duke then countered this with an even more generous bonus scheme from Ogden's. Capitalizing on his ample war chest, Duke had Ogden's offer to its customers among the retailers the company's entire net profit on its British business for the next four years, and about $1 million (200,000 pounds) a year in addition. The final sentence of this circular attracted a great deal of sympathetic attention: "To participate in this offer we do not ask you to boycott the goods of any other manufacturer."[13]

As the battle between Imperial and Ogden's raged in Britain, it also reached into distant parts of the world. E. J. Parrish, the Durham native whom J. B. Duke had sent to Japan to represent the American Tobacco Company, reported that his colleague in Calcutta, India, was being bothered by "cheap cigarettes [made] by Wills and others." Parrish advised the home office: "We have no doubt the English Combination is disposed to force things in India, the Straits and China. We have no doubt the A[merican] T[obacco] Co., with our help, will be able to make it very interesting for England's manufacturers in that territory."[14]

Both in Britain and the Far East, as well as South Asia, the Americans succeeded, in Parrish's words, in making things "interesting" for the Imperial company. As a countermove against the Americans, Imperial made noises about invading the American market, and reportedly began considering sites for factories in the United States in the summer of 1902.

In Britain itself, however, Imperial's bonus scheme for retailers came close to backfiring. This was because of its requirement that those signing up for it had to exclude all competing brands from Ogden's and the American Tobacco Company. Grumbling increased among retailers that Imperial's bonus agreement seemed designed not only to defeat Duke but also to establish a monopoly for Imperial of the retail trade in tobacco in Great Britain. Angry mass meetings of retailers in London and other large cities inspired Imperial to reconsider its bonus policy.[15]

Over the bitter opposition of Harry Wills, the original promoter of the bonus plan, Imperial's directors moved to modify the restrictive terms of the agreement. Harry Wills, according to the historian of the Wills company, was so displeased that he considered resigning from Imperial's board; he decided, however, to stay on in order to push his view that the "only course open to Imperial was to amalgamate with the Americans."[16]

Using his own money, Harry Wills dispatched his personal assistant and brother-in-law, Hugo Cunliffe-Owen, to Paris to talk with a prominent cigarette-paper manufacturer who was also well known to J. B. Duke. Cunliffe-Owen persuaded the Frenchman to travel to New York, again at Harry Wills' expense, to make discreet overtures to Duke about a possible compromise or deal.

On another front, when Imperial's directors were meeting in London in July, 1902, Thomas Fortune Ryan, a key ally of J. B. Duke, joined the meeting, probably at the invitation of Sir William H. Wills. Recalling that meeting some years later, a senior official in Imperial described how, after Ryan had spoken pleasantly to the group for a few minutes, Sir William "with a genial air, rose from his seat and drew Mr. Ryan aside to a sofa in a corner where the two men engaged in what seemed to be an amiable conversation...."[17] Sir William also invited Ryan to his home and saw him on several occasions.

As a result of all these delicate maneuvers, Ryan cabled J. B. Duke who, accompanied by W. W. Fuller (an old Durham friend who was chief legal counsel for the American Tobacco Company), returned to London for a series of crucial meetings with Imperial's top leaders, including several members of the Wills family. The outcome of these meetings would be the termination of what might be called the Anglo-American tobacco war and the establishment of the British-American Tobacco Company.

There were formidable obstacles to any meeting of minds between J. B. Duke and his British counterparts. Both sides had undoubtedly to overcome a great psychological barrier in the form of stereotypical thinking. Duke, as noted earlier, had initially characterized the British people whom he had observed on his first visit to London in 1901 as "back numbers" who were "narrow minded & slow." He said nothing, as so many Americans of that time most certainly would have added, about the British being cold, and snobbish to boot. That Edwardian England had more distinct and more rigid class divisions than did the United States was, in fact, quite true.

The British, on the other hand, had in mind different but just as numerous stereotypes about Americans. One British historian suggests, in fact, that "upstart American cousins were still figures of fun in British business circles" in the early 1900s. He goes on to admit that "an enlightened few" realized, however, that the United States' growing railroads, mass production methods, and steel-making capacity were "symbols of the world's new leading industrial power."[18] It would require developments during World War I, however, to drive home that last point. And in the meantime, British scorn for the alleged brashness, ruthlessness, and general uncouthness of American businessmen found a ready target in the person of J. B. Duke. And that was quite unfair. In the first place, he was not a brash person. While his formal education had been quite limited, all the evidence suggests that he was a soft-spoken, even-tempered person, one whom a later business acquaintance (Roy Hunt of the Aluminum Company of America) characterized as a "courteous Southern gentleman" who seemed "very friendly and very keen."[19] As for Duke's alleged "ruthlessness," in light of Imperial's tactics in the great tobacco war of 1901–1902, it seems highly debatable that Duke was any more "ruthless" than his British counterparts.

Despite stereotyped thinking on both sides, a most important deal was made, and one factor that made it possible may have been that J. B. Duke and the Willses, especially Sir William H. Wills, had more in common than they had realized before they got to know each other. Take the Wills family first. The historian of the Wills company points out that the family's Puritan beliefs in the seventeenth century led them to become religious dissenters. "Congregationalism taught them," the historian argues, "a sense of responsibility to those less fortunate than themselves, and their religious nonconformity was the mainspring of their political radicalism...." ("Radicalism," in this context, meant that they had greater sympathy with gradual steps toward political democracy in Britain than did the landed gentry and aristocracy that generally belonged to the Tory party.) Towards the end of the nineteenth century certain members of the increasingly wealthy Wills family became Anglicans, that is, part of the Established or official church in England; but "this had little effect on their outlook on life." Their most apparent personal characteristics were a certain "sobriety and distaste for personal extravagance, which sometimes appeared as petty meanness...."[20]

The exception to the family code and pattern was Sir William Henry Wills (who became Lord Winterstoke in 1906). A "convivial and popular" man, he purchased a country estate in 1852, when his fortune had reached a size to allow that; and one of his most treasured possessions was a large motor yacht. Unlike his many Wills cousins and nephews, he was something of a man of affairs, serving for a number of years as a Liberal member of Parliament. Sir William and other members of the Wills family made substantial gifts to various institutions in Britain, such as hospitals and libraries, and the family played a key role in the establishment of a university in Bristol.

The Willses began to have money, of course, a considerable period before Washington Duke and his family did. It is noteworthy, however, that the patriarch of the Duke family imbued a strong sense of Methodist social responsibility in his family; their benefactions for various charitable causes—such as orphanages, African-American as well as white colleges and churches, and other such causes—began to become significant in the 1890s. The Dukes not only played the major role in bringing Methodist-related Trinity College to Durham in 1892, but they also became in subsequent years the principal financial supporters of the college. That relationship would climax in 1924 when J. B. Duke's princely benefactions made possible the organization of Duke University around Trinity College.

As for political "radicalism," Washington Duke, as mentioned earlier, chose to become a Republican soon after the Civil War. A synonym for that party in the Reconstruction South was "Radical"— because Republicans such as Washington Duke and his sons dared to accept the idea of political equality for African-American males. In the eyes of the white majority at that time, the Southern Democrats, the Dukes, by abandoning the "White Man's Party," had committed the ultimate racial and political heresy.

In short, J. B. Duke and the Wills family had more in common than might have been initially apparent to them. Whether they actually were able to transcend stereotypical thinking, on both sides, is not known, but, at the least, they were able to cut a deal and then to launch successfully a pioneering, multi-national global enterprise. A series of meetings between J. B. Duke and Fuller, on the one hand, and a deputation from Imperial led by two members of the Wills family and their lawyer, on the other hand, resulted in a peace treaty late in September, 1902. Duke sold Ogden's to Imperial for about $15 million (3 million pounds); since the American Tobacco Company had only paid a bit more than $5,347,000 for Ogden's in 1901, the sale of the firm to Imperial no doubt pleased J. B. Duke. More importantly, the American Tobacco Company agreed to withdraw altogether from the British market and not to re-enter it. Imperial, in turn, agreed to stay out of the United States market (including Cuba). Each company acquired the trading rights in one another's brands and patents in its own home markets, including the right to use respective trade markers. Through the sale of Ogden's, the American Tobacco Company acquired a substantial minority interest (second only to that of the

Wills family) in Imperial, and also the right to name three directors to the board. And, as the historian of the Wills firm put the matter, "like the division of the world [between Spain and Portugal] by Pope Alexander VI in the fifteenth century, trade in the world outside the [United Kingdom] and the U. S. A. was to be served by a new company—British-American Tobacco — to be owned in the proportions of one third by Imperial and two thirds by the American Tobacco Company...." Moreover, the new company would be headed by J. B. Duke and headquartered in London.[21]

There are obvious questions to be asked about this global deal and the new company. First, why did the American Tobacco Company acquire two-thirds ownership? The answer is that J. B. Duke had been much bolder than his British counterparts about acquiring or building overseas tobacco factories and related facilities—in Japan, Australia, Canada, China, Germany, and elsewhere. The British firms, on the other hand, tended to rely largely on the export trade for their foreign markets and therefore had many fewer assets to put into the new British-American company.

With the American Tobacco Company owning such a preponderant share of the British-American company and with J. B. Duke as its leader, why was it registered in Britain and headquartered in London? The most frequently suggested reason for that is that President Theodore Roosevelt went on the warpath against the first of his anti-trust targets early in 1904. By being based in Britain, the new company was safely beyond the reach of any such anti-trust action. The only problem with this explanation is that no one really knew just how successful Roosevelt's anti-trust move would be; therefore, there might be an element of "reading backwards" (from 1904 or even 1911) in that explanation. There is also the possibility that J. B.Duke, having gained so much of the substance of what he wanted, was quite happy to have his new British partners gain symbolic satisfaction. Too, it is quite likely that he had already discovered that there was much to be said for a rich man's life in Edwardian England. In other words, Duke may well have already realized that spending some time regularly in London was not something to dread but rather to enjoy. After all, as one British historian notes, in England "businessmen were the new aristocracy, respected for their contribution to the nation's industrial power."[22] Leading businessmen were regularly made baronets and some even elevated to the peerage. While there were certainly people in the United States who also respected businessmen, those who did not—especially among pundits, intellectuals and academics—made a lot more noise and received much public attention.

The British-American Tobacco Company, with a complete absence of organizational models for it to emulate, was obliged to develop systems of international management that were largely its own creation.[23] While a number of others obviously contributed to this trail-blazing process, J. B. Duke clearly played the most crucial role. By adopting a managerial structure which delegated operational decision-making to functionally specialized departments, Duke and the American Tobacco Company had been able in the 1890's to channel some of their high-volume production in the United States to foreign markets; they simply grafted an export department on to the existing administrative system.[24]

Also, the strategy of corporate acquisition that Duke used so successfully within the United States was also used in foreign markets where tariffs or competition—or both —made it desirable. Duke's "willingness to employ acquisition as a market strategy in the international sphere," according to a recent historian, "was of vital importance as a means of accelerating the growth of a global cigarette industry."[25]

To illustrate some of J. B. Duke's overseas methods and strategies, a close look at markets in Japan and China might be illuminating. Asian markets tempted Duke (and other tobacco manufacturers in the West) not only because their vast populations had long used tobacco in one form or another—and in the case of China, tobacco was regarded as a relatively benign alternative to opium—but also because the famed bright-leaf tobacco of America was quite different from the huge crops of tobacco grown in China, India, and elsewhere in Asia. J. B. Duke, along with some other pioneers in the American tobacco industry, played a major role in creating a world market for one of the most important agricultural exports of the United States.

Japan attracted American tobacco salesmen in the late nineteenth century. When the Japanese government, which had a monopoly on the importation of leaf tobacco, imposed a prohibitive duty on imports of manufactured tobacco products in 1899, Duke had the

American Tobacco Company purchase a controlling interest in one of the leading Japanese tobacco firms, Murai Brothers Company. It then proceeded to manufacture and sell its products in rough-and-tumble American style. Duke picked a veteran tobacco man from Durham, Edward J. Parrish, to go to Tokyo in 1899 as the representative of the American Tobacco Company and vice-president of the Murai Company, of which Kichibei Murai was president.

Dignified and courteous in an old-style Southern manner, Parrish worked harmoniously and effectively with his Japanese colleagues. He assured the New York office that the "Messrs. Murai and Matsubara [secretary of Murai company] are even more anxiously concerned about the business... than ever before." Remembering J. B. Duke's hard-working habits, Parrish added: "We all get to [the] office at 8:30 every morning : office hours begin at 8:30 with the understanding of an hour for lunch, and after 5:30 any one could feel at liberty to go home. Parrish felt satisfied that he and his coworkers in Tokyo were agreed on one thing:

"We must have the *cigarette* business of Japan, and even if we cannot make much profit...."[26]

A great believer in the merits of bright-leaf tobacco, Parrish advised the Leaf Department in the New York office that the Murai company would always want about half of its purchases of leaf to be "of the Henderson, Oxford [North Carolina] types—old tobacco belt tobacco." The Japanese, according to Parrish, like "a mild, mellow smoke," and he subsequently amplified this by explaining that the "Japanese people do not eat much meat, or strong food like we Americans, their principal diet being rice, fish, vegetables &, and therefore a strong cigarette attacks their stomachs."[27]

Building a new factory modeled closely after the plant of W. Duke, Sons and Company in Durham, the Murai company advertised and promoted its goods with all the verve and vigor that the Dukes had earlier displayed in the American industry. "We are preparing to advertise our leading brands by street parades in principal cities with banners and music and Sandwiched men distributing circulars," Parrish informed the New York office. An exposition at Osaka, Japan, afforded the company an opportunity to make a splash, and Kichibei Murai reported on it: "I am glad to say that everything we have exhibited is beautifully made, and that the fact that we used special care over our exhibits is clearly seen if we compare our things with the small exhibits of [the rival] Iwaya and Chiba companies, which are right next to ours." Murai noted that the company's ten or more "free smoking stands" scattered around the exhibition grounds were quite popular and always crowded. His greatest praise, however, was reserved for the "Advertising Tower" which he thought was "beautifully finished" and made a "quite gigantic" show. "I felt delightfully when I myself was on the top of the tower and looked down upon the whole of Osaka city," Murai declared. "The electric illumination of the tower at night is so beautiful that not only myself but all who have a chance to witness the scene will be surprised by the great advertisement of our company."[28]

Not all was sweetness and light in the fiercely competitive Japanese cigarette business. One of Murai's popular brands of cigarettes was named "Hero." A sharp rival company, capitalizing on the Japanese difficulty with the English letter "l" which usually resulted in an "r" sound, came out with a brand called "Hallo." Though the rival allegedly admitted that "morally he [was] guilty, but not legally," the rival brand was not withdrawn. Attacks by competitors on the Murai company as "unpatriotic" and "foreign" did not prevent Parrish and his Japanese colleagues from building a most profitable business.

J. B. Duke, though he never visited Japan, took a keen interest in the affairs of the Murai company. Not only were various officers in the American Tobacco Company periodically dispatched to Japan, and Murai officials brought to New York, but Duke conveyed advice and recommendations about many aspects, large and small, of the Murai company's affairs. When he summoned Parrish to come home on a visit in 1903 — a visit for which Parrish prepared elaborately by collecting detailed data on every conceivable aspect of the business in Japan — Duke invited Parrish, Mrs. Parrish, and their daughter to Duke's Farm for a weekend. "When Mr. Duke was through asking the many questions that an ordinary man would not have even thought of, and of making suggestions that only Mr. Duke is capable of making," Parrish reported to the senior Murai, "he said that he would answer your letter himself, and that he would have a still more extended talk with me relative to these matters, before I returned to Japan." Parrish then went on for eight typewritten pages to convey Duke's ideas about various aspects of the business in Japan.[29]

When the Japanese government established a state monopoly on tobacco manufacture in 1904 and purchased the Murai company (for a fair price), Duke and his associates in the British-American company shifted more of their attention to China. James A. Thomas, a native of North Carolina and another veteran of the tobacco trade, became the key representative in China after a stint in India and Singapore. Thomas, who became a close friend of the Dukes, later wrote two memoirs about his career in the Far East. He recalled his first interview with J. B. Duke, who had unintentionally acquired a considerable mystique by the turn of the century: "I went into Mr. Duke's office with as much awe as if I were meeting the President of the United States, wondering all the while what he would say.... After being in his presence for five minutes, I felt as though I had known him all my life. I realized that I could tell him in detail what I was undertaking in the Far East, because I was certain that he would be interested and would give me the benefit of his great mercantile knowledge."[30]

Thomas recounted many incidents that illustrated J. B. Duke's keen interest in China and his great business acumen even in such an exotic context. Thomas noted, too, that the global organization that Duke headed "developed a remarkable *esprit de corps* which he nursed continually." On one occasion, Duke asked Thomas how many men he had working under him in the Far East who could take his place if that necessity should arise. When Thomas in a few minutes handed Duke a list of twelve names, the latter considered a moment and declared that if Thomas had trained twelve men to take his place, he deserved a raise in salary, which he promptly received.[31]

One of the most interesting points made by Thomas in his account of J. B. Duke is that Duke "put the same amount of energy and business ability into the Far Eastern trade that he did into the domestic business." In fact, Thomas recalled that Duke once told him that he "expected soon to have the domestic business so thoroughly organized that if it were not for the Far Eastern trade he would have nothing to do."[32] The formation of the British-American Tobacco Company in 1902 presented Duke with certain new challenges, but he faced them with the benefit of having already had considerable experience with a global market.

"Corporate culture" was a concept that undoubtedly did not exist in the abstract in 1902—though the reality was very much a fact in the case of the American Tobacco Company and Britain's Imperial Company. Moreover, there are some clear indications that J. B. Duke was quite aware of the problem arising from differing corporate cultures and promptly set about trying to do something about it. When the deal creating the British-American company was finally made, the first thing Duke did was to send a cable to his father: "Have just completed great deal with British manufacturers covering world [and] securing great benefit to our companies." A bit later Duke graciously declared to Sir William H. Wills: "I strongly believe that the business combination made by your Company and mine, will prove to be very advantageous to both companies, and its consummation, I feel sure, was largely due to your practical wisdom and foresight."[33]

To celebrate the consummation of the British-American deal, Duke hosted an elaborate banquet at the Carlton Hotel, one of London's most elegant hotels at the time. In preparing for the affair, he is reported to have turned to two of his American associates, with a smile, "Fuller, you take charge of the grub" and "Cobb, you get the wines."[34] With Sir William H. Wills on his right hand and William C. Whitney on his left, Duke presided over a handsome celebration. Under the heading "A Millionaire's Dinner Party," the *Illustrated London Mail* reported that Duke's guests "constituted a remarkable gathering, including as they did thirty members of the most prominent Tobacco Houses in England and America." The menu was said to have been "beautifully designed, and printed in gold and bound with white silk...."[35]

More important than the banquet for the future operation of the new British-American Company were Duke's actions concerning an Imperial officer whom Duke clearly selected and groomed as a future leader of the British-American company. Exercising his uncanny knack for spotting men with ability and character, Duke also made a most diplomatic move when he saw to it that Hugo Cunliffe-Owen be put in line for higher office in the British-American company. Brother-in-law of Harry Wills as well as former personal assistant to him, Cunliffe-Owen started out as secretary of the British-American company but soon became vice-chairman and eventually, and for many years, chairman. In the early years of the company's existence, Duke made a particular point of arranging for Cunliffe-Owen to spend considerable time in New York as well as in the Far East, so that he had a thorough familiarity with various aspects of the company's complex corporate culture. In fact, one British historian suggests that Cunliffe-Owen's considerable experience in the United States inclined him towards aspects of management that prevailed there. For example, he felt strongly that the British-American company should not revert to the type of family dynasty that characterized the domestic tobacco industry in Britain; consequently, he discouraged his sons from pursuing careers in the British-American company. More generally, this historian continues, "the company's trailblazing approach to international markets reflected far more readily the aggressive character of Duke, and his financial adventurism, than the more conservative approach that generally prevailed with the tobacco trade in Britain."[36]

As adroit as J. B. Duke proved to be in launching a pioneering multi-national and globespanning organization, all was not sweet harmony. A revealing example of conflicting priorities or viewpoints arose in 1904. Harry Wills, vice-chairman of British-American, wrote J. B. Duke concerning an employee (who had earlier worked for the Wills firm and then for Imperial) whose failing health necessitated his retirement. When Harry Wills proposed that British-American pay a pension to the employee in view of his services to the company, Duke was not sympathetic to the idea. "While I would prefer to agree with you in judgement about any matter," Duke wrote, "I cannot see any obligation resting on BATCo. to pension" the employee. "It is true that I am not familiar with a pension system," Duke continued, "because it has never been adopted in any of the companies with which I have been associated, nor in others which I have known.... It strikes me that it is scarcely to be expected that BATCo. should begin a pension list when it is scarcely more than a year old.... Our expectation is that our employees will, from their salaries, make savings sufficient to take care of them when they become old or disabled." Duke concluded: "At any rate, in as much as there is not a single person car-

ried on the pay-rolls of any of our American companies who is not
actively engaged in the service of that company, I do not see how I
could favour the inauguration of a pension system in the B.A., especially in its infancy.... I know you wanted me to write you frankly my
views on the subject, and I have done so."[37]

While the employee in question went back on the payroll of Imperial, Harry Wills decided soon after 1904 to resign as vice-chairman and a director of British-American. Although Duke hoped then
to have Cunliffe-Owen named as Harry Wills' replacement, that had
to wait a while, and Sir William H. Wills (chairman of Imperial) and
William Ogden became joint vice-chairmen of British-American.

Although the new company had gotten off to a flourishing start on
the whole, J. B. Duke decided in the summer of 1905 to relinquish
the chairmanship. The reasons for this are not altogether clear, but
from a purely personal point of view this was one of the low points
of Duke's life. His beloved father, Washington Duke, died in May,
1905, and this loss devastated Buck Duke. As if that were not enough
of a blow, the ill-fated marriage of Duke to Mrs. Lillian McReady was
ending less than a year after it had occurred because of her infidelity,
as was to be established in court. Duke's suit for divorce was scheduled to begin in September, 1905, and for a man who hated personal
publicity as much as Duke did, it promised to be an agonizing ordeal
and a field day for the tabloids. (This will be more fully discussed in
a subsequent chapter.) An acute case of erysipelas in his foot bothered Duke, especially since he was accustomed to robust health. Both
psychologically and physically, then, J. B. Duke suffered unaccus-
tomed woes, and in August, 1905, Duke yielded the British-American chairmanship to his long-time chief auditor and associate in
American Tobacco, W. R. Harris.

A few months before Duke took this action, he arranged for a
young man whom he had selected to be one of his closest associates,
George G.. Allen, to become a director of British American. A native
North Carolinian, Allen, like Duke, lacked formal higher education;
but after going to work for American Tobacco as a quite young man
in 1895, Allen was spotted by Duke as a winner and became someone whom Duke relied upon increasingly for the remainder of his life.
So not only did Duke have Allen strategically placed in British-Amer-

ican, where, as one historian notes, Allen was gradually to become "a central feature of BATCo.'s management structure," but also by August, 1905, Duke had the satisfaction of seeing Cunliffe-Owen become vice-chairman of the company.[38]

The British-American Company quickly became highly profitable. Annual profits rose rapidly above the $5 million mark, which meant generous returns to the two parent companies, American Tobacco and Imperial. In the financial year ending in September 1911, the annual dividend provided a return of 37.5 percent.[39]

Duke resumed his chairmanship of British-American in 1912 and remained in the position until 1923. After the outbreak of World War I in 1914, however, he operated from New York and left much managerial responsibility in the hands of Hugo Cunliffe-Owen. World War I impacted Duke's life and business career in many ways. While he had maintained close ties with North Carolina after his move to New York in 1884, circumstances after 1914 vastly increased and strengthened his links with the Piedmont Carolinas.

6

KEEPING TIES TO CAROLINA—AND A MANSION ON FIFTH AVENUE

Although J. B. Duke never again lived in Durham after moving to New York in 1884, he also never lost touch with his birthplace and home state. The strongest tie, of course, was through his father, who lived until 1905. But the original facilities of W. Duke, Sons and Company in Durham became an important component of the American Tobacco Company, meaning that J. B. Duke also had business reasons for regular visits home.

Historians and literary critics argue that, of all Americans, natives of the South, both white and black, have a peculiarly strong sense of place, an identification with their home-places and home region. A good bit of evidence suggests that J. B. Duke was no exception to that general pattern, although he early became and remained markedly national in his political outlook and globally cosmopolitan as far as his business interests were concerned. A person who consistently believed that his actions were more important than his words, Duke never spouted off, as did so many southerners of his generation, about what the South needed. The incantatory phrase "New South," so beloved by regional boosters and politicians, was not in his vocabulary. Yet few southerners actually did more than he to help transform the South—or at least the Piedmont Carolinas—from an agrarian backwater to a vibrantly industrialized area.

"One of the most persistent impulses in the life of the South since the Civil War," a prominent historian has declared, "has been the desire to develop an industrial economy."[1] The reason for that "persistent impulse" was not hard to find, either, for the widespread poverty that ravaged the South after 1865 led to the region's falling far behind the rest of the nation in most of the positive aspects of modern life. "In every measure of human progress and welfare," as another historian notes, "the South lagged far behind the rest of the nation."[2] Southerners hoped fervently that industrialization might mean escape from such poverty and backwardness.

Although tobacco manufacturing brought industry to Durham, as to a number of other towns in the North Carolina Piedmont and in Virginia, Durhamites were too canny to pin all of their hopes on one product, and the clamor for a textile mill, the postwar South's foremost symbol of industrialization, began early in Durham. Pointing to the large crops of cotton grown in eastern North Carolina, and some even in Durham County, the Durham *Tobacco Plant* asked: "Why should not this staple be manufactured here, where there will be no freights [freight charges] to get cotton...." Besides, the newspaper noted, southern cotton mills were reported paying profits in the range of 15 to 25 percent annually.[3]

Sure enough, Durham got its first textile mill in 1884 when the Blackwell company's Julian S. Carr joined with some capitalists from Greensboro to start the Durham Cotton Manufacturing Company. One textile mill was not enough, however, and the Durham newspapers hammered away at the argument that more cotton factories would benefit many people above and beyond the stockholders. "There is money in these enterprises for the owners, work for our laboring people, and general advantage to the community at large," the *Tobacco Plant* asserted.[4]

Even before a severe, nationwide depression began in 1893, southern farmers were in economic distress because of low prices for their crops. Bemoaning the "depressed condition of farming" in 1889, the Durham *Recorder* argued: "Durham needs more enterprises right now. Let's be like Noah of old: in his great wisdom he entered the Ark and was on the safe side."[5]

To learn about the distress of farmers, the Dukes did not have to rely on newspapers, for their incoming mail contained pathetic and first hand evidence, some of it from kinfolk. When Washington Duke sent Christmas checks to his numerous nephews, nieces, and other kin, a nephew in Tennessee, who had received a check for $1,000, wrote that he rested "mighty good on Xmas eve night...," but with corn at thirty cents a bushel and cotton at five cents a pound he would make "nothing after expenses paid."[6] Letters from farmers who sought jobs came regularly to the Dukes. One such letter nicely epitomized the farmers' plight: "'Tis said "Cotton is King.' If so 'the Lord help us.' I am in the center of a cotton belt and the price has made everything here depressing. Can't you make me an offer of a position of some kind, some place, some where?"[7]

Neither the plight of poor farmers nor the exhortations of newspapers, however, led the Duke brothers and their partner George Watts to go into textile manufacturing. Rather, the lure was the large profits that could be made. Yet the fact that they launched their textile-manufacturing venture in Durham should be emphasized. Opportunities for capitalists to invest their money abounded in the 1890s, with Wall Street in its unregulated, wild-and-wooly glory as the Mecca for a large number of rich men. Closer to home, a South Carolinian tried to lure the Dukes to build a cotton mill there, with the promise of a free twenty-five-acre site, immunity from town taxes for ten years, and 60 percent of state and county taxes rebated for the same period. Ben Duke replied, "Sorry I cannot."[8]

The Dukes showed great skill in 1892 when they picked the right man to manage their new textile enterprise in Durham. Thirty-six-year old William A. Erwin had already had considerable experience in textile manufacturing, came with strong recommendations, and for many years as the general manager and secretary-treasurer of the Erwin Cotton Mills displayed remarkable skill at his job. Since the Dukes were only beginning to enjoy the monetary rewards of the American Tobacco Company in 1892, they began their textile venture modestly, with the company initially capitalized at $125,000. They moved gradually, however, toward the "very large mill" they had in mind, and eventually, after much expansion, the Erwin Cotton Mill Company was capitalized at approximately $10,000,000. With Erwin Mill Number One in Durham expanding and making a profit (55 percent of the capital in 1901), the Dukes and their associates in 1903 launched Erwin Mill Number Two on the Cape Fear river in Harnett County, which is south of Durham and then a relatively undeveloped part of North Carolina. There the mill village was first named Duke but, after Duke University was organized in the mid-1920s and to avoid confusion, the names was changed to Erwin. An even larger textile mill, which became Erwin Mill Number Three in 1906, was developed at Cooleemee, which lay to the west of Durham near Salisbury, North Carolina. Despite serious problems that drastically reduced textile-manufacturing profits from about 1908 to 1911, a prominent textile selling agent in Philadelphia declared in 1914 that "of all the mills in the South[,] the Erwin Cotton Mills Company has a place entirely by itself."[9]

Although the Duke brothers' most significant involvement in North Carolina's textile industry was in connection with Erwin, they also played key roles as large investors in various other cities in Piedmont North Carolina, including Roxboro, Concord, Greensboro, and Spray. Moreover, in addition to the cotton mills, Duke money went into banking and railway ventures that were related to the mills. In Durham some of the Dukes' cash went into the establishment in 1889 of the Fidelity Bank. Even as southern agriculture virtually went under in 1893, Ben Duke reported that Fidelity Bank earned "about 16 ½ percent net...."[10] The Bank of Harnett, launched in 1904 near the mill village on the Cape Fear, also proved to be profitable.

Banks were not the only institutions to grow out of the tobacco and textile enterprises of the Dukes and their associates. Building a short railway in 1898 to haul lumber out of Harnett County, the Dukes eventually expanded the line to run the approximately sixty miles from Durham to Dunn and Duke (later Erwin). Named the Durham and Southern Railway and capitalized at $1,000,000, the railroad proved to be not only a profitable investment but also an important transportation facility for the growth of an hitherto undeveloped section of the state. Since Ben Duke always kept a home in Durham (even after acquiring a mansion on New York's Fifth Avenue), he helped to watch over the Durham and Southern, as he did the Erwin Mills. In 1918 he noted that the railroad had been "a profitable enterprise, never having paid dividends of less than 7 percent upon its capital stock since the year 1909."[11]

Railroads, banks, and textile mills in North Carolina were thus spawned by money that originally came from the tobacco industry.

They were significant economic developments in themselves, especially the textile mills. Despite the social problems that came with them and the low wages they paid, the mills played their part in the South's gradual twentieth-century movement toward economic parity with the rest of the United States. "Augmentation of the incomes of the mass of the population was not the goal directly sought [by individual investors]," a distinguished economist has written about the South's industrial experience, "though this was achieved almost in proportion as enterprise succeeded."[12]

In the last analysis, perhaps the most important consequence of the Duke brothers' involvement in cotton mills was that it led them straight into the new electric-power industry. Before that happened, however, the family became significantly—and, as it turned out, permanently—involved in Methodist higher education.

Because Washington Duke deeply loved the Methodist church, he and his family became interested in Trinity College. It was North Carolina Methodism's college for men that traced its antecedents back to a modest school begun in 1838 by Methodists and Quakers in Randolph County, some fifty or so miles west of Durham.[13] Surviving the Civil War, but barely, Trinity almost went under in the 1880s, but at the last minute it was saved by three Methodist businessmen, one of whom was Durham's Julian S. Carr. Ben Duke, for his part, gave the nearly bankrupt college $1,000 in 1887 and was soon elected to the board of trustees. He certainly did not know it at the time, but with that $1,000 Ben Duke had, in fact, cast into the church-and-college pond a pebble that would end up causing some sizable waves.

When Trinity acquired in 1887 a twenty-nine-year-old, Yale-trained president, John F. Crowell, that led to some profound changes. Certainly the most important change resulted from Crowell's conviction that if Trinity intended to grow and prosper, it would have to relocate from its bucolic isolation in Randolph County to one of North Carolina's more flourishing industrial towns. The upshot of this was that Washington Duke, determined to outbid Raleigh for the college, promised $85,000 for the college if it came to Durham. (The gift was widely hailed as the largest single philanthropic gift of money up to that time in the state's history.) Julian S. Carr offered to give the land for Trinity, and in the fall of 1892 Trinity opened for business in its new buildings in Durham.

Naively thinking that Trinity was now on Easy Street and that his big dreams about university status might soon be realized, Crowell actually had to face daunting problems. There was no money to pay the modest salaries owed to the small faculty and no money to buy the coal needed for heating the buildings. There was some friction growing out of the move from Randolph County and unhappiness among some of the Methodist trustees about Crowell's having introduced the new game of football into the state. Crowell soon resigned, and Washington Duke became thoroughly disenchanted by his brief experience with higher education. Approaching seventy-five, he is reported to have driven with a visitor in his buggy out to see the college and, upon arriving there, declared: "Well, there it is. I never expect to give another dollar to it, and I wish I had never put a dollar in it."[14]

Fortunately for Trinity, Washington Duke soon changed his mind. In Trinity's grim winter of 1892–1893, however, it was apparently Ben Duke who decided that, having brought Trinity to Durham, the family simply could not just sit by and watch it collapse. After conferring with his brother Buck and his sister, Mary Duke Lyon, Ben Duke offered on behalf of the three of them to give the college $7,500 per year for three years if the college would raise an additional $15,000 in each of the years. With the prompt acceptance of the offer by the two Methodist Conferences in North Carolina, Trinity College gained breathing space, at least.

The naming of John Carlisle Kilgo as Crowell's successor as president of Trinity quickly reawakened enthusiasm about Trinity on the part of the Dukes. Kilgo became, in fact, a key link in the chain that tied the Duke family to Trinity College. A spellbinding Methodist preacher and controversial fighter for the causes in which he believed, Kilgo thoroughly captivated the Dukes, and especially Washington Duke. He was not given to advertising his views, but Washington Duke apparently shared the reaction of another man who wrote to Kilgo: "My appreciation of your ability is unlimited. When I listen to your speeches and sermons I am so afraid you will quit it makes me nervous."[15]

Ben Duke was just as mesmerized by Kilgo, not only as a preacher but also as a college administrator, as was his father. Ben Duke believed that "the hand of God must have been in Kilgo's selection as President of the Institution," for he was "one of the greatest and best men in every way I have ever known. . . ." Ben Duke vowed that he looked "for great things for the College in the future." In the meantime, he and his father authorized Kilgo, in pursuance of one of the family's pet interests in the college, "to put our campus and grounds in splendid shape." "We wish," Ben Duke explained "to make it an attractive place not only for the students, but a pleasant park for the citizens of our community."[16]

While J. B. Duke obviously remained very much on the periphery as far as Trinity College was concerned, Ben Duke served on the executive committee of the trustees and became closely involved with many phases of the college's life. At age forty, he was generous with the time, worry, and service he gave. Though he came up with cash at all sorts of crucial junctures and to meet specific needs, he encouraged his father to give the larger donations to Trinity at this stage. Accordingly, Washington Duke in 1895 informed the trustees that he would give $50,000 toward the endowment for professorships, about which Kilgo spoke so often and urgently, if others would come up with an additional $75,000. Though the $75,000 never came in, Washington Duke was undaunted and informed Kilgo in 1896 that he (Washington Duke) would give $100,000 to Trinity on the condition that it would "open its doors to women, placing them on an equal footing with men."[17] He gave no explanation for this stipulation, though he may have meant it as a memorial to his deceased daughter, Mary Duke Lyon. Moreover, during Crowell's final year as president, Crowell had urged the establishment of a full-fledged coordinate college for women in connection with Trinity. While that dream was a full generation away from realization, Kilgo and the trustees happily accepted Washington Duke's conditional gift and promptly proceeded to admit women students, though the college lacked adequate facilities for them.

Washington Duke was by no means through with his generosity toward Trinity, for in 1898 he informed Kilgo that, "moved by a desire to build up our people and advance the Kingdom of Christ," he wished to give another $100,000 to the college's endowment.[18] And he gave another $100,000 in 1900, while Ben Duke had given $50,000 in 1899. The significance of these Duke gifts to Trinity in the early years is pointed up by the fact that the state's appropriation to the University of North Carolina for 1899–1900 was $25,000, and the university's total income from all sources for that year was $48,000.[19]

James B. Duke, no doubt encouraged by his father and Ben Duke, made his first major gift to Trinity in 1902 in the form of a handsome new library—and for good measure, he added $10,000 for books to go in the new building. When the time came for dedicating the new library, however, J. B. Duke stuck by his usual policy of refusing to make a public speech. Instead, he sent as his representative Walter Hines Page, a native Tar Heel who had become a prominent publisher and editor in New York. According to Page, J. B. Duke instructed him to tell them, "every man to think for himself." Page accordingly dedicated the new library "to free thought, reverent always, always earnest, but always free."[20]

J. B. Duke, usually acting in tandem with his brother Ben, made other gifts to Trinity in the first decades of the twentieth century. Enough has been said, however, to make two points clear: 1) Washington and Ben Duke took the lead in supporting Trinity College, while J. B. Duke dutifully followed their suggestions; 2) financial support from the Dukes gave Trinity College a stability that it had long sought but had never been able to find. By the time of World War I, it had grown to be—thanks to able leadership from Crowell, Kilgo and William Preston Few; a small but well-trained and ambitious faculty; and financial support from the Dukes—one of the strongest liberal arts colleges in the South.

While Trinity College early became and remained the Dukes' "prime beneficiary," they also gave to several other Methodist colleges in North Carolina and to a few non-Methodist institutions, such as Guilford College, the Quaker school near Greensboro. Just as Ben Duke deferred to Buck Duke in major business moves, Buck deferred to Ben in the family's charitable giving in North Carolina, which began in Durham but soon spread outward. The Oxford (N.C.) Orphanage, the "Colored School" at Kittrell (later Kittrell College), rural and poor Methodist churches across the state, and "worn-out" Methodist preachers—all were recipients of gifts from the Dukes. The monetary gifts grew larger as the years passed and the family grew richer, but Washington Duke had clearly imbued his family with the idea and spirit of regular and consistent giving.

While J. B. Duke was rarely , if ever, seen on the Trinity Campus, he most definitely made regular visits to Durham, primarily to visit his father. In September, 1904, eighty-three-year-old Washington Duke, having been in declining health for some time, summoned Ben and Buck in New York to "come and spend a few days with him."[21]

The sons promptly went to Durham, and the probable consequences of the visit were indeed unfortunate. No doubt Washington Duke as well as his sons believed that his death was fast approaching. Only circumstantial evidence exists to prove the point, but it seems likely that the aged father had somehow learned about his youngest son's longstanding relationship with Mrs. Lillian McRedy and that Washington Duke extracted a promise from his son that he would marry her. It also appears quite likely that J. B. Duke, for instinctive reasons perhaps, had not actually wished to marry Mrs. McRedy, whom, after all, he had known intimately for more than a decade. Yet, to J. B. Duke's ever-lasting regret, he did marry her, in a quiet ceremony in the home of her aunt in Camden, New Jersey, on November 29, 1904.[22]

Washington Duke was spared the knowledge of how grim a mistake his forty-eight-year-old son had made, for the sensational and headline-making divorce case happened after the the patriarch of the family had died. Late in January he fell in his home and broke his hip. J. B. Duke, on a combined honeymoon and business trip to Europe, rushed back to Durham. Although Washington Duke seemed to rally in the early spring, he died on May 8, 1905, at the age of eighty-four. A few months earlier he had a long talk about death with John C. Kilgo and concluded, "The only thing that makes me hate to die is I do not want to leave the boys."[23]

As if the death of his beloved father were not enough of a blow for J. B. Duke, he and his new wife began to quarrel bitterly about her aversion to residence at Duke's Farm. Then in the summer of 1905 J. B. Duke learned, through messages intercepted by servants, that his wife was in communication with another man. After consulting his lawyers and arranging for surveillance of Mrs. Duke by private detectives as well as by one or two executives in the American Tobacco Company, Duke arranged to be summoned to London on British-American business. During his absence, abundant and incontrovertible evidence of Mrs. Duke's clandestine affair with an aging man-about-town, one Frank L. Huntoon, was gathered by the detectives and Caleb C. Dula, a vice-president of American Tobacco. As a result, in September, 1905, Duke sued for divorce on the ground of his wife's alleged adultery.

The bitter contest that followed provided abundant grist for the mills of the sensation-mongering tabloids of the day. And as never before or afterward, J. B. Duke's private life was in the limelight. In addition to much testimony from servants and the private detectives, the evidence against Mrs. Duke included telegrams as well as "personals" that Huntoon placed in the advertising columns of the New York and Paris editions of the New York newspapers; these were Huntoon's messages to Mrs. Duke during her honeymoon trip to Europe. "Oh, memories that bliss and burn!," one of these strange advertisements proclaimed. "This separation is killing. Please don't wear low-necked dresses. Shall enjoy your house until Octopus [J. B. Duke] returns, when that pleasure shall cease."[24]

The New Jersey court found the evidence against Mrs. Duke overwhelming and granted J. B. Duke a divorce in May, 1906. Since the trial brought out the fact that he had given his wife, over the period of their acquaintance, over $250,000 in securities and other property, there was no financial settlement. Though the first Mrs. J. B. Duke tried unsuccessfully to press her claims at various later times, the subject was, understandably, one that J. B. Duke did his best to forget. Those around him did likewise. When his close associates of the last period of his life, George G. Allen and William R. Perkins, arranged for a North Carolina-born newspaper-man, John W. Jenkins, to write the first biography of James B. Duke, which was published after the subject's death, it contained only one terse paragraph concerning the disastrous first marriage.[25]

Unfortunately for J. B. Duke, trouble also came at him from the federal government. In 1907 the federal courts found a subsidiary of the American Tobacco Company, one that had a near-monopoly on licorice paste, guilty of violating the Sherman Anti-Trust Act. Then in 1908 the federal government began the legal action which the leaders of the American Tobacco Company had feared at least since the Northern Securities case of 1904. The Department of Justice, increasingly zealous about enforcing the Sherman antitrust law of 1890, moved directly against the gigantic American Tobacco Company in the Circuit Court for the Southern District of New York. In a suit in equity against twenty-nine individuals and sixty-five corporations, the government sought either to force the dissolution of the tobacco combination or to enjoin it from operating in interstate commerce.[26]

Like J. P. Morgan in 1904, J. B. Duke was both outraged and appalled by the federal government's move against the American Tobacco Company. Yet there is evidence that some of the deep satisfaction he had earlier found in putting together the vast combination and rationalizing various facets of the industry had waned after he and his associates had won most of the competitive contests. Testifying in the antitrust suit early in 1908, Duke insisted, not altogether convincingly, that the continuous program of expansion on which the American Tobacco Company had embarked after 1890 had been motivated by both prudence and a desire for additional profitable investments rather than by any idea on his part of eliminating or lessening competition. When asked why the company had wanted to produce every variety of tobacco product, Duke replied "because after one went out of fashion we would have another style ready for the public to take up...."[27]

As for his company's alleged desire to swallow or destroy all potential rivals, Duke maintained, "I never bought any business with the idea of eliminating competition, it was always [with] the idea of an investment....." He admitted, however, that the case of the Union Tobacco Company in 1899 had been special because, as he put it, "we had an idea for instance of getting in with ourselves a lot of rich financial people to help finance our properties."[28] Pressed about his company's secret purchase around 1903 of several formerly independent tobacco companies, Duke gave this answer: "Our crowd had about all they could handle and we concluded that the best way would be...to let them [the secretly purchased companies] continue an interest in it and they could manage it." Duke argued that he and his associates had "wanted them to push and drive hard against us." In fact, he admitted in a significant statement that "one of the mistakes the American Tobacco Company made in the beginning [was] that we didn't keep a separate organization for all of the principal businesses we bought." The company would have gotten "better service and better management," Duke believed, and "we would have had competition and would have built and extended the business."[29]

When queried about the alleged advantage of competition, Duke insisted that business not only grew more in such competitive circumstances but also made more money. "I know it in the case of the cigarette business," Duke continued, "because when we had so nearly all of it, [business] was cut in half in four or five years and as soon as we had competition we built it up again."[30]

Duke's own testimony about the economic advantages of competition contrasted glaringly with one large, undeniable fact: by 1906, on the eve of the federal government's legal action against the Duke-led companies, the tobacco combination controlled approximately four-fifths of the production in all lines of tobacco except cigars.[31] After voluminous testimony and the presentation of a veritable mountain of documentary evidence, the lower federal court, in a three-to-one decision, found the American Tobacco Company guilty of violating the antitrust law but exempted the United Cigar Stores, the Imperial Tobacco Company, and the British-American Tobacco Company. Except for those three companies, the other parts of Duke's vast combination were prohibited from engaging in interstate trade "until conditions existing before the illegal contracts or combination were entered into are restored."[32]

Both the federal government and American Tobacco appealed the ruling, and in May, 1911, the Supreme Court of the United States rendered a landmark decision of great importance. It ruled not only that the three companies excluded by the Circuit Court fell within the ban of the Sherman law but also that the tobacco combination had to be dissolved. Holding that the enforcement of an injunction against operation in interstate trade or the appointment of a receiver would be too prejudicial to the interests of both the stockholders and the American public in general, the Supreme Court declared:

> lst. That the combination in and of itself, as well as each and all of the elements composing it, whether corporate or individual, whether considered considered collectively or separately, be decreed to be in restraint of trade and an attempt to monopolize and a monopolization within the first and second sections of the

Anti-Trust Act. 2nd. That the [Circuit] court below, in order to give effective force to our decree in this regard, be directed to hear the parties, by evidence or otherwise, as it may be deemed proper, for the purpose of ascertaining or determining upon some plan or method of dissolving the combination and of recreating, out of the elements now comprising it, a new condition which shall be honestly in harmony with and not repugnant to the law.[33]

Ironically, the man who had put together the great combination turned out to be the principal unscrambler of the eggs. That is, J. B. Duke, aided by his lawyers, spent months of incessant labor hammering out a plan of dissolution. With some modifications urged by Attorney General George W. Wickersham, the plan was approved by the court and issued as a decree on November 16, 1911. Beyond the severance of the more autonomous parts of the tobacco empire from the control of the American Tobacco Company, the business of that company itself and its closely related subsidiaries was divided into three major parts—a new, much-shrunken American Tobacco Company, a reorganized Liggett and Myers Tobacco Company, and a reorganized P. Lorillard Company.[34] Those three firms plus the R. J. Reynolds Tobacco Company were destined to dominate the domestic tobacco industry in the years ahead, and, in the terms of the economists, a monopolistic situation had been replaced by an oligopolistic one.

Both angered and frustrated by the Supreme Court's decision in 1911, J. B. Duke proceeded to divorce himself completely from the domestic tobacco industry. While he continued to be much involved with the British-American Tobacco Company and, in fact, resumed the chairmanship in the London-based company in 1912, he more than ever turned his attention to the electric-power industry in the Piedmont Carolinas with which he had become involved in 1905.

By the time of the Supreme Court's decision against American Tobacco, J. B. Duke had fully recovered from the psychological and even physical decline which he suffered after his father's death and his own humiliating divorce. One of the explanations for his recovery was his second marriage in 1907. Too, the Ben Dukes helped him recover. They acquired in 1901 a residence at 1009 Fifth Avenue; it faced on

East 82nd Street and was (and is) directly across the avenue from the main entrance to the Metropolitan Museum of Art. When J. B. Duke's first marriage fell apart, the Ben Dukes took him in at 1009 Fifth Avenue. Subsequently, they arranged for the distraught Buck Duke to meet the woman who became his second wife.

Vacationing at an elegant resort on Lake Toxaway in the North Carolina mountains in 1906, the Ben Dukes met and were charmed by a strikingly handsome, dignified widow, Mrs. Walker P. Inman. She had lived in Atlanta with her late husband and son but was born Nanaline Holt in Macon, Georgia, in 1871 (making her fifteen years younger than J. B. Duke). Like so many southerners after the Civil War, she had experienced genteel poverty in her youth, but her first husband had left her with a modest competence, and she frequently travelled to New York and to such resorts as Lake Toxaway.[35]

Struck by the beauty and poise of Mrs. Inman, Ben Duke saw to it that his brother soon met her, and Mrs. Inman and her mother took up temporary residence in a New York hotel. Ben Duke also probably had something to do with the fact that the publisher of *Town Topics*, the gossip sheet of New York's wealthy Society, instructed his staff to be "careful of anything said about Mrs. Inman of Atlanta." There was to be "nothing unpleasant."[36]

James B. Duke married Nanaline Holt Inman in a quiet ceremony on July 23, 1907, and a new era began in the private life of the man who built the tobacco empire. Though J. B. Duke never really cared for the social pattern that was an inevitable part of life on Fifth Avenue in that era, the new Mrs. Duke enjoyed many aspects of that life, and she apparently preferred it, in fact, to Duke's Farm or any place in the South. Primarily for her, therefore, J. B. Duke acquired a lot on the northeast corner of Fifth Avenue and 78th Street. He then commissioned the firm of Horace Trumbauer, a well-known architect in Philadelphia, to draw plans for the proposed mansion. Trumbauer's office often depended on the great talent of Julian Abel, a pioneer African-American architect whom Trumbauer had befriended, and the firm had designed outstanding residences for the Wideners, Elkinses, and Stotesburys in Philadelphia, as well as numerous important public buildings there and elsewhere in the nation.

At a time when wealthy people were building residences cheek-by-jowl on Fifth Avenue north of 28th Street, the famed thoroughfare was a grand hodgepodge of styles. A few of the ornate mansions were faithful replicas of famous chateaux or palaces in France and Italy, but most were hybrid affairs that borrowed and mixed features from Versailles, Venetian or Florentine *palazzi*, and the English castles and manor houses. One critic described the Renaissance, Medieval, Byzantine, and other types of mansions as "palatial plagiarisms."[37]

When it came to architects and their plans, J. B. Duke was very much a hands-on client. His extensive building experience, not only in his business but also at Duke's Farm, made him knowledgeable and sometimes exacting about building plans. The classically restrained mansion in white marble, built in 1909–1910, that the Trumbauer firm designed was, at least, in part, a tribute to Duke's good taste.[38]

Along with their mansions on Fifth Avenue, the Duke brothers and their wives enjoyed other aspects of New York high life. The "Diamond Horseshoe" of boxes in the Metropolitan Opera House, especially in the heyday of such singers as Enrico Caruso and Geraldine Farrar, was a glittering showplace. The J. B. Dukes paid $1,250 for "Mr. Belmont's box" on alternate Thursdays in 1909.[39] Renting a box and actually attending the opera were, of course, two different matters, and whether J. B. Duke joined his beautiful wife for such operatic evenings is not known. At any rate, he moved easily and confidently in those circles that did matter to him; on one occasion he sent 2,000 of the "best Havana cigars" to J. P. Morgan and on another John D. Rockefeller, Jr., invited him to visit the family's gardens on the estate at Pocantico Hills.[40]

For all their mansions on Fifth Avenue, boxes at the Metropolitan Opera, and paintings by such British artists as Gainsborough and Hoppner, the Duke brothers may have had one true distinction among the residents on "Millionaires' Row": they regularly imported food-stuffs, especially freshly ground cornmeal, from Durham. Chicken and hams also came up from the South, and on one occasion there was even a barrel of turnips.[41] When they were in Durham, shipments to them from New York were of a quite different nature. The evidence suggests that neither J. B. nor B. N. Duke drank much in the way of intoxicants, but apparently they did enjoy champagne.

Since North Carolinians were participating in a great prohibitionist crusade around 1908, Ben Duke ordered from New York a case of "Pommery sec [champagne] — vintage 1900," six bottles of gin, and two of dry vermouth [martinis!] — all to be sent in "plain packages (that is packages that will not show contents)."[42]

When the Duke brothers began around 1906 to rent private railway cars for their trips to the Piedmont Carolinas, mostly in connection with the affairs of the electric power company, their executive secretary emphasized to the Pullman Company that "a liberal supply of champagne and cigars" would be required. To be sure that the eight persons in the party on one occasion had the beverages and smokes that they would want for the six-day trip, the secretary requested "two cases of Pommery Sec Pints, instead of one case, and *two* hundred and fifty Principe de Gales 'Sobranos' [cigars]...."[43] Although in his younger days J. B. Duke had enjoyed chewing tobacco, New York (and Lillian McRedy) helped to end that habit; instead he took to mild cigars and in his later years was seldom seen without one.

The happiest thing to happen to J. B. Duke occurred on November 22, 1912, when his wife gave birth to a daughter whom they named Doris. Perhaps because he was of an age (56) when many men become grandfathers, J. B. Duke found a special satisfaction and joy in his beautiful, fair-haired daughter. Preoccupied though he had been for so long with his business affairs, he actually possessed the same strong family feeling that Washington and Ben Duke had always taken the time to cultivate and demonstrate. After the birth of his daughter, J. B. Duke also began to think of things other than his business affairs — and his beloved Duke's Farm.

Initially, when J. B. Duke got ready to build his Fifth Avenue mansion, he also planned to build an elaborate mansion on Duke's Farm, a residence that would match the splendor of his richly landscaped estate. The Supreme Court's decision in 1911, however, apparently so disturbed J. B. Duke that he abruptly halted the construction that was already underway on the Duke's Farm mansion. Instead, he contemplated the purchase of a great mansion in Mayfair, London's most exclusive West End area.

As mentioned earlier, J. B. Duke resumed the chairmanship of the British-American Tobacco Company in 1912. Consequently, he envisioned more frequent and perhaps longer periods of residence in London. He clearly had become accustomed to and even quite comfortable with a rich man's life in pre-World War I England. Mrs. Duke apparently shared in the viewpoint and was no doubt highly pleased when arrangements were made for her to be presented to King George V and Queen Mary at the Court of St. James. That was something that many monarchy-obsessed and socially ambitious Americans then regarded as the ultimate social achievement. Wearing "white and gold brocade with pearls and diamonds embroidered upon the corsage," a court mantle or cape of "geranium red velvet lined with gold tissue," and ropes of pearls, Mrs. Duke no doubt made a striking picture when presented. Not even to please his lovely wife, however, would J. B. Duke don the purple silk knee breeches and other such vestments that were prescribed for his appearance at the royal presentation. He swore that with his thin legs and large stomach, the outfit would make him look like a "caricature of a brownie," and he arranged for the American ambassador to send some other man to escort Mrs. Duke.[44]

The British-American Tobacco Company was doing a flourishing business. So much so, that J. B. Duke laid the cornerstone for a large, new headquarters building for the company in Westminster, near the Houses of Parliament. Before the building could be completed, however, and before J. B. Duke exercised his option to buy Crewe House, the Mayfair mansion, World War I began in August, 1914. That calamity sent the J. B. Duke family scurrying back across the Atlantic to the United States.

Despite his aversion to costumed pomp, J. B. Duke returned to America in 1914 thoroughly Anglophilic and convinced that the United States should sooner or later enter the war on the side of the Allies. Yet his unhappiness about many features of the Progressive Era, which had climaxed in the Democratic administration of Woodrow Wilson, led him for the first (and only) time in his life to publish an article in a national periodical, the *North American Review*. Just who inspired Duke to such an uncharacteristic action is not known; and while the ideas expressed in the article resonate with Duke's staunch, McKinleyite Republicanism, neither is it known who helped polish the prose. At any rate, he declared in the article that it was "not a pleasant contemplation, but it is the simple truth that since 1904 the whole course of national political affairs, so far as it has been influential at all, has been—with one solitary exception—toward the depression of business, the hindering of business prosperity, [and] the curtailment of the income of the capitalist and the laborer alike." The exception which Duke noted was the Federal Reserve Banking Act, but his guarded approval of that was greatly overshadowed by his denunciation of the Wilson administration's lowering of the protective tariff rates and by what Duke perceived as the continuation of the war against large businesses which he traced back to 1904 and the beginning of President Theodore Roosevelt's antitrust fight.[45]

Duke continued to attack the economic policies of the Wilson administration even after the United States entered World War I in 1917. With the unshaken faith of an old-fashioned capitalist and Old Guard Republican, he argued that the railroads would perform more efficiently if left in private hands rather than being run by the federal agency set up to control them in the wartime emergency. And he insisted that "enormous and unparalleled inheritance taxes and surtaxes" were raising comparatively little revenue while they "hurt all our enterprises and the individuals who are engaged in and dependent upon them." The federal government, Duke charged, was "pulling down the pillars of our business temples."

The income tax, made constitutional by the ratification of the Sixteenth Amendment in 1913 and made telling in its impact by the higher rates occasioned by American military preparation and then entry into the war, came in for special attack from many of the country's wealthy people. J. B. Duke was no exception, and he argued that the government could not hope to sell its bonds to "those whose incomes are too largely taken by taxation." The draft law Duke applauded, though he asserted that it should go further and include "for purposes of labor, every man, woman, and child over sixteen years of age and mentally and physically fit."[46] Responding to the wartime program for the production of essential grains and other foodstuffs, Duke devoted all possible acreage on Duke's Farm to such purposes.

Duke's conservative views on government and public policy had no discernible impact on the course of events in wartime America. He therefore quickly turned to and remained in his more natural sphere of entrepreneurial capitalism. Moreover, the electric power industry in the Piedmont Carolinas with which he had become involved as early as 1905 loomed larger and larger in his life and consumed ever greater amounts of his time and money.

The house Washington Duke built for his second wife in 1852 and where Mary, Benjamin N., and James B. Duke were born. Though Washington Duke is shown seated on the porch, the photograph was apparently taken around 1900, about a quarter of a century after he and his family left the homestead for Durham.

Washington Duke in about 1880, when he turned sixty.

Young Buck Duke at about seventeen, when he went away to business school.

James Buchanan Duke in about 1881, when he was twenty-five.

Ben, Washington, and Buck Duke (left to right) shown in a cropped corner of a group photograph taken at a barbecue in Duke (later Erwin), N.C., in the early 1900s.

Buck Duke at a fishing camp in eastern North Carolina in the early 1900s. (Reproduced from an original at the Duke Homestead.)

"Boulder-style" stonework used in the early development of Duke's Farm in New Jersey.

More formal style of stonework employed in the later phase of development at Duke's Farm.

Two of the numerous fountains at Duke's Farm.

A greenhouse designed by Horace Trumbauer at Duke's Farm. It was later incorporated into Doris Duke's Gardens of the World.

Nanaline Holt Inman (Mrs. J. B.) Duke, *circa* 1915.

James B. Duke's mansion on the corner of Fifth Avenue and East 78th Street, New York.

Architect's drawing of the proposed mansion at Duke's Farm, construction on which J. B. Duke halted in 1911 and never resumed.

James B. Duke and his almost-seven-year-old daughter Doris in a photographer's studio in Newport, Rhode Island, in the summer of 1919.

Two views of White Oaks, James B. Duke's home in Charlotte, North Carolina, where he and his associates gave a final review to the indenture creating the Duke Endowment in early December, 1924.

Benjamin N. Duke and James B. Duke in the early 1920s.

James B. Duke, *circa* 1924, when he established the Duke Endowment.

7

ELECTRIFYING THE
PIEDMONT CAROLINAS
Part I

When James B. Duke agreed in 1905 to make substantial investments in the electric-power industry in the Piedmont Carolinas, he could have not have known that he had embarked on what would be the most creative economic endeavor of his life. Moreover, of all his entrepreneurial activities, the electric-power company that eventually bore his name would have the most positive, long-lasting, and far-reaching impact on his native region and its economic health.

At some point during the two decades in which Duke was involved with the power company —probably in the early 1920s — he came to realize that it would never be the "cash cow" that the tobacco industry had been for him (and numerous others). He confessed to a friend that, because of various circumstances, there simply was not the money to be made in the electric-utility business that there had been in tobacco. Yet, money-making, per se, was not Duke's prime purpose in his zealous effort to build up and protect the power company. Encouraging the industrialization of the Piedmont Carolinas and providing a stable, dependable support-base for a perpetual charitable trust that he envisioned were his true purposes.

Contrary to an oft-told tale, the involvement of J. B. Duke in hydroelectric developments in the Carolinas was not altogether the result of Dr. W. Gill Wylie's being asked to treat J. B. Duke's erysipelas-inflamed foot. While he was indeed a bold entrepreneur, Duke never invested his money capriciously or on the spur of the moment. Because of the Duke brothers' involvement in textile manufacturing, they and W. A. Erwin, the general manager of their textile operations, were well aware of significant developments that were underway in the 1890s concerning hydropower and industrial electrification. One of the nation's earliest and, at that time, most widely noted ventures in the industrial use of electric power occurred in Columbia, South Carolina. There, in April 1894, a cotton mill began to utilize seventeen electric motors of 65 horsepower each, and the alternating current that ran them was furnished by a hydro-station located on a river about a thousand feet from the mill. At $15 per horsepower, the Columbia mill was reported to be utilizing the cheapest power in the nation.[1] The Duke brothers were well aware of such developments, and in addition to hiring their own engineer to look over possible water-power sites in the Carolinas and to advise in the new field, they also had Erwin's faithful assistance.

As a result of these activities, Erwin reported in late 1899 that he was "making a special effort quietly to learn the status of the Catawba River [Great] Falls, which is unquestionably the biggest thing in the South...." A little over a year later, in 1901, he managed to acquire the coveted site for a little less than $42,000; then he obtained additional properties at Great Falls that brought the total cost to $90,000.[2]

After several years of scouting out power sites in the Carolinas, Erwin concluded, quite prophetically, that the "main trouble with all these powers" was the erratic flooding and drying up of rivers in a region where periods of heavy rainfall often alternated with prolonged droughts. The one exception, Erwin believed, was "the Great Falls of the Catawba, where the river never rises above eleven feet, and [which] would give practically an invariable steady power." It was, Erwin declared, "the greatest property... in the United States on this account," as well as because of the "low cost of development it would require...."[3] To secure and hold their land and water rights, primarily along the Catawba River, the Duke brothers incorporated the American Development Company.

Preceding the Dukes in his interest in hydropower development on the Catawba, Dr. W. Gill Wylie was a native South Carolinian who became a distinguished and well-to-do medical leader in New York

City after the Civil War. Having grown up near the Catawba, Wylie believed that, except for the Penobscot River in Maine, it offered the best opportunities for hydro development of any river east of the Rocky Mountains. After being involved with some relatively small hydroelectric projects near Anderson, South Carolina, Wylie and his brother in 1900 undertook to finance the building of a more substantial hydrostation on the Catawba River at India Hook Shoals near Rock Hill, South Carolina. When the engineer with whom Wylie worked to launch the project withdrew after early delays and frustration, Wylie replaced him with a most promising and already experienced young engineer, William States Lee, Jr., who was also a native South Carolinian and a graduate of the South Carolina Military Academy (later the Citadel).[4]

Although Wylie attempted to interest the Duke brothers in his project at India Hook Shoals, he only succeeded in gaining a modest investment from Ben Duke—and it was J. B. Duke whom Wylie needed to recruit for the larger plan that Wylie envisioned. From various experiences that Wylie had with the small hydrostations near Anderson, he had hit upon the idea of providing more reliable and more economical electric service by building a series of hydroelectric plants on the Catawba and linking them together with high-voltage transmission lines. In this way, Wylie figured, a series of dams and reservoirs along the Catawba (which became the Wateree River in South Carolina) could utilize a large part of the 700-foot fall which occurred through its 130-mile length from Hickory, North Carolina, down to Camden, South Carolina.[5]

W. S. Lee became the first and most enthusiastic convert to Wylie's ambitious plan. Lee noted that a few miles below the original Catawba plant at India Hook Shoals were the (Duke-owned) Great Falls, with a "head" or fall of 160 feet; then below that part of the river was Wateree, with a fall of 72 feet. To build power plants at these falls and tie them in with the original Catawba plant would, in effect, be laying the foundation of a great superpower system. "I didn't know where the money was coming from to finance the scheme...," Lee later declared, "but I didn't trifle or neglect the details while waiting for something to happen...." Lee noted that he "worked just as hard on the super-power idea as if I had unlimited capital at my command." He stated that he had surveyed every mile of the Catawba River and had his plans all worked out in minute detail before knowing how the scheme was going to be financed. It even occurred to him, Lee confessed, that nothing might come of the plan, but he was utterly convinced of its practicality. "It was something that just had to be done... and it was a job for some man who would give his heart and soul [and a large chunk of his money] to it."[6]

That rich man willing to commit to and underwrite the Wylie-Lee version of a "super-power system" turned out to be J. B. Duke, of course. When Dr. Wylie was called in to treat J. B. Duke's inflamed foot in late 1904 or early 1905, he finally had an opportunity to talk with Duke about his vision for the development of the Catawba and the great ability of W. S. Lee. After that discussion, J. B. Duke—who was by no means a total novice about hydro-electricity for he had his own small generating plant at Duke's Farm—asked Wylie to invite Lee to come to New York with the surveys, preliminary plans, and other data that he had been so carefully assembling.

J. B. Duke undoubtedly gave Lee a courteous hearing when he came with Wylie for the interview. Lee later recalled that Duke, after posing sharp questions and carefully examining Lee's plans and diagrams, asked what the estimated cost might be. "I told him about $8,000,000," Lee noted. "I thought that was about the biggest amount I had ever heard of, but it seemed to attract him."[7]

Lee quickly realized that utilizing hydroelectric power for industry—and, specifically, textile mills—was the aspect of the plan that most interested Duke. Since long-distance transmission of electricity at high voltage was still in the early stages, many investors were fearful of the economic risks involved. Lee discovered that Duke, because of his keen interest in promoting the industrialization of the Piedmont Carolinas, was willing to take the risk if practical plans were prepared. On that point, Lee was ready, for he had prepared a map showing transmission lines that linked the existing Catawba plant at India Hook Shoals and projected plants at Great Falls and at Mountain Island, which was on the Catawba to the northwest of Charlotte and more than fifty miles north of Great Falls. Lee, giving practical application to Wylie's original vision, aimed at continuity of service through linking the various plants together. There was also another site, Wateree, down the river some eighteen miles below Great Falls, that Lee envisioned as part of the system.

J. B. Duke asked Lee and Wylie many sharp questions, which he always preferred to reading documents. "I know that in many cases he never had studied or heard of the things brought up," Lee recalled, but "readily grasping the idea, his mind passed on to the next step." Disdainful of committee meetings or conferences involving what Duke regarded as too much talk—"town meetings" he termed them—he quickly made up his mind and verbally issued many important instructions. "He had a wonderful power of making decisions," according to Lee. Sometimes they "seemed to be almost off-hand," but "they were as accurate as they were swift." Lee concluded his admiring appraisal: "Generally, he had gone into the matter thoroughly, had the points fixed in his mind and was sure of his ground. He merely thought faster, more accurately, and grasped the points of a situation more quickly than most men. And, once he had decided, he acted promptly."[8]

Thus, after J. B. Duke's interviews with Wylie and Lee and after several years of cautious preliminary investigation, the Duke brothers were ready by the spring of 1905 to plunge into the electric utility industry. The Southern Power Company was incorporated in New Jersey with an authorized capital stock of $7,500,000. By March 1906, $6,000,000 worth of stock had been issued in exchange for $1,097,794 in cash (mostly from the Dukes); the entire $850,000 worth of the capital stock of the Wylies' Catawba Power Company; a demand note from that company to the Southern Power Company for $118,579; and property, real estate, and water rights valued at $3,933,607 (mostly paid for by the Dukes).[9]

Locating its home office in Charlotte, the Southern Power Company lost no time launching its construction program at Great Falls—and extensive construction would not stop for any significant duration until the Great Depression of the 1930s. By April 1907, the 24,000 kilowatt plant at Great Falls, with a total cost of a bit over $1,612,000, was ready to go into service. A 44,000-volt transmission line delivered power first to Charlotte, and then later the lines were extended to Gastonia, Shelby, and other towns in the Piedmont.

Entrepreneurs take risks, and in the beginning, selling the idea of electric power to the established textile manufacturers in the area was not always easy. Aside from the initial and short-run expense in changing equipment and procedures, many people remained frightened of electricity. An engineer for the Southern Power Company tried to convince one textile manufacturer of the feasibility of electric power. After listening for a quarter hour, however, the manufacturer ended the discussion by asserting, "You must be drunk or a damned fool if you think I will bring electricity into my mill to kill my people."[10]

To overcome such fear and skepticism and to encourage the mill owners to use electric power, the Dukes invested heavily in a large number of textile mills in both Carolinas. Even before the launching of the Southern Power Company, the Dukes had taken the lead, and put up the lion's share of the necessary capital, in establishing a large textile bleaching and finishing plant in Greenville, South Carolina. After 1905, however, their investments in the textile mills around Charlotte, Spartanburg, and Greenville began to increase dramatically.

When James W. Cannon, the founder of what grew to be one of North Carolina's largest textile enterprises, approached J. B. Duke about investing in his mill, Duke sent word that if Cannon would "go to the site of one of our water power developments, say Great Falls for instance, and build a large plant,...he [Duke] would be glad to become interested, and largely interested with you." Duke thought that the plant "should be a very large one, operating not under 100,000 spindles, and possibly 200,000 to 250,000 spindles." The mill might well produce "plain sheetings" and do so in such large quantities as to become known in the whole country as "the largest and best in this line of production." A vast amount of capital would be required for building on such a scale, but Duke believed that "the money could be provided without much difficulty."[11]

Although Cannon did not go to Great Falls, another large textile mill did locate there, and the Dukes invested substantially in it. Later, James Cannon's son, Charles A. Cannon, asserted that Kannapolis, home of the extensive Cannon Mills, could never have been built without the Southern Power Company. His mother had nervously inquired, "Now, are you sure that this electric power will be a success?" And his father had confidently replied, "Yes, Mr. Duke will make it a success."[12]

The electrification of the textile factories of the Piedmont Carolina in the early years of the twentieth century paralleled developments across the country. One historian has called electrification probably "the most sweeping and complex technological change in American manufacturing over the past century...." While the fundamental breakthrough occurred in the 1890s, the speed of electrification was held back, according to this historian, by a number of technical and economic factors, the most serious being "the general unavailability of cheap electricity." This problem was solved by the growth of the electric utility industry, a development that gathered full force after 1905. By 1914, utilities generated over half of all the electricity in the nation, and by 1967, over 90 percent.

The same historian observed that the emergence of this new, specialized industry with its central power stations stimulated the electrification of manufacturing plants, replacing the coal/steam combination that had supplied most of the power requirements during the last half of the nineteenth century. The overriding reason for the adoption of electrical systems was the expectation, and then realization, of large cost savings. Electrification was the sort of technical advance that reduced all costs—labor, capital, and materials.[13] The Dukes, whether they realized it or not, were key players in a revolutionary change in the American economy.

Even before the plant at Great Falls was fully completed, the company began building another hydroelectric plant at Rocky Creek on the Catawba, just below Great Falls, and another at Ninety-Nine Islands on the nearby Broad River in South Carolina. The Rocky Creek plant went into service in 1909 and Ninety-Nine Islands in 1910. In that latter year, the company began constructing small, strictly auxiliary coal-burning steam stations, one at Greenville, South Carolina, and another at Greensboro, North Carolina. More expensive to operate than the hydro plants with their free "white coal," the steam plants were primarily for standby use and emergency situations.

As early as 1911, therefore, the Southern Power Company had linked together four hydroelectric plants—Catawba, Great Falls, Rocky Creek, and Ninety-Nine Islands. In 1910, the editor of *Electrical World*, credited the Southern Power Company with "stimulating a whole population [in the Piedmont Carolinas] from a condition of former commercial and industrial apathy to an activity comparable... to that which characterized a new Western State."[14]

To credit the power company alone with awakening a "whole population" from a deep, southern slumber was an overstatement. A writer in *Electrical World*, however, was on more solid ground when he hailed "The Great Southern Transmission Network." He began by asserting that there had quietly grown up in the South "what is today by far the most extensive interconnected transmission system in the world." Observers in the electric utility industry had been aware for some years, the writer continued, that "splendid work" was being done in the development of the waterpowers of southern Appalachia and the Piedmont. But the linkage of the various networks into what already approximated, and one day would become, a united whole was "a comparatively new phase of the situation."[15]

This then-unrivaled "system of systems" referred not only to the Southern Power Company's network of generating plants with interconnected transmission lines but also to the fact that J. B. Duke and W. S. Lee moved quite early to establish transmission links with other utility companies in the Southeast. Linkage with the fledgling Carolina Power and Light Company in eastern North Carolina and northeastern South Carolina came early (1912). The Georgia Railway and Power Company undertook the building of a large development at Tallulah Falls in northern Georgia. Anticipating a surplus of power, the Georgia company agreed readily to the Southern Power Company's offer to buy 2.5 million kilowatt-hours of electricity a month. In order to make the delivery to the Southern Power Company, a double-circuit, steel-tower transmission line had to be built in 1913 from Tallulah Falls to Easley, South Carolina, a distance of forty-five miles. The two companies split the cost.[16] This farsighted arrangement would turn out to be critically important for the Southern Power Company when disaster, in the form of unprecedented flooding on the Catawba River, struck in 1916.

J. B. Duke and W. S. Lee pushed such technological breakthroughs as the industry's first double-circuit 100,000-volt line in 1909, but others also played important roles in the Southern Power Company's early history. Charles I. Burkholder, for example, was a native of Illinois and engineering graduate of the University of Wisconsin. Joining the company at age twenty-four in 1906, he remained with it for his entire career and developed great expertise in transmission line operation.

J. B. Duke, showing his uncanny knack for selecting and keeping top-flight subordinates and colleagues, brought twenty-one-year old Norman Cocke into the company in 1906. A native Virginian and graduate of New York Law School, Cocke would not only eventually head the company but also play a prominent role in the civic and educational life of North Carolina. Another young Virginian whose ability J. B. Duke spotted early on was Edward C. Marshall. A great-grandson of Chief Justice John Marshall, young E. C. Marshall began his business career at age eighteen (in 1895) with the Seaboard Railway. He soon took a job with the American Tobacco Company in New York, and in 1907 Duke asked Marshall to become the power company's auditor. He subsequently held several top management positions before becoming president of the power company in 1949.

J. B. Duke enjoyed the company of hard-working, talented people like Lee, Burkholder, Cocke and Marshall. Norman Cocke later recalled one occasion when he was talking with J. B. Duke about some needed extensions. When Duke asked where the money to pay for the work was coming from, Cocke replied, "We're going to get it from you." "No you ain't," Duke retorted. "I'm like the farmer who had a young steer that he wanted to break to a yoke, so he got a double yoke and he put his head through one side of it, and he put the young steer's head through the other. And the steer lit out and he ran all around the yard, and this fellow couldn't stop. He hollered to his son and said, 'Come here, Bill, and head us off, durn our fool skins!' That's what I want somebody to do for me," Duke laughingly concluded, "head me off."[17]

Although the Duke brothers sometimes complained privately about the vast amounts of capital consumed by their power projects in the Carolinas, they never failed to provide the money as it was needed. On some occasions, they sold their stock holdings in other enterprises to plow more capital into the power company and its related enterprises. To facilitate the industrialization that was J. B. Duke's goal and also to use some of the ever-increasing amounts of available electric power, he launched an electric interurban railway, the Piedmont and Northern, in 1910–1911. The South Carolina branch of about one hundred miles linked Anderson, Greenwood, Greenville, and Spartanburg with Charlotte; and the North Carolina division ultimately had about fifty miles of track, with the main line running between Charlotte and Gastonia, along with several shorter branch lines. Carrying both passengers and freight, the Piedmont and Northern, with its proud slogan, "A Mill to the Mile," became another important factor in the economic life of the region. The last of North Carolina's electric railways to switch to diesel engines (in the 1950s), the Piedmont and Northern had a proud, efficient history of its own until it was merged with the much larger Seaboard Coast Line Railroad in 1969.

The Duke brothers, together with W. S. Lee and Edgar Thomason, a longtime official of the railroad, were the key figures in the building of the "P. & N." One example of the role of the Dukes came in 1913, while J. B. Duke was occupied in London as chairman of the British-American Tobacco Company, and Ben Duke in New York coped with the financial needs of the electric railway. When Lee informed Ben Duke that work on the railroad would require $250,000 in the next ten days, Ben Duke advanced $100,000 and cabled his brother in London for $150,000. A few weeks later, when Lee needed additional funds and proved unable to arrange a loan in New York, Ben Duke went to work on the original subscribers to the syndicate that he and J. B. Duke had organized to back the railroad and managed to get most of them to increase their subscriptions. "I feel very much gratified that we could handle the matter in this way," Ben Duke declared, "rather than borrow so much money at a time like this." I figure that we will get in say, $1,250,000 from these increased subscriptions...." He concluded, somewhat wearily: "I hope no new and unexpected thing will turn up that will require additional money for I am about worn threadbare. I have had to pay out over a million dollars since January lst for enterprises that I did not know the first of the year I would be called upon for." Over $600,000 of that money, Ben Duke noted, had gone for power company purposes, but he hoped that "the storm is now over and that we can take things more quietly."[18]

That particular cash crunch no doubt passed, but the capital needs of the power company remained an ongoing problem. The significance of the manner in which those needs were met should be emphasized, for the autonomy enjoyed by the Southern (and then the Duke) Power Company was rare among electric utilities. The expensiveness of so much of the machinery and equipment that were needed by the utility companies led most of them to pay for equipment with company stocks and bonds. In this manner, General Electric set up one of the first major holding companies, Electric Bond and Share, in 1905. Even earlier, the Thompson-Houston Company set up United Electric Securities to own the holdings of companies that paid for equipment with securities. There were other reasons that led to the emergence of the electric utility holding companies, but the main point is that by 1932, the eight largest holding companies controlled 73 percent of the investor-owned utilities.[19] Not only were crucial decisions concerning the utility companies made in northern cities quite distant from where the utilities actually operated, but the holding companies were not regulated or supervised by any governmental agency. That is, they were not regulated until the New Deal's Public Utility Holding Company law was enacted in 1935. As for profits, the biographer of Samuel Insull, a major figure in the history of the electric utility industry, has succinctly noted that "financing utilities was many times as profitable as running them."[20]

The unusual autonomy of the Southern (Duke) Power Company, made possible by the fact that the Dukes—and especially J. B. Duke—furnished the capital, was merely one source of the company's efficiency, reasonable rates, and high morale. Enough has been suggested concerning the economic impact of the company to explain why the rumor that began to spread around 1912 that J. B. Duke might transplant himself permanently to London inspired deep consternation in the minds of business-oriented Carolinians in the Piedmont.

That J. B. Duke was considerably irritated by the forced dissolution of the American Tobacco Company in 1911 and that he was seriously considering the acquisition of a mansion in London are matters that have already been discussed in a previous chapter. Before the outbreak of World War I in August 1914 inspired Duke's hasty return to the United States, a prominent South Carolina businessman, worried about the possible allure of London for J. B. Duke, wrote him a letter that inspired an unusually articulate and significant response. The businessman, having missed seeing Duke in both Charlotte and New York, expressed his "very sincere hope that your residence abroad is going to be only temporary." He continued: "We need you in the United States, and particularly in the South." The great obstacles that had to be overcome in the development of the South's "wonderful latent resources" simply required "men of the broad constructive abilities which you possess to so marked a degree." Duke's personal interest in "our electric power and transportation matters" and in the "direct introduction of our Southern goods to the Orient" had been "highly gratifying." The South Carolinian concluded by declaring that he wished to assure Duke that "I feel very keenly the loss that it will mean to us if your personal interest and activities should be devoted elsewhere."

J. B. Duke, who generally delegated the task of responding to letters to his executive secretary, could hardly ignore such a gracious tribute as the South Carolinian had paid him. Accordingly, he personally replied in a rare articulation of his priorities and inner thoughts. "It is true," Duke noted after expressing thanks for the letter, "that it has become necessary for the protection of my own interests that in the future I devote a considerable portion of my time in the British Empire and the Continent of Europe." That fact alone, however, "does not mean that I have in the slightest degree lost interest in my native land and it people, especially that part lying south of the Potomac and embraced in the States of North and South Carolina." Duke continued, "I have always felt that this particular region had, by reason of its natural resources and climate conditions, the possibility of becoming one of the most favored and desired spots on this Continent or elsewhere." Duke believed that the "one thing necessary ... to bring this about is capital directed by intelligent effort." He went on to say:

> With this end in view I have within the past five years invested and caused to be invested in the two states above named, approximately twenty-five million dollars. I have invested this money along lines calculated to do most for the general good of the two states and the prosperity of the people; that is, in the

development of water powers running to waste and in the improvement of transportation facilities. Those investments can be made profitable and even exceedingly attractive if we can secure the co-operation of your people (in supporting them with their business); but without this they are doomed to failure....

J. B. Duke concluded his rare letter with a combination of sentiment and mild threat. He could never, he declared, "lose a sentimental interest in the land that gave me birth; but my financial interest in the future must necessarily be limited by the appreciation shown and the cooperation afforded those investments already made.... To sum up briefly, my future investments in your state and elsewhere in the South will depend upon the encouragement I receive at the hands of your people and not upon my place of residence or the investments I have made in foreign countries."[21]

People in the Piedmont need not have worried. J. B. Duke was one Tar Heel who had never totally left home, and events were transpiring to bring him closer to his native region than ever.

8

ELECTRIFYING THE PIEDMONT CAROLINAS
Part II

Just as everything seemed to be going so well for the power company, disaster struck in July 1916. Unprecedented rains falling on the eastern slopes of the Blue Ridge Mountains in western North Carolina caused the trouble in two destructive stages. First, in early July, the remnants of what was then called a tropical cyclone passed inland over the Gulf coast and thoroughly soaked the western Carolinas, filling the streams and rivers. Then, on July 15–16, the remnants of another tropical cyclone moved inland from the Atlantic coast and in a twenty-four-hour period dumped over nineteen inches of rain on the mountainous area where the Catawba originates.[1]

"Greatest flood since Noah," declared old-timers near the Catawba. A young employee who had just been hired in the Dukes' New York office, which maintained direct and constant links of communication with the power company and all its plants, reported that a stenographer emerged from an inner office with a dazed look. Then he announced woefully that they had all best look for new jobs because the "rains have been so heavy down there...at the Catawba river, that the company's washed the hell down the river."[2]

Governor Locke Craig reported to the North Carolina legislature, "There has been no such swell of waters since the country was settled by white people.... The sides of mountains were torn loose. The valleys were flooded by raging torrents. Trees, crops, buildings, roads, railroads and the land itself were swept away.... The rich bottom lands of the Yadkin, the Catawba and tributaries were turned to desert wastes."[3]

On the Southern Power system, the Rocky Creek plant just below Great Falls suffered the greatest damage. After river debris settled on the plant's roof, it caved in, and the raging river swept through the plant. The original Catawba plant at India Hook Shoals went out of service on July 15, 1916, and could not resume service until December. A number of other plants were knocked out for periods ranging from six days to two months.[4]

The power company's loss, both in equipment and from lost kilowatt hours of service to customers, ran into the millions of dollars. But by purchasing power from every available source — and the earlier linkage with the Georgia Railway and Power Company proved invaluable — and by carrying dangerous overloads on its own plants, the company slowly struggled to its feet. "Every useful and available member of the organization was put to work," a veteran employee recalled, "and sleep was at a premium until the restoration...of the plants was completed."[5]

Although J. B. Duke well knew that he could not check the rains from the sky, he rushed south from New York, alarmed as well as angry about the large losses. Traveling around from plant to plant inspecting the damage, he no doubt made frequent use of his favorite expletive, "Well I'll be dinged." E. C. Marshall, in whose home Duke frequently stayed when in Charlotte, finally confessed: "Mr. Duke, I don't blame you for being mad. If that were my money floating down the river, I would be mad too.... We just don't know how to cope with the river and the flood." Duke grunted his assent to the explanation but added that he meant to find out how to cope with such problems and that he expected the others in the company to apply themselves promptly to the same task.[6]

W. S. Lee, Charles Burkholder, and other first-rate engineers in the company quickly proceeded to carry out Duke's directions. Their solution proved to be perhaps the most impressive and imaginative single project yet achieved on the Catawba River: they would build a series of three massive interlinked dams on the headwaters of the Catawba and create a vast reservoir behind the dams. Not only would the dams help to avoid future flooding such as had occurred in 1916, but the reservoir could also be utilized to increase stream flow on the lower Catawba during the low water of dry spells. The project would prove to be a giant step for the company in taming, enhancing, and thus harnessing the entire Catawba River.

The first phase of the large-scale project began in 1916, promptly after Duke's stern pronouncement following the flood. The company selected a site in mountainous Burke County at the small town of Bridgewater, about eight and a half miles west of Morganton, North Carolina. There they would build the Bridgewater plant and reservoir, which would be named Lake James in tribute to James B. Duke. Because the tracks of the Southern Railway ran alongside the Catawba and east of the town of Bridgewater, the engineers realized that to build a high dam across the Catawba at that point would be impracticable. Therefore they hit on the solution of building three separate dams, all within a radius of two and half miles from the railroad station at Bridgewater—one dam on the Catawba itself and two on tributaries that fed into it. Because topographical and geological conditions at the three sites precluded the use of masonry dams, the company built earthen dams, one of which was said to be among the highest in the world at that time. Altogether, the project represented a remarkable and highly creative feat of engineering. W. S. Lee and Richard Pfaehler, a young engineer who worked with Lee on the project, were understandably proud of what Southern Power had accomplished at Bridgewater and wrote several detailed accounts of the project for the leading journals in engineering.[7]

The Bridgewater plant began operation in 1919, but the critical test for the flood-control aspect of the project came in 1940. In August of that year, the highest flood on record occurred at the upper reaches of the Catawba, a flood even worse than the one in 1916. As a result of the Bridgewater reservoir (Lake James), however, the flood stage at Morganton in 1940 was 14.5 feet below the 1916 mark. At other points on the river, the 1940 levels were similarly reduced.[8] While the plan for releasing water from Lake James to increase the flow of the lower Catawba during dry spells proved to be highly effective and beneficial to the company, not even that arrangement would prevent a desperate situation for Duke Power when rains refused to come in the long hot summer of 1925.

While the Western Carolina Power Company (a subsidiary of the Southern Power Company) was building the Bridgewater plant and reservoir. J. B. Duke organized another company, the Wateree Power Company, to build the Fishing Creek and Wateree plants, the latter to become the largest plant on the system up to that point. One should note that J. B. Duke believed in carefully looking ahead and acquiring land and water rights as early as possible, long before the public announcement of a project. The Wateree Power Company was incorporated in 1909, but the construction on the Wateree plant did not begin until November 1916. In May 1917, moreover, J. B. Duke incorporated the Wateree Electric Company in New Jersey. This step was important in the history of the company, for the Wateree Electric Company gradually became the owner of a number of power companies that J. B. Duke and his brother had organized, including the Great Falls River Company and the Wateree Power Company, among others. In November 1924, The Wateree Electric Company changed its name to the Duke Power Company. The Southern Power Company, however, kept its name and separate identity until December 1927—more than two years after J. B. Duke's death—when it too became part of the Duke Power Company.

W. S. Lee and the growing cadre of first-rate engineers recruited by the company were unconcerned with corporate structure and names. The engineers, and the hundreds of those who worked with them, built dams, reservoirs, and generating plants with remarkable alacrity. No sooner was the Fishing Creek hydro-station, located about two miles north of Great Falls, substantially completed (and while work on the Bridgewater project was also underway), than work on the largest plant so far built on the Catawba began in February 1917. This was the Wateree plant, about eight miles north of Camden, South Carolina, and the farthest downstream Duke plant on the Catawba-Wateree River. The huge plant cost $5.25 million; began operation in September 1919; and had an installed capacity of 56,000 kilowatts, which was more than one-third of the Duke system's total capacity at that time.[9]

J. B. Duke liked the company of many of the able engineers and others in the Charlotte headquarters. Moreover, he particularly liked being around large construction projects involving stone, water, and other materials. Consequently, he made frequent trips to Charlotte and from there to construction sites at Bridgewater, Wateree, and elsewhere. In Charlotte he had no office of his own but, as Norman Cocke later recalled, Duke would arrive at the power company's office around 7:30 or 8:00 a.m. Interested in the loads at different plants, he would often remain for long periods in the central operating office. Sometimes he would just drop in on W. S. Lee or Cocke or Marshall.

On some days, Duke would have a simple picnic lunch prepared so that his chauffeur-valet, Fred Crocker, whose services he had acquired in England, could drive him and one or two others out to one of the power plants or construction sites. One young engineer, newly employed by the company, met Duke with trepidation, for the word had been passed around that "Mr. Duke was a dangerous man to talk to, that he remembered everything you told him, and he might bring it out two or three years later in an embarrassing way." Sometime after the introduction, Duke invited the young man to ride out with him for an inspection of a new coal-burning steam plant. After the nervous engineer managed to have someone telephone a heads-up alert to the plant, he and J. B. Duke set out in the latter's old chauffeur-driven Rolls-Royce. As the car topped a hill near the plant and the engineer saw that both stacks were clear with no black smoke coming out, he felt one spasm of relief. But as Duke's actual inspection of the plant began, the engineer's tension mounted. After going through turbine, pump, and boiler rooms, questioning all along, Duke walked outside and, to the engineer's great consternation, proceeded to walk into an opening at the base of a chimney, where soot was gathered with a small electric machine. The area turned out to be perfectly clean. Returning to the car and sharing sandwiches and a thermos of coffee with the engineer, Duke looked straight at him and said, "You have fine plant here. I like the way you run it." As the young engineer began to glow, Duke added, "Why don't you run the others like this?"[10]

Duke frequently went out to the dam and power plant at Wateree during their construction between 1917 and 1919 and often visited in the home of the resident engineer, A. Carl Lee, younger brother of W. S. Lee. Smoking the small, mild cigars that he liked, Duke would sit in a large rocking chair after dinner, occasionally hold the Lees' baby daughter, and talk about his own young daughter, Doris, who had been born in November 1912. Duke told Mrs. Lee that on one occasion he had been emphasizing to Doris that he had always been a Methodist, her grandfather had been a Methodist, and he hoped she would be one also. When Doris looked up at him and asked, "Daddy, what's the difference between a Methodist and a Presbyterian?," Duke had to do some quick thinking. "Doris, it's time for you to go to bed," he hastily announced. "You go to bed and tomorrow we'll settle all that." The next day Duke promptly sought out a Presbyterian minister in Charlotte, absorbed a few of the fine points of theology and church history, and then tried to explain the denominational difference as best he could to his bright, inquisitive young daughter.[11]

Giving concrete expression to J. B. Duke's intensifying interest in the power company and his native region, he decided in 1919 to acquire a home in Charlotte. His fondness for the business-minded and ambitious city had grown steadily since the establishment of the power company, so he purchased a house in the new, close-in suburban section known as Myers Park and near homes of the E. C. Marshalls and other power company officials. Duke remodeled the house extensively and handsomely landscaped its ample grounds; he also installed a fountain on the lawn that threw a jet of water more than eighty feet in the air. The house itself was spacious and comfortable, rather than pretentious, but the fountain and the grounds were Duke's special joys. Always a keen lover of trees, he admired the stately white oaks on his property and especially liked coming with his family from New York to Charlotte in the early spring. That was when, he declared, the white oaks "bloomed." (They did not actually bloom but budded out in a showy manner.)[12]

By the time Duke acquired his home in Charlotte he was sixty-three years old and obviously mellowing, even if in no way losing his zeal for work or his keen sense of business. Bertha (Mrs. E. C.) Marshall, had been a girlhood friend of Nanaline Holt (Mrs. J. B.) Duke in Macon, Georgia, and she became a good friend also of J. B. Duke. The Duke she saw socially in Charlotte was a man who "loved to laugh and...to enjoy watching people's grass grow and he would go in and ask them how they grew their dahlias or chrysanthemums or violets or whatever...." When Bertha Marshall and Nanaline Duke met and proceeded to chat, as they frequently did, J. B. Duke laughingly declared, "You women go ahead and knock each other. I never have time to sit down and listen to women talk." He sat there laughing, however, and when a lull occurred in the women's conversation, he said, "Go ahead and say some more."[13]

Entertaining small groups for dinner in his Charlotte home, Duke often had movies shown in the living room after dinner. There were home movies of young Doris and some of the silent spectacles then coming out of Hollywood too. On one occasion when there was conversation rather than movies, Mrs. Marshall made some laughing comment about J. B. Duke's shoes. All his life he had had trouble with his feet and his shoes, and the difficulty probably began with the rough, heavy brogans that he had to wear as a boy. Needled by Mrs. Marshall's remark, Duke laughed and proceeded to remove a shoe, demonstrating the built-up support of his arch and explaining that the comfortable shoes were one of six pairs made in Italy some twenty years earlier. "I would not wear those awful looking shoes you have with that nice slender foot," Mrs. Marshall retorted. "I thought you had deformed feet."[14]

Though the whole episode was silly and light-hearted, Mrs. Duke probably did not care for such undignified behavior as the removal of a shoe in public. She frequently accompanied her husband to Charlotte, where Doris was enrolled for a while in a kindergarten conducted in the rear of a neighborhood grocery store.[15] The Dukes occasionally attended Sunday morning services in some of the Methodist churches in Charlotte, to which J. B. Duke made substantial contributions.

Just as Washington Duke had heard Sam Jones, a famous evangelist, preach a generation earlier, J. B. Duke in Charlotte went to hear Billy Sunday, a well-known evangelist of the early twentieth century. In fact, Duke invited Billy Sunday to his home. When Duke asked him why he indulged in so many gymnastics in the pulpit, the evangelist replied, "Oh, Boss, you know how it is. If I'd get up there and just preach a dry sermon, I'd never get these people in there." Chuckling, Duke authorized one of his associates to give Sunday $1,000 from him.[16]

Many such aspects of life in Charlotte appealed to Duke, but New York and such exclusive resorts as Newport, Rhode Island, were more to the taste of Nanaline Duke. After leasing different houses in Newport for several seasons, in 1922 J. B. Duke purchased a "cottage" there for his wife, who always insisted that she was not a "picnic girl." She certainly did not have to "picnic" at Newport, for the mansion that Duke bought, "Rough Point," had been built by Frederick W. Vanderbilt in 1886 and was one of the great houses of the famed resort. Just as Mrs. Duke often accompanied her husband to Duke's Farm and Charlotte, he dutifully put in appearances at Newport. But he growled some, too; "I like those old ladies at Newport," he told Bertha Marshall, "but I don"t want to sit by them [at dinner] every night."[17]

On one occasion when Mrs. Marshall was visiting the Dukes at Newport, she and Mrs. Duke slipped away for a cigarette. Duke, who never liked to see women smoke, later confronted his wife with the accusation, "You've been smoking." Crossing her fingers no doubt, she quickly replied, "I can prove by Bertha Marshall that I haven't." To the relief of Mrs. Marshall, Duke dropped the subject.[18]

For all of Mrs. J. B. Duke's enjoyment of certain expensive things, she, like Mrs. Ben Duke, was quite capable of counting pennies and watching expenditures. Both women had grown up in a time and place — the post-Civil War South — where poverty, however genteel, was the general rule, and all the money in the world could hardly eradicate indelible childhood memoirs and attitudes. When Nanaline Duke complained privately to Bertha Marshall about certain of J. B. Duke's expenditures connected with the Charlotte residence, the latter promptly retorted, "Now, you just let him alone. Look at all those beautiful diamonds he has given you. This [residence in Charlotte] is his diamond bracelet.... Let him enjoy himself."[19]

Mrs. Marshall was only partly right: J. B. Duke's real "diamond bracelet," in the sense of affording him great pride and pleasure, was not so much the residence in Charlotte as it was the great dams with their great cascades of water and the electric power system as a whole. Just precisely when he began to explore in his own mind the idea of using a substantial part of his stock in the power company as the basis for a large philanthropic project for the Carolinas no one can say for certain. But almost from the time that William R. Perkins became Duke's legal counselor in 1914, Perkins had in one of his desk drawers an early rough draft, made for Duke, of what eventually became a decade later the indenture creating The Duke Endowment.[20]

The beginning of Ben Duke's protracted illness around 1915 was another development that influenced J. B. Duke, for it forced a modification of the old division of labor between the two brothers. While J. B. Duke had always taken the lead in the family's business affairs, Ben Duke for a quarter-century had specialized in the family's charitable concern for many institutions in North Carolina, particularly for the Methodist church and Methodist-related Trinity College. Starting around 1915, however, J. B. Duke directly assumed certain annual philanthropic responsibilities that were relatively new to him.

Bishop Kilgo as well as Ben Duke helped nudge J. B. Duke toward the acceptance of more philanthropic responsibilities. Kilgo, after visiting the Duke brothers in New York and at Duke's Farm in the summer of 1915, reported enthusiastically to Few: "I feel that I used the opportunity for its full value, and if there had been nothing except the companionship I should have written down the trip as one of life's highest points. But as things turned out, it became a mountain peak event in my life." Kilgo added, in unhappy words for the historian, that it was all too lengthy for him to try to relate in a letter.[21]

J. B. Duke soon assigned his own landscape architects to the preparation of plans for the Trinity College campus, and he provided a special fund of $10,000 for the grounds. Starting in 1915 he commenced the practice of making an annual contribution to supplement the funds of the two Methodist conferences in North Carolina for their "worn-out preachers" and the widows and orphans of deceased preachers. He requested Trinity College to disburse $10,000 annually for that purpose, a chore that President Few performed happily and gracefully just before Christmas each year. In addition, Duke began giving $25,000 annually to the Board of Church Extension of the Methodist Episcopal Church, South; $15,000 of the gift was earmarked for the building of rural churches and $10,000 for assistance with the current expenses of such churches. In 1920, J. B. Duke requested Trinity College to administer these funds also and explained to the Board of Church Extension that he made the change not through any dissatisfaction but simply because "I have always been very closely identified with Trinity College, and not only would like for them to handle it for me, but think it would help the college by its so doing."[22]

As for the power company and its relationship to philanthropic plans, many of J. B. Duke's closest associates were always struck by the fact that he took neither salary nor expenses from the company during the two decades he was so closely involved in it. More significantly, Duke was not interested in his and his family's receiving dividends from the vast blocks of stock they held in the various companies that made up the Southern Power system. A typical example of this came in 1911 when Ben Duke learned that no dividends would be paid on the preferred stock he held in the Southern Power and Great Falls companies. "We have more than earned the dividends," the Duke's executive secretary and treasurer of the power companies explained, "but it seems to be the same old story, namely that we have been spending so much money for extensions and new acquisitions that we have not sufficient money in the bank to pay the dividends without cramping ourselves. I took the matter up with Mr. J. B. Duke and his decision was that we should not attempt to pay the dividends on the 1st of April."[23]

Both J. B. Duke and B. N. Duke advanced the equivalent of the dividends to certain kinspeople or friends who held small quantities of the power company stock and who might have needed the income. The principal owners of the company, however, were not building the vast Southern Power system for the quick enrichment of themselves and their families. Rather, the Dukes themselves expected to find the necessary capital for the cash-devouring enterprise. In the spring of 1917, Ben Duke, his wife, and his two children had loans out to the Southern Power Company and one other related company that totalled $1,020,000. By August 1917, Ben Duke's son Angier was selling the family's American Tobacco preferred stock as well as other stock in order to gain additional cash for the power company.[24]

As sound as J. B. Duke's business judgment usually was, he was by no means infallible. One venture in which he invested considerable capital and effort failed rather dismally—his attempt to utilize his power plants on the Catawba for the important and lucrative manufacture of fertilizer. Duke noted that at certain times when good rains produced high water (but not too high) on the Catawba, his generating plants were from an early date capable of producing more electricity than there was a market for. He understood that electricity, unlike tobacco or textiles or many other commodities, could not be stored, and waste bothered him. He liked to remind his engineers and other associates in the power company that before the plants were built, only water flowed down the Catawba-Wateree to the ocean. But once the plants were installed, water wastage represented loss in dollars.

By 1908 Duke, working closely with W. S. Lee, began investigating ways to put that surplus power to use. One way to solve the problem might be to manufacture aluminum, a process requiring large amounts of electricity. The catch in Duke's case was, however, that his surplus electricity was only intermittently available. Thus Duke and Lee continued an intensive and far-reaching search for an electrochemical use of the surplus electricity. After considering various other possibilities, they decided to utilize the fixation of atmospheric nitrogen to make fertilizers and explosives.[25]

After considerable investigation, J. B. Duke, who obviously had to educate himself quickly about a complex new process and industry, purchased the United States or North American rights to several European patents. Then he and Lee built an experimental plant on the Catawba just above Great Falls. The plant site was named Nitrolee and began operations in May 1911. It soon encountered problems, however. An Austrian chemical engineer whom Duke employed to help run the plant later explained that the principal problem was that surplus power was only sporadically available for the plant's operation. Thus the company was unable to set a regular schedule of production and to negotiate firm contracts for the sale of nitric acid. Because of these complications and other developments, the Nitrolee plant was shut down in 1916.[26]

Not one to be easily deterred, J. B. Duke set to find other water-power sites where abundant and cheap electricity could be produced and then used to make nitric acid for fertilizer or gunpowder. In pursuit of that goal, J. B. Duke—accompanied by W. S. Lee, George G. Allen, Ben Duke and various others—proceeded in September 1912 to travel by a special train to the Pacific Northwest in search of likely waterpower sites. An unanticipated diversion into Canada, however, would lead to one of J. B. Duke's boldest entrepreneurial gambles.

9

A MASSIVE ENTREPRENEURIAL
GAMBLE IN CANADA

J. B. Duke had gambled on the Catawba River in 1905, for he had built hydroelectric plants before the market for their electricity was fully developed. That gamble, however, paled in comparison to the risk he later took when he set out to build what would be the world's largest hydrostation at that time in a remote region of northern Canada where there was then virtually no market for electricity. That the gamble ultimately paid off handsomely should not blind one to the sheer audacity of the undertaking in the first place.

In a sense, Duke's involvement in the Canadian venture was a serendipitous development, one that he had neither planned nor foreseen. In a search for large and undeveloped water-power sites, he set off in September 1912 with Ben Duke, W. S. Lee, George G. Allen, and various others. Travelling in private railway cars, the group headed for the Pacific Northwest, going via up-state New York. Prior to departure from New York City, however, Charles Bryan, a friend of the Dukes who was a native of New Bern, North Carolina, helped to persuade J. B. Duke to alter his itinerary. Involved with a fertilizer-producing company, Bryan hoped to tie up with Duke and wanted him to check out, among other things, a power site in a remote region of Canada owned by Thomas L. "Carbide" Willson, a pioneer inventor in the electrochemical field who was also allied with the fertilizer-producing company.[1]

Willson's power site was on the Saguenay River, which is located about a hundred miles north of Quebec City. A tributary of the mighty St. Lawrence River, the Saguenay is itself a most spectacular river that runs approximately ninety miles before joining the St. Lawrence. The Saguenay is fed by Lake St. John, which is roughly circular, twenty-five miles in diameter, and covers 410 square miles at high water. Adding immeasurably to the advantageousness of a possible Saguenay power source for industry was the fact that in the relatively short stretch of about thirty miles below Lake St. John, the Saguenay completes its 300-foot fall to sea level. Then in the remaining fifty-two miles to the St. Lawrence River, the Saguenay runs through a broad, deep fjord that is navigable by ocean-going ships. In other words, while the Saguenay was in a remote, undeveloped region, there was easy and economical access to the market-rich eastern seaboard of the United States. J. B. Duke probably did not know all of these geographic facts when he arrived on the Saguenay in September 1912—but he had a remarkably quick mind plus the invaluable assistance of W. S. Lee.

Arriving on a train from Ottawa at the riverside village of Chicoutimi, Duke and his party boarded a steamboat to take them upstream about six miles to the head of tidewater. There they were met by wagons and drivers who took them to see "Carbide" Willson's dam on the Shipshaw River, which is a tributary of the Saguenay. Duke was not impressed by what he saw, but he had yet to see the upper Saguenay itself. To do that, he and others had to walk about two miles through rough country. Reaching an overlook, where the vast river broke thunderously through dramatic gorges, Duke and Lee separated from the party and went down to the bank of the Saguenay to examine it close up and critically. Duke was there less than thirty minutes, Lee later recalled, before he made his decision. "Lee, I'm going to buy this," Duke announced.[2]

Duke's idea of buying the power sites on the upper Saguenay was conditional, however. As early as 1910, an American engineer who studied the economic potential of the Saguenay had noted that the Saguenay's flow varied from roughly 170,000 cubic feet per second during the spring flood to some 22,000 cubic feet per second during the low-water period of late winter, giving a ratio of approximately eight to one. To more nearly equalize the flow of the river over the course of the year, the engineer recommended that the level of Lake St. John should be raised, which would require the permission of the Quebec government.[3]

Having studied that 1910 report, along with other such documents, W. S. Lee shared the information with Duke, and both men, from the beginning, assumed that any development they undertook on the Saguenay would have to involve the raising of the level of Lake St. John. Unlike numerous others who had long envisioned discrete power sites on the Saguenay, Duke and Lee, already veterans of comprehensive river development on the Catawba, had more ambitious plans in mind. But they could hardly have realized what a long, arduous process would be required before they could realize their dream.

Continuing on to Seattle after the visit to the Saguenay, Duke saw nothing that could rival the potential of what he had seen in Canada. Upon returning to New York, therefore, Duke had his lawyers prepare two contracts: one with "Carbide" Willson gave Duke a one-year option to purchase Willson's Chute-à-Caron power site on the Saguenay, with Duke free to negotiate on his own for the remaining stretch of the river up to Lake St. John; the other contract with the Interstate Chemical Company stipulated that Duke would test at an experimental plant in North Carolina the so-called "Willson Process" — a method for producing high grade fertilizer that involved, in part, the action of electrically-generated heat on pulverized phosphate rock. If Duke should be satisfied with the results of the experiment, he would then put up $8 million to form a new company and Interstate would be obligated to supply an additional $2 million.[4]

While Duke kept his promise about a full and fair test of the Willson Process, he was all along primarily interested in the power sites on the Saguenay. When complications developed about the exact floodage rights of Willson's site at Chute-à-Caron, Duke shifted his attention farther up the Saguenay and set out to buy the great power site and necessary land and water rights that would eventually become part of the vast development at Isle Maligne. He not only began negotiations in November 1912 with Colonel Benjamin Scott, one of the owners of the upper site, but Duke also returned briefly with Scott to the upper Saguenay. Serious complications arose, however, because Scott and the other owners of the upper or Isle Maligne site had never acquired floodage rights from the hundreds of small farmers and others whose holdings would be impacted by the damming of the river. Although Scott and his agents promptly set about trying to gain the necessary rights, it was a daunting and time-consuming task, so much so that by late April 1913 when Duke left for London and his British-American responsibilities, he was apparently disenchanted about his prospects on the Saguenay. Or was he just being cannily patient?

W. S. Lee, Ambrose Burroughs (Duke's chief attorney in the matter) and one or two other Duke lieutenants anticipated further negotiations, and sure enough, after Duke returned to New York he signed a contract on November 1, 1913, to buy the upper Saguenay for $1.5 million. Benjamin Scott's share of this payment, however, was conditional upon his ability to secure all of the back water or floodage rights considered necessary for the hydro-electric scheme.[5] As for "Carbide" Willson's power site on the Saguenay at Chute-à-Caron, Duke ended up acquiring it and the "Willson Process" at a bargain price ($377,000) because not only did Willson owe a debt of $150,000 to Duke that he (Willson) was unable to pay, but he also had incurred other debts that left him in a most vulnerable financial position.

Just as "Carbide" Willson lost out on any hope of participating in the Saguenay development, so also did the Interstate Chemical Company. Faced with the prospect of bankruptcy, Interstate appealed for emergency aid from J. B. Duke, but he refused to bail out the company. A subsequent lawsuit that went through various appeals and dragged on for several years completely vindicated Duke's position.[6]

As Benjamin Scott and his agents negotiated to obtain the necessary floodage rights along the upper Saguenay—and particularly the all-important right to raise the level of Lake St. John—Duke became involved in complex negotiations looking toward linking up with industrial companies that might utilize some or all of the electricity that would be generated on the Saguenay. Duke and Lee, as stated earlier, envisioned comprehensive development of the 300-foot fall or head from Lake St. John to tidewater. At Isle Maligne, ten miles below the lake on what was known as the Grand Discharge, Lee planned to harness the initial 110 feet of fall in a giant hydrostation. Then twenty-one miles downstream at Chute-à-Caron Lee envisioned an even larger plant that would harness the remaining 200-foot fall. If constructed properly according to Lee's plans, the two dams might together generate upwards of 800,000 horsepower, giving Duke the largest single-company hydroelectric facility in the world at that time.[7]

Duke's promising negotiations with E. I. DuPont de Nemours Powder Company of Delaware began in 1913. Needing steadily increasing amounts of nitric acid for their manufacturing activities, the DuPonts were happy to consider working with J. B. Duke. At first, negotiations involved joint activity in both manufacturing and power generating on the Saguenay, but the anticipated collaboration finally boiled down to the DuPont company's agreeing to buy 120,000 horsepower (of the initial 250,000 horsepower projected) from the Isle Maligne plant.

These promising negotiations with the DuPonts hit a roadblock, however, when Duke and his agents proved unable to secure permission from the government of the Quebec province to raise the level of Lake St. John, an absolutely crucial part of the development scheme worked out by Duke and W. S. Lee. Consequently, the DuPonts pulled out of the venture altogether, and, with World War I churning the Atlantic economy, Duke had to put his bold Canadian project on hold until the early 1920s.

Duke next acquired a valuable ally in his Saguenay venture when he began to team up with Sir William Price late in 1919. One of the top newsprint producers in Canada, Price Brothers already had extensive power and plant capacity on tributaries of the Saguenay, and Duke added to those holdings when he sold timber lands and a power site on the Shipshaw river to Price Brothers. Subsequently, the powerful newsprint company agreed to "become interested in the development of the water powers of the Saguenay River" by subscribing to one-fourth of the development company's stock and contracting to buy a large block of power (200,000 horsepower) from the projected Isle Maligne station.[8]

Not only had Duke solved at least part of his problem about building a market for a huge amount of electricity, but in teaming up with

Sir William Price he had also acquired a valuable political ally. Circumstances in Quebec, and particularly in the Saguenay region, had changed considerably by the 1920s from what they had been in 1914–1916. The worldwide economic depression of 1920 had a devastating impact in the province of Quebec. Prices of both manufactured goods and agricultural commodities plummeted. "Mills closed, fields lay fallow, and a renewed wave of emigration to the United States took shape," one historian notes, "as the young and under-employed sought out desperately needed work outside the bounds of the homeland province."[9]

In the more prosperous years around 1915, Duke's proposed project on the Saguenay had received a decidedly mixed reception among the inhabitants of the region, with many merchants in favor of it and many farmers opposed. By 1922, however, opposition to the project had virtually disappeared. Moreover, a new premier in Quebec announced that his government was determined "to open our doors wide to capitalists" in the search for economic progress and to pay "particular attention to the further development of all our natural resources."[10]

The upshot of all this was that by late 1922, with Sir William Price playing a key role, Duke finally won the coveted permission to raise the level of Lake St. John. Ten years after making his bold decision to buy and develop the prime power sites on the Saguenay, J. B. Duke had finally gained a green light. This meant that he would put W. S. Lee, Frank Cothran, Richard Pfaehler, and other similarly experienced Duke Power engineers back to work on what would be one of the world's largest hydroelectric plants (at that time) on Isle Maligne in the Saguenay.

Although the highly talented engineers brought two decades of experience in building dams and hydroelectric plants on the Catawba River, they faced a new challenge on the Saguenay. Its natural flow was six to seven times that of the Catawba, and the Isle Maligne's projected output , as finally worked out by Lee and his colleagues, would be 540,000 horsepower. By way of contrast, Southern (Duke) Power's eight hydro plants in 1920 had a combined capacity of some 314,000 horsepower. The Wateree plant, largest on the Catawba at that time, was designed to generate a maximum of 90,000 horsepower.

Since Isle Maligne was inaccessible in so far as rail transportation was concerned, the Duke team had to build a railroad before construction on the power station could be started. Accordingly, an eleven-mile railway running from Isle Maligne to Hebertville, the nearest station on the Canadian National Railway, was completed by late 1923. Working in below-freezing temperatures during the winter, Duke's engineers and workman then proceeded to build the massive dam and generating plant, a feat of which they were justifiably proud and about which they wrote several articles for leading engineering journals.

Duke, however, continued to face a big problem. With Price Brothers contracted to buy less then half of the Isle Maligne's projected output, who would buy the remainder? Manufacturing aluminum required abundant electricity, but Duke failed in his efforts, which continued on an off-and-on basis after 1908, to find and gain control of a large source of bauxite, the main source of industrial aluminum. After pursuing various schemes—including the possibility of selling Saguenay power to New England utilities—Duke in late 1924 began a series of conversations with Arthur Vining Davis, head of the Aluminum Company of America (ALCOA). By the spring of 1925, those negotations resulted in Duke's exchanging his as-yet-undeveloped power site at Chute-à-Caron, the potential of which was even greater than that of Isle Maligne, for a one-ninth interest (about $17 million) in a reorganized Aluminum Company of America. Furthermore, Davis agreed for ALCOA to purchase 100,000 horsepower from the Isle Maligne plant.[11]

With J. B. Duke's Isle Maligne complex, a new industrial era dawned on the Saguenay. In the somewhat purple prose of one historian, "Canada's poverty-stricken agrarian Cinderella had been transformed by the fairy godmother of hydroelectric power into a princess, consort to a warrior-prince of American merchants, J. B. Duke."[12] The warrior-prince did not live to see the results of what he had initiated, however. While he would undoubtedly have been pleased by the many thousands of industrial jobs that became available to the French Canadians in the hitherto impoverished region, he never intended to transfer the focus of his later interests from the Carolinas to Canada. The entrepreneurial challenge presented to him by the untamed Saguenay in 1912 had simply been irresistible to him. Having gambled big time and won, he turned again to where his heart had always been, at least in good part—the Carolinas and home.

10

CREATING CAROLINA PHILANTHROPY IN PERPETUITY
Part I

The dictionary defines "entrepreneur" as one who organizes, manages and assumes the risk of a business or enterprise. Accordingly, J. B. Duke's last great venture, his creation of The Duke Endowment, was in some ways his boldest feat of entrepreneurship, for he set out to design a perpetual philanthropy on a princely scale for the benefit of Carolinians. While the element of risk was certainly different from that in his earlier business ventures, he had no model for the multifaceted philanthropy that he envisioned and could proceed only with the hope of acting wisely. He began pondering his philanthropic scheme at least a decade, and possibly even earlier, before he actually announced it in December 1924. There were problems connected with the Duke Power Company, however, that had to be solved before he could execute his philanthropic plan.

With Ben Duke unwell from 1915 onward, J. B. Duke increased his involvement with Trinity College as well as with other charitable causes long favored by the family. At Ben Duke's suggestion, J. B. Duke agreed to become a trustee of Trinity College in 1918, but allergic to what he called "town meetings," he chose not to attend the trustees' meetings. Happily absorbed in his work, J. B. Duke was not an easy person to pin down for a conference, and Few had to exercise considerable ingenuity to communicate with or convey information to him. In early 1919, however, after a particularly forceful and graceful letter to J. B. Duke, Few managed to secure an interview. Duke had earlier, once in 1916 and on one or two other occasions, referred vaguely to his long-range philanthropic plans in conversations with Few, but in 1919 matters became more specific. In a frustratingly short letter after the conference, Few wrote: "As I have thought of your plan, it grows in my mind. I think it is really a sounder idea than that around which any other large benevolence in this country with which I am familiar has been built. I have done a good deal of thinking concerning your suggestions, and I should be glad of an early opportunity to talk with you again."[1]

A few weeks later, Few followed up with more specific suggestions for implementing the ideas that J. B. Duke had advanced. "If you and your lawyer find that the property cannot be administered under the charter of Trinity College," Few noted, "I would suggest that you create a separate corporation, perhaps to be called the James B. Duke Foundation or Fund, as you might prefer." The trustees of the foundation could be self-perpetuating and be seven in number, the seven members, in fact, of the executive committee of the Trinity trustees. Since there was a vacancy coming up on the executive committee, Few hoped that J. B. Duke might be willing to fill it. "To carry out your ideas as I understand them," Few continued, "I think the charter of the Foundation ought to provide that the income is to go to Trinity College, Durham, N. C., and the building of rural Methodist churches and the supplementing of rural preachers."[2]

This makes clear that Duke had revealed to Few something of his plan for basing his philanthropic foundation on a substantial portion of Duke's equity in the electric-power company. At that point, however, the beneficiaries of the projected foundation were apparently to be limited to Trinity College and to certain Methodist causes. Nothing had thus far been said, in other words, about Trinity College's fulfilling a dream that went back to the 1890s of becoming a university; or about aid to other educational institutions; or about aid in the areas of health care and child care. In fact, Duke himself may not have yet included these other charitable objects in his thinking.

As Few was about to discover, however, Duke was simply not ready to act in the matter, mainly because the stock of the power company was not paying what he regarded as adequate dividends and could not do so until the rates could be adjusted upward. Too, Duke continued to be fully absorbed in the affairs of the fast-growing power company in the Carolinas and in the vast project he had undertaken on the Saguenay River in Canada.

As Duke and his lawyers battled to gain a rate increase from the North Carolina Corporation Commission in the early 1920s, President Few, whose hopes for Trinity had soared in 1919, struggled with acute budgetary problems that were rooted in the sharp inflationary spiral that afflicted the country around 1918–1919 and then the brief but severe depression of 1920–1921. While both Duke brothers increased their annual support for the college because of the emergency, Few desperately wanted a long-term solution in the form of an endowment. Overworked and badly stressed by college problems, Few had to be hospitalized in the summer of 1920; he continued to be unwell on and off through the winter of 1920–1921, finally developing pneumonia. Convalescing from that in the spring of 1921, he had some time for thinking, and a number of ideas, many foreshadowed by past efforts or proposals, finally fell into place in his mind.

In coming up with his initial blueprint for a new institution, one that Few suggested should be called "Duke University" and that could be organized around Trinity College, Few revealed that he had quite correctly read J. B. Duke's mind. That is, Duke strongly preferred to "think big" — and Few was doing just that. Furthermore, while Duke had deep roots in and affection for his native region, there was nothing parochial — and certainly not sectional — in his outlook. Few, accordingly, spoke of hoping to build a "national" or "major" university, one that would strive to be of the utmost possible service to its home region while at the same time being national in outlook and welcoming students and faculty from other regions. (By "national" or "major" university, Few actually meant research university, but that term was not in use in the 1920s.)

Few's blueprint was no hastily conceived scheme designed to lure a large benefaction. Rather, it was the carefully considered synthesis of a number of ideas that had long been evolving and of developments in Trinity College that were already underway.[3] Also one should particularly note that the idea of naming the new, enlarged institution "Duke University" came from Few. His principal reason was that there were already in the United States alone a Trinity University in San Antonio, Texas, and several other Trinity Colleges. In Great Britain and elsewhere in the English-speaking world there were numerous other educational institutions named "Trinity." Not wishing to share a name with so many others, Few turned to the name that various people first began to suggest in the 1890s, but there is not a shred of evidence that any member of the Duke family had ever shown any interest in changing the institution's name.

At any rate, as a result of his brainstorm in 1921, Few drew up the following statement that he hoped J. B. Duke would sign:

> I wish to see Trinity College, the law school & other schools expanded into a fully developed university organization. It has been suggested to me that this expanded institution be named Duke University as a memorial to my father whose gifts made possible the building of Trinity College in Durham, and I approve this suggestion. I desire this university to include Trinity College, a Coordinate College for Women, a Law School, a School of Religious Training, a School of Education, a School of Business Administration, a School of Engineering (emphasizing chemical & electrical engineering), a Graduate School of Arts & Sciences, and, when adequate funds are available, a Medical School. I desire this enlarged institution to be operated under the present charter with only such changes, if any changes at all, as this enlargement may require. To this university that is to be thus organized I will give _____ millions of dollars. I agree to pay in within _____ years _____ millions of dollars either in cash or good securities.[4]

After having gained Ben Duke's enthusiastic approval of the proposal, Few traveled to New York to confer with J. B. Duke. He, however, was still not ready to commit himself so definitely and refused to fill in the blanks that Few had left in the document or to sign it. J. B. Duke did, nevertheless, gave some sort of general approval to the scheme, for when Trinity's trustees met in June, 1921, Few alluded briefly to a possible reorganization looking toward university status. To one or two close friends, Few referred to "great plans which I think in due course will be completely realized" and to "our reorganization for the future." Conferences about the matter between J. B. Duke and Few followed, but there is no record of what was said or agreed upon.[5]

Few's plan for the university included a medical school, "when adequate funds are available." The qualifying phrase was important, for Few had been learning about medical education and its extremely high cost from the most authoritative teacher on the subject in the country, Dr. Abraham Flexner. Author of a report for the Carnegie Foundation that helped revolutionize medical education in the United States after 1910, Flexner began advising Few in 1916, when Trinity's president resumed thinking about something that had interested his predecessors intermittently since the 1890s. With no four-year medical school in North Carolina, there was a growing awareness in the state of the critical need. Nor was there, in fact, a first-class medical school anywhere in the South at that time.

After the distraction caused by the nation's involvement in World War I had passed, Few again picked up the idea of a medical school but hoped to avoid the financial burden that Trinity would have to bear if it alone tried to build a four-year school. He therefore came up with a bold, imaginative scheme whereby a new medical school in Durham could be linked with both Watts Hospital, an idea which George W. Watts supported, and with the existing two-year, preclinical medical school at the nearby University of North Carolina. The Rockefeller-backed General Education Board was also eager to help a soundly conceived and well-financed medical school in the South and indicated that it would consider supplying half of the $6 million needed if Few could obtain the other half.[6]

In 1922 Few's bold plans were frustrated by objections from those who hoped that the University of North Carolina might build its own medical school (which it would not be able to do until after World War II) and by some who claimed to see, in the linking together of a church-related institution and a state-supported one, a possible violation of the principle of the separation of church and state. Though Few had failed in his early efforts to secure a medical school, the episode was important in educating J. B. Duke not only about the great cost of medical education but also about the larger situation concerning health care in the Carolinas.

One of Few's strongest supporters in the effort to secure a four-year medical school was Dr. Watson S. Rankin, the secretary of the State Board of Health. One of the most respected public health officers in the nation, Rankin keenly recognized the acute need for a full-fledged, high-quality medical school, but he also warned that such a school would not by itself alleviate the widespread shortage of doctors in much of North Carolina. Still one of the most rural states in the nation, as well as one of the poorest, North Carolina faced daunting deficiencies in the area of health care. Rankin had come to believe that the main remedy for the shortage of doctors in rural areas and small towns would be the establishment of a system of local, community-supported hospitals. He had closely studied a system of government-supported community hospitals in the sprawling, agricultural province of Saskatchewan in western Canada; as a result, he had become a veritable apostle on behalf of not-for-profit, local hospitals as an essential step toward better health care for Carolinians.[7]

Rankin's ideas, relatively novel and advanced in the United States at that time, clearly had a great influence on J. B. Duke. And in deciding to work with and through Rankin, Duke showed the same knack for spotting uniquely talented and dedicated persons that he had displayed throughout his career. He treated them — men like W. S. Lee, W. A. Erwin, and Watson Rankin — fairly and generously, thereby winning their lifelong loyalty.

Unlike Ben Duke, J. B. Duke had, for the most of his life, little direct experience with higher education in general or Trinity College in particular. Yet in deciding to work with W. P. Few to build a great university, J. B. Duke also showed the same shrewd ability to select and then work fruitfully with an outstandingly able person.

As the outline of what would become The Duke Endowment gradually took shape in J. B. Duke's mind, it is clear that, in part, he was institutionalizing for posterity, on a princely scale, a pattern of family giving — to higher education (especially Trinity College), to orphanages, and to the rural Methodist church. This was the pattern that Washington Duke had initially inspired in the late nineteenth century and for which Ben Duke had taken the major administrative responsibility between 1890 and 1915.

One of the most creative and original aspects of The Duke Endowment, however, would be in its provision in the area of health care. In assisting communities in the Carolinas to provide hospital care for indigent Carolinians, both white and black, and to build not-for-profit community hospitals, The Duke Endowment would perform one of the classic and most valuable functions of America's private foundations: finding a great social need and trying to show how it might be at least partially met. A good generation or more before the state or federal governments would acknowledge any responsibility in the matter of local hospitals, The Duke Endowment's Hospital Section began in the mid-1920s to point the way. When the federal government enacted the Hill-Burton legislation after World War II to spur the building of community hospitals, The Duke Endowment's pioneering efforts in the Carolinas served as both inspiration and model.

Since that important part of the Endowment was actually not derived from the family's traditional pattern of giving, J. B. Duke himself must be credited with including the health-care area in the Endowment's work. He, in turn, owed a large debt to Watson Rankin, whom Duke would subsequently select to design and direct the work of the Hospital Section.[8]

President Few's abortive effort in 1922 to build an unconventionally supported medical school was not, therefore, a total loss, for it had brought J. B. Duke into contact with Dr. Rankin. Duke continued to be stymied in his philanthropic planning, however, by the fact that his electric power company was simply not making an adequate profit, and he desired a more satisfactory and stable financial base for his projected philanthropy.

Aside from the huge losses incurred in connection with the 1916 flood on the Catawba, the power company, like many other businesses, was hurt by the war-induced inflation and the depression that struck in 1920. The power company, therefore, applied for a rate increase from the North Carolina Corporation Commission late in 1920. The importance of the commission's hearing on the matter was underscored not only by the crowded courtroom but also by the presence of J. B. Duke, making a rare appearance in Raleigh, along with W. S. Lee, Norman Cocke, and others. In presenting the power company's case, attorney Zebulon V. Taylor declared that up to that point the company had invested almost $47 million in North Carolina alone. The earnings in the previous years, however, had not aggregated 3.81 percent and during the previous five years the earnings of the company had not reached the 5 percent mark. The time had come, Taylor concluded, for the company to show better returns on the investment if it wished to expand and gain additional capital.[9]

With the Corporation Commission calling for a continuance of the case until mid-January 1921, the debate now shifted to the state legislature, and a classic example of how politics influences and often distorts rate regulation now unfolded. Josephus Daniels, powerful editor of the Raleigh *News and Observer*, and his Democratic allies in the legislature had hailed the relatively new (1913) principle of state regulation of electric utilities. (After the North Carolina Democrats had smashed their Republican and Populist opponents in the torrid "white supremacy" campaigns of 1898 and 1900, the Democrats maintained an almost unchallengeable control of the state government and its agencies.) Yet so bitterly did Daniels and his allies oppose J. B. Duke, a well known Republican and capitalist, that they clamored for—and almost got—a state law that would leave all existing contracts between Southern Power and its larger customers (mostly textile mills) outside of any rate adjustments that the Corporation Commission might be willing to make for Southern Power.

While the owners of some cotton mills recognized the seriousness of the power company's plight and sympathized with its need for higher rates, other mills, including the Cannon Mills of Kannapolis, North Carolina, did not and fought tenaciously to protect the low rates in their existing contracts. In a public hearing before the state senate's committee on the Corporation Commission, the attorney for the mills (that is, those who supported passage of a law that would protect their existing contracts) argued that the owners of the mills had entered into contracts with the power company in good faith and had scrapped their former equipment because they were offered electric power at an attractive price. Further, the attorney declared that the legislature of 1913, which extended the powers of the Corporation Commission to cover utility rates, had never dreamed that the power would be used to abrogate contracts.

The principal attorney for the power company, W. S. O'B. Robinson, countered that the company had also entered into contracts with good faith and had not sought to be relieved of them until the state's supreme court had ruled that all rates of the power company were subject to review by the Corporation Commission and that contracts would not hold as against rates fixed by the commission. Other lawyers, as well as W. S. Lee, also spoke, but a newspaper reporter observed the J. B. Duke sat quietly during the discussion. Only after the hearing ended did he remark, "I think our boys made the best speeches."[10]

The bitter legislative battle raged for many weeks, and the *News and Observer* and the *Charlotte Observer* took diametrically opposite positions. The former wielded its greatest influence and power in the still-predominantly agricultural eastern portion of the state, while the latter championed the interests of the rapidly industrializing Piedmont. "There will be little sympathy for the demands of the power companies to be allowed to make larger profits," Daniels's newspaper declared. "The emergency demands that in behalf of the people the grave responsibility which a previous Legislature entrusted to the Corporation Commission be recalled to the extent that it may under no circumstances be employed to permit the annulling of existing contracts...."[11]

The *Charlotte Observer*, on the other hand, hoped that the public would soon better understand "the influences of prejudice and animosity" that the Southern Power Company had to live down before it could attend to its "program of continued development work in the waterpower and interurban [railway] territory of this part of the South." The Charlotte newspaper avowed that it saw the matter "not as a fight on Duke and his power company, but as a fight against the industrial interests of this part of North Carolina." It was a situation in which "Industrial North Carolina should at least match interest with Political North Carolina."[12]

After an unusually intense political battle, the measure to force Southern Power to maintain its existing contracts with textile mills passed the state senate but failed by one vote in the lower house. The *Charlotte Observer* rejoiced in the outcome of what it described as one of the greatest fights in the legislative history of North Carolina. "It is a very easy matter for legislation to tie the hands of capital," the

Charlotte paper noted. Yet "no faction or combination of factions, however animated, whether by personal prejudice or political animosities, could strike [J. B.] Duke to the ground and not kill the most momentous factor that has yet been created in this part of the country in the development of textile and related industries, and in promotion of the prosperous conditions which follow the establishment and operation of these industries." Another positive outcome, the *Charlotte Observer* believed, was the "establishment by the Legislature of a righteous vindication for the Corporation Commission."[13]

The *News and Observer* saw the matter differently, of course, and as the debate shifted back to the Corporation Commission and its hearing on Southern Power's application, Josephus Daniels fired off a steady barrage of fiery editorials. "The people of North Carolina are threatened with a monopoly in power, in lights, in electric transportation, in gas by reason of the methods of the Southern Power Company," the Raleigh editor asserted. "The Corporation Commission must protect the people or Monopoly and Extortion will have them by the throat."[14]

Daniels seemed to have forgotten, or perhaps not fully understood, that along with state regulation of utility rates came the grant of a monopoly to a utility within a certain specified area. The cry of "monopoly," however, was irresistible to those Democratic partisans who wished to call up memories of the original American Tobacco Company. Despite all the angry rhetoric, the Corporation Commission in July 1921 granted at least a part of Southern Power's request. Hoping to achieve a return of 6.8 percent on investment, the company asked for a wholesale price of 1.4 cents per kilowatt-hour. The Corporation Commission, however, granted a rate of only 1.25 cents, subject to change upon any subsequent petition and additional data from the power company. Although no doubt glad to win even a partial victory, J. B. Duke and his associates were determined to pursue their requests for additional rate increases.

In the immediate aftermath of the 1921 rate increase, limited though it was, Duke authorized the construction of two new hydro plants on the Catawba River (Dearborn and Mountain Island). In addition, to help meet the Piedmont's insatiable appetite for electricity, the company added units to the existing steam plants at Mount Holly and Eno Station (near Durham).

After that, however, J. B. Duke finally issued an ultimatum: he announced that if the power company could not obtain what he and his associates considered a fair return on investment, then Southern Power would build no more plants in the Piedmont. With the company applying to the Corporation Commission for an increase in its wholesale rate to 1.4 cents per kilowatt hour (the amount requested but denied in 1920–1921), J. B. Duke issued a rare public statement in October 1923: "I am ready to spend more money, to build more plants to create more power for the future development of the Carolinas," Duke explained, "but I am not willing to spend it on the basis of the returns which the Southern Power Company is now allowed." He noted that the company had averaged a return of not more than 4 percent since it was started, and those small earnings had always been plowed right back into the company, along with additional millions.

"I have put approximately $60,000,000 of my own money into the Southern Power Company so far," Duke continued. "I have never taken a cent out of it, and never intend to." What he was to invest in the company in the future depended on the attitude of the people toward the undertaking, as revealed through their representatives in Raleigh, the three members of the Corporation Commission. "We will lay the situation before the Corporation Commission," Duke stated. "Our books will be submitted to that body. . . . We will let the records speak for themselves." If the Commission granted the requested increase, then the company was prepared to build another plant costing $10 million to supply the demand for electric power that already existed. "Otherwise, I am through," he concluded.[15]

Predictably enough, Josephus Daniels responded to Duke's statement with flaming editorials in the News and Observer, beginning in October 1923. Daniels charged, among other things, that J. B. Duke, a die-hard monopolist from way back, was out to monopolize electric power in the Carolinas; that much of the so-called investment in the power company was actually "watered stock"; and that since J. B. Duke seemed to think that he was either superman or king, the Corporation Commission might as well abdicate.[16]

The Durham Herald somewhat meekly observed that "it is a pity that the News and Observer is not willing to allow the Corporation Commission to pass upon the [rate] case in accordance with the facts." To which the Raleigh paper replied that it merely wanted the Commission to consider all the facts, including "the use Mr. Duke has made of monopoly in the past and to determine whether, in light of the record, he ought to be confirmed in monopoly of so vital a thing as power."[17]

As influential as Josephus Daniels was in Democratic circles, there were others, besides the *Charlotte Observer*, who dared to take him on. W. O. Saunders, a salty newspaperman in Elizabeth City in the northeastern corner of North Carolina, called on J. B. Duke in his New York office. Saunders asked when Duke was going to bring his power lines into eastern North Carolina, which lagged glaringly behind the Piedmont, and "give us coast country folks some of the cheap power that [your] great superpower system is feeding to scores of towns and cities in the Piedmont section today."

Duke replied that there was indeed plenty of power potential on the Roanoke River in eastern North Carolina. He thought, however, that Josephus Daniels should develop it. Daniels, Duke continued, is a "big, constructive man, always wanting to do something for the people." Let Daniels build a monument to himself, Duke suggested, by harnessing the Roanoke and "putting it to work for eastern North Carolina, just as the Southern Power Company has put the mountain streams of the Carolinas to work for the west."

If there was any bitterness in Duke's words, Saunders reported, he did not betray it by any look or tone, but "there was a sly twinkle in his eye." In the meantime, the Elizabeth City editor noted, Duke was spending millions on hydroelectric projects in Canada. "But Mr. Duke meets with less opposition in Canada than in his native North Carolina. Canadians seem glad enough to let him take their waste waters and turn them into power to be sent over the border to run New England mills. But in North Carolina he meets the constant opposition of Mr. Daniels and the *News and Observer*."[18]

A mill owner in Gastonia who, like quite a few other mill owners in the Piedmont, supported the power company's request for a rate hike, found Daniels's opposition to the hike odd in light of the fact that since 1917 the *News and Observer* had raised its advertising rates approximately 60 percent and its subscription rate nearly $3.50. Would Daniels be willing to go back to 1917 rates?[19]

Taking a more serious approach, *Natural Resources*, a publication of the State Geological and Economic Survey, declared that the greatest danger to the further development of North Carolina's water power lay in the fact that "the politician had added the word 'kilowatt' to his vocabulary." The publication reported that North Carolina then ranked fifth among the states in water power development and second only to New York in the states east of the Mississippi. The forecast was that North Carolina would need an additional 120,000 horsepower in the next two years and an additional 469,000 horsepower for the next five years. At a conservative cost estimate of $100 per horsepower, that meant a capital investment of $12 million in two years to be followed by $46 million in the five following years. In other words, North Carolina in seven years would need more horsepower than had been installed in the whole state up to that point. *Natural Resources* next asserted that the Southern Power Company had not only played the leading role in the past in the state's development of hydropower, but "its activities constitute[d] the best hope of the immediate future." *Natural Resources* concluded that there was nothing in the big, pending rate case that could be brought into politics "except through sheer recklessness, demogogism or wickedness."[20]

W. S. Lee testified that in North Carolina in 1922, power sales had increased about 22 percent over 1921 sales; in 1923, the increase was almost 14 percent over 1922; and the estimate was a 24 percent increase for 1924. "If North Carolina goes ahead as it reasonably should," Lee declared,"we've got to build one or two power plants a year to keep up with the business or somebody else has to do it."

As to average earnings on invested capital in the Piedmont territory served by the company, Lee noted: "I don't think there are any [companies] but what are earning 12 or 15 percent on the invested capital and some of them are going much higher than that." He reminded the Commission that Southern Power had employed an independent engineering consultant to evaluate its property. Moreover, in the 1920–1921 hearing, the protestors (later to be called intervenors) had called for an outside investigation of the power company's books and records. That request was granted, and those who were opposed to the rate hike had employed accountants to check the company's books and engineers to inspect the physical properties. After all that had been done, not a word of testimony was heard from the protestors. Under the rate approval of 1921, the company maintained and the Corporation Commission agreed that the return was 5.91 percent on investment. Under the rate proposed in 1923–1924, there was similar agreement that the return would be 6.86 percent.[21]

J. B. Duke won the desired rate increase in January 1924. In the Corporation Commission's order approving the new rate, it declared, among other things, that the power company was undertaking in good faith to supply a service for which there was an ever-increasing demand. Within the previous two years Southern Power had added 200,000 horsepower to its system, and those additions alone constituted a greater volume of electricity than was produced by all the other companies in North Carolina combined. Those new power units were capable of turning the wheels of more than four hundred cotton mills of ten thousand spindles each. The company was "entitled to a fair return for such service," the Corporation Commission concluded, "and such rate of return as will justify the continuing investment of such sums of capital as may be necessary to continue to meet the increasing demand for power for new industries in the territory it serves."[22]

J. B. Duke had finally won a crucial battle, and his power company would not again face such a critical struggle about its rates until the difficult, indeed perilous, 1970s. Duke's motivation in his zealous effort to build up and protect the power company was not to acquire personal wealth. Indeed, he once commented to his friend Bertha (Mrs. E. C.) Marshall that he had come to realize, just when he did not say, that there simply was not the money to be made in the electric utility business that there had been in tobacco. In lavishing so much time, money, and attention on the power company, J. B. Duke sought, primarily, to facilitate the industrialization of the Piedmont Carolinas and to provide a stable financial base for his projected charitable trust—his Grand Design for perpetual philanthropy in the Carolinas.

11

CREATING CAROLINA
PHILANTHROPY
IN PERPETUITY
Part II

As J. B. Duke had promised, the Corporation Commission's approval of the rate increase in early 1924 led Southern Power to launch a large expansion of its power plants. With demand for electricity, particularly for textile mills, steadily increasing in the Piedmont, the power company had to scramble to stay ahead. It began constructing three new hydrostations and one new steam plant in 1924–1925 and the latter year began planning the first large-scale coal-fired steam plant in the system. Construction of that plant in 1926 would mark an important shift from hydro to steam power, from the Catawba's free "white coal" to fossil fuel that had to be mined from the earth and imported some distance from the Piedmont.

That there was a ready market for all the new output of electricity immensely gratified J. B. Duke, for more than one reason. Aside from wanting a fair return on investment, he had hoped to spur industrialization in the Piedmont Carolina. By the 1920s statistics revealed that the power company was indeed helping to achieve that goal.

"One of the most persistent impulses in the life of the South since the Civil War," a prominent historian has declared, "has been the desire to develop an industrial economy."[1] Certainly a basically important precondition for the pursuit of that goal was the mania for cotton mills that swept over the region from the 1880s well into the twentieth century. Another well-known historian has described the shift of the cotton textile industry from New England to the South's Piedmont between 1880 and 1930 as "the most important migration ever experienced by a major branch of American industry...."[2]

Why did that shift occur? Discounting fervent southern hopes and prayers (and mountains of boosterish rhetoric), one finds that two of the most frequent and widely accepted explanations of the shift point to lower labor and transportation costs for the southern textile mills. While both of these explanation are undoubtedly valid, another historian has pointed out that if the Piedmont South had not developed an adequate and cheap source of power, cheap labor and lower transportation costs would have been meaningless. "Electric power, generated and transmitted over long distances," according to this historian, "was a major factor in the shift of the cotton industry to regions previously associated with an agrarian economy."[3]

The argument continues by noting that New English textile manufacturers relied mostly on local generation of electricity at the mill sites. In the Piedmont Carolinas, on the other hand, the textile mills after about 1905 "rented" most of their power from a centralized system, with its generating plants located on the Catawba and a few other rivers of the Piedmont. Since "rented" or hired power allowed for lower capital expenses, reduced operating costs, and increased flexibility in locating textile mills, the southern mills gained a distinct economic advantage over those of New England and thus encouraged a continued migration of the cotton textile industry to the South.[4]

When J. B. Duke led in the establishment of the Southern Power Company in 1905, the cotton textile industry was well established in the Piedmont Carolinas, which already had over 20 percent of the nation's spindles, and half of these operated in a hundred-mile radius of Charlotte. Then, however, the typical southern mill got its power from steam engines. As discussed earlier, Duke, W. S. Lee, and others in the power company set out to change that arrangement and achieved remarkable success fairly quickly. As early as 1913, southern textile mills consumed more cotton than those of New England. Then in the 1920s, the southern mills clearly achieved national supremacy:

in value of product, 1923; in total spindles and total wages, 1927; and in the number of looms, between 1927 and 1931.[5]

Unfortunately, many historians and other writers have long tended to denigrate the cotton textile industry. Instead of recognizing that industrial economies must develop gradually over time, these historians bemoan the fact that the South did not more quickly move into diversified manufacturing and high technology. And in countless books that emphasize southern workers' low wages and long hours, the authors tend to ignore or gloss over the fact that the wages, as low as they were indeed, were still better than those that could be made from tenant farming. One has to wonder also if the working hours of southern farmers, whether tenants or landowners, were any shorter than those of the mill workers.

The most influential historian of the late-nineteenth and early-twentieth century South, C. Vann Woodward, in a chapter tellingly titled "The Colonial South," paints a largely negative and gloomy portrait of the region's struggle for industrialization in that era. Admitting that there were gains in the South's cotton textile production, he nevertheless argues that the industry "did not escape the general pattern of colonialism [i.e. subordination to northern capital] to which other industries of the region were prone to conform." Noting that the chief products of the southern mills were yarn and coarse cloth, much of which got shipped north for final processing, he adds that the investment of northern capital and the "dependence upon northern commission houses for selling and even for financing brought the cotton mills into line with the colonial trend." While skewering J. B. Duke as "the master of the tobacco monopoly," Woodward nowhere mentions the Southern Power Company or even hydro-electricity— probably because they did not fit into his thesis about colonialism.[6]

The growth of the southern textile industry, however, did not result from a wholesale migration of plants or capital from the North. A study in 1922 revealed that almost 84 percent of southern spindles were owned or controlled by southern capital.[7]

J. B. Duke did not, of course, live to see Charlotte become one of the nation's preeminent banking centers. He would have quickly understood, however, that such could not have happened if the city had not first become a center for financing cotton textile manufacturing, a circumstance made possible at least in part by the Southern Power Company's phenomenal growth.

Fortunately for Duke and the Carolinas, he did live long enough to get his Grand Design for perpetual philanthropy in the Carolinas at least launched, and movement toward that goal quickened after the rate increase in early 1924. What might be called the "starter dough" for what grew to be the great loaf of The Duke Endowment was the Duke family's longstanding involvement with Trinity College. While J. B. Duke began his philanthropic planning with that family sponsorship of Trinity College as his main focus, he displayed his characteristic independence by going far beyond that tie with Trinity in his endowment scheme. And, also quite characteristically, he liked to think and operate on a large scale.

J. B. Duke had always taken great interest and pleasure in construction work, and he was probably more personally excited about the prospect of extensive building at Trinity College than in any other aspect of the development there. One of the most commendable aspects of the Dukes as benefactors of Trinity College had been, in fact, that they had never attempted to interfere in any way with the internal operation or academic side of the institution. While their monetary gifts supported the whole college, in every sense, their personal involvement had always been limited to buildings and grounds—and especially the latter because of their penchant for horticulture and landscaping.

As early as 1923 Duke picked the architectural firm that he wished to design the new buildings that he planned to give to Trinity, and the head of the firm, Horace Trumbauer of Philadelphia, began corresponding with President Few. Then Few and one his key advisors in the area of buildings and grounds made a tour of eastern and midwestern college and university campuses in the spring of 1924. Admiring the Tudor Gothic buildings they studied at Bryn Mawr, Yale, Chicago, and elsewhere, Few and his associate conferred with J. B. Duke and Trumbauer, and all agreed by September 1924 that the Tudor or Collegiate Gothic style was their first choice for the new stone buildings to be constructed in Durham.[8] "Personally, I have no doubt that Mr. Duke, when he once makes up his mind definitely to go ahead, will see that a most creditable job is done," George G. Allen assured Few in September 1924.[9]

Fortunately for Trinity and the Carolinas in general, J. B. Duke finally had stopped concentrating on building dams and generating electric power long enough to "go ahead" with his philanthropic plans. In late October 1924 Robert L. Flowers, vice president for finance at Trinity and Few's right-hand man in administration, went to New York and began sending Few some interesting letters marked "personal and confidential." Conferring at great length with George Allen, W. R. Perkins, and Alex Sands, Flowers discovered that he faced a real challenge in explaining various aspects of Trinity College to New York businessmen who were just becoming acquainted with it. "I think everything is going all right," Flowers assured Few. "From what they tell me, Mr. J. B. Duke is right behind the thing now. Mr. B. N. is greatly interested." Later in the same day Flowers sent off another dispatch: "Mr. J. B. is undecided how to have the trust fund administered." Up until that time and during five years or so of the preliminary planning, the idea had been to have the executive committee of Trinity's board of trustees administer the fund. Now Flowers reported a highly significant new development: "They have been to confer with the Rockefeller Foundation and at present they are very much inclined to have fifteen trustees of the fund." Flowers thought it might be unfortunate for Trinity to have the trustees of the foundation and those of the reorganized college two widely separately. Still, the personnel for the foundation's board would be the important thing, and both Allen and Perkins, according to Flowers, were eager "to get in touch with the college."[10]

One of J. B. Duke's fellow millionaires, Andrew Carnegie, had written extensively to advise wealthy individuals to dispose of their fortunes carefully and wisely during their lifetimes. Ben Duke, unlike J. B. Duke who read little besides certain business reports, may have read Carnegie's advice, and Ben Duke certainly urged his younger brother to proceed expeditiously with his proposed philanthropy. And Flowers reported that, "Mr. J. B. is pushing things just as fast as he can."[11]

Flowers proved to be quite correct about J. B. Duke's "pushing things" rapidly, for early in December 1924 Duke arrived in Charlotte with his wife, his daughter Doris, George Allen, W. R. Perkins, and his nephew-in-law, Anthony Biddle, who was married to Ben Duke's daughter Mary. They were soon joined at Duke's home in Charlotte by several top officers of the power company and one or two others. For an apparently brief part of the time, Few and Flowers joined the group. J. B. Duke announced that he had been working on his philanthropic plans for a number of years and that he now wanted the group to remain assembled until the job of polishing the indenture, the legal instrument that would create the perpetual trust, was completed. Stopping only for meals, the group reportedly met until well into the evening for about four days and discussed, section by section, the lengthy draft by W. R. Perkins.[12]

Unfortunately, documentary evidence concerning what went on in this conference in Charlotte does not exist. Almost forty years after the event, one of the participants could recall no substantial alterations or additions to the indenture that the group made. "Of course, Mr. Duke…was a positive man," this participant noted, "and when he made a positive assertion very few people controverted it."[13] If this memory was correct, and forty years is an especially long time where remembering correctly is concerned, the fact that J. B. Duke's associates did not scrutinize the indenture more critically was indeed unfortunate, for there were, as will be discussed, a number of questionable matters and at least one major blunder, with immediately unfortunate consequences, that might easily have been avoided.

Since there is so little evidence concerning the conference in Charlotte, one can only speculate, but one possible explanation for the reported lack of critical comment may have had to do with an idiosyncrasy of J. B. Duke's: over the years he had found that the quickest way for him to get at the hard-core essence of a business letter or report was to have George Allen, Alex Sands, or whomever was assisting him at the time read the document aloud to him, presumably skipping any prefatory or extraneous matter. Several of Duke's close associates noted that in that manner he could absorb and process information more rapidly than most people. So much did Duke like that procedure, in fact, that he memorialized it in the Endowment indenture by including the request, which has been faithfully honored, that the indenture, with long sections of numbingly legalistic language, be read aloud to the assembled trustees during at least one meeting each year.

That aural method of receiving and processing information apparently worked well for J. B. Duke. For many people, however, the eye works better than the ear for the absorption of complex, important data; and as any teacher knows, not a few people actually doze off if certain types of material are read aloud to them for any length of time. At any rate, one must certainly wonder it a person as intelligent and experienced as was William P. Few might not have caught certain unfortunate passages in the indenture concerning Duke University if he had been given an opportunity to read the passages carefully and think about them.

At any rate, J. B. Duke had taken philanthropic action the likes of which the poverty-stricken South of that era had never known. He did not formally sign the indenture creating The Duke Endowment until December 11, 1924, at his legal residence in New Jersey, but news of it leaked to the newspapers two days earlier. While the nation at large paid ample attention to the development, the largest impact of the news was in the Carolinas where all of the beneficiaries were located. Securities worth approximately $40 million, mostly but not exclusively in the Duke Power Company, were turned over to the trustees of the Endowment, and the annual income was to be distributed among four educational institutions, nonprofit community hospitals and orphanages for both races in the two Carolinas, and the rural Methodist church in North Carolina. First of all, however, the trustees, after dividing among themselves 3 percent of the annual income as compensation for their services, were instructed to set aside 20 percent of the remaining annual income to be added to the principal (or corpus) until an additional $40 million had been accumulated. (This was accomplished in 1976.) The remaining 80 percent of the annual income was to be distributed in the two Carolinas as follows: 46 percent to four educational institutions, 32 percent to nonprofit community hospitals for both races, 12 percent for certain purposes of the rural Methodist church in North Carolina, and 10 percent for orphanages of both races.

Just as Trinity College had been the principal beneficiary of gifts from the Duke family from the 1890s onward, so was "[a]n institution of learning to be known as Duke University" designated as the recipient of 32 percent of the Endowment's annual income. Moreover, to help establish the new university, the trustees were authorized to expend $6 million from the corpus of the trust. Then in clumsy, legalistic, and quite superfluous language that immediately led to long-lasting misunderstanding, W. R. Perkins and J. B. Duke put this sentence in the indenture: "However, should the name of Trinity College...be changed to Duke University" within a three-month period, then the $6 million should go to that institution.

Journalists and others quickly seized on this section of the indenture and interpreted it, understandably enough, as a blatant case of J. B. Duke's "buying himself a university" or bribing a small college to memorialize himself and his family. Since the idea of organizing a university around Trinity and naming the enlarged institution "Duke" had originated with Few, the popular interpretation was hardly fair to J. B. Duke. Yet he and his lawyer were solely responsible for the clumsy language that inspired that interpretation. To no avail, Few issued explanatory statements and privately confessed that he "was sorry that the legal phrasing in the indenture of Trust seemed to put Mr. Duke in a bad light."[14]

The sad fact, of course, is that truth seldom if ever catches up with error, especially if the falsehood may be turned to witty, amusing ends. H. L. Mencken's *American Mercury* magazine specialized in sophomoric attacks on J. B. Duke and his alleged presumption in thinking that he could build himself a university from scratch. Other journalists for many years ignored Few's patient efforts to set the record straight and kept alive the story of J. B. Duke's "buying" himself a university. An additional twist was soon added with the allegation that J. B. Duke had first tried to "buy" Princeton (sometimes Yale or some other college) but failing there, turned to a small college in the South that was unknown to so many in the East. Strangely enough, students and even some faculty members at Duke University itself have for many decades passed along the story about J. B. Duke and Princeton. (The story has also had a long, vigorous life at Princeton.) Most of this silly, groundless mythmaking arose out of ignorance not only about President Few's part in the naming of the university but more especially about the Duke family's long, close relationship with Trinity College.

The misguided emphasis on the name change also obscured another important point. J. B. Duke had agreed to underwrite what Few called a "major" or "national" university. It was, in fact, to be a research university, and it was to be organized around, to have at its core or heart, as Few preferred to say, an older liberal arts college. That latter entity was to be the university's college of arts and sciences, and it was named, and still is in the early twenty-first century, Trinity College. Understanding the truth, however, is often too much to ask of either some journalists or a large portion of the public.

There were, in fact, even more serious problems in the indenture having to do with Duke University, but only gradually—and after J. B. Duke's death—would they come to light. In an early portion of the indenture, the Endowment trustees are given the power to withhold annual payments to any and all of the beneficiaries except Duke University. Thus singled out for a special status, Duke University, in a later section of the indenture, loses some of that special protection when the trustees are given the power to withhold annual payments even to Duke University under certain circumstances. Even though such withholding has never happened, the mere fact that the Endowment trustees possessed such a power vastly increased their own influence and power in relation to Duke University and its affairs. Several Endowment trustees—and particularly George G. Allen, W. R. Perkins, and Perkins's son, Thomas L. Perkins—would use their powerful position in ways that were not always in the best interests of Duke University.[15]

As for the name-changing hullabaloo that began in late 1924 and continued, there is no evidence that J. B. Duke lost a moment's sleep about it. He had long before developed a tough hide, possibly too tough for his own good, when it came to what journalists (and some politicians) had to say about him. He believed, whether rightly or wrongly, that he had more important things to do than worry about his image or misunderstanding on the part of the public.

While Durham, the home first of Trinity College and then Duke University, was at the eastern edge of the territory served by the Duke Power system, the other three educational beneficiaries were located much closer to the hub of that system. Given the largely Protestant and biracial character of the population of the Carolinas in the 1920s, the selection of the schools also reflected a gesture in the direction of ecumenism as well as racial liberalism. Davidson College, a Presbyterian institution near Charlotte, was to receive 5 percent of the annual income as was Furman University, a Baptist institution in Greenville, South Carolina. Johnson C. Smith University, an institution in Charlotte for African Americans, was to receive 4 percent.

The 32 percent of the net income that was earmarked for health care provided, at the "uncontrolled discretion" of the trustees, for assistance to not-for-profit hospitals for both whites and African Americans in the Carolinas. At a time when Dr. Rankin and others calculated that, on average, it cost $3.00 per bed per day to provide ward service in Carolina hospitals, the trustees were authorized to pay $1.00 "per free bed day" provided by the hospital. Any residue left over after the provision designed to assist in free care was to be used to help those communities that wished to acquire and equip nonprofit hospitals, preferably in the two Carolinas but possibly also in those states contiguous to them (Virginia, Tennessee, and Georgia) if surplus funds should become available.

As in the case of the name-changing clause in the indenture, a truly cautious participant in J. B. Duke's Charlotte conference in December 1924 might well have questioned the wisdom of specifying the precise amount ($1.00 per free bed per day) to help toward hospital care for poor people. The assumption was, obviously, that $3.00 would remain the average cost for a ward bed for the indefinite future. While giving one-third of the cost was a significant boost for charity care at that time, what would happen if hospital costs began to climb, as they did so relentlessly during and after World War II? The fact was, however, that J. B. Duke had spent his adult life in a period of marked price stability. True, there had been a sharp, unsettling burst of inflation in the United States from about 1918 into 1920, but it had receded more quickly than it had come after the national economic recession of 1920–1921. J. B. Duke and his advisers apparently made the mistake of thinking that the dollar would retain a more or less fixed purchasing power in the long years ahead. The able staff of the Endowment's Hospital Section, however, with the backing of the trustees, would later have no difficulty in finding other creative ways to help in the health-care area even after both inflation and then the joint federal-state program of medical assistance for the poor (Medicaid) entered the picture in the 1960s.

While the Endowment's provisions in the health-care area represented J. B. Duke's own, novel addition to the family's philanthropic pattern, the 12 percent of the annual income designated for the rural Methodist church in North Carolina harked back to the institution that originally inspired Washington Duke and then his sons to become philanthropists. To help build and maintain rural Methodist churches in the state, there would be 10 percent of the annual income, the remaining 2 percent was to be used to supplement the church's payments to superannuated (or "worn-out") preachers and to their widows and children. For the institutions that served the white and African-American orphans and half-orphans of the two Carolinas there would be 10 percent of the annual income.

Far back in 1893, Ben Duke had acted for the family in disbursing about $13,500 for charitable purposes. In 1924 J. B. Duke apportioned the income from a perpetual trust worth $40 million—and that amount would be vastly increased by the terms of his will. The striking point, however, is not so much the difference in the sums of money but the continuity in the purpose and nature of giving.

The creation of The Duke Endowment was certainly not an inevitable development, for many rich individuals have found countless other ways to dispose of their wealth. J. B. Duke was perfectly free to do whatever he wished with his fortune. The Endowment did have, however, a lot of family history behind it and was, as mentioned earlier, the culmination of a deeply rooted, long-standing tradition and pattern of giving that Washington Duke had begun, Ben Duke largely supervised for many years, and J. B. Duke, after adding his own emphasis on health care, institutionalized for posterity on a princely scale.

As for the trustees of the Endowment, J. B. Duke wanted them to be a carefully selected, working group, the majority of whom he suggested should be either natives or residents of the Carolinas. He declared in his indenture that the trustees should "make a special effort to secure persons of character and ability" as their successors, that they should meet at least ten times each year, and, as mentioned, that they should be paid for their service from a fixed percentage of the annual income.

He went on to explain in the indenture that he had carefully planned for much of the profit from the power company to be used for the social welfare of the communities which it served. Therefore he recommended that the securities of the power company be "the prime investments for the funds of this trust," to be changed only in "response to the most urgent and extraordinary necessity." (As the only alternative to the securities of the power company, Duke approved certain types of governmental notes and bonds.) One reason for dropping the original plan to make the executive committee of Trinity's trustees also the trustees of the Endowment was made clear by Duke's next phrase, for he requested that the Endowment's trustees "see to it that at all times" the power company "be managed and operated by the men best qualified for such a service." In other words, he intended for the trustees of the Endowment, which would hold a controlling share of the power company's stock, to maintain a close, direct supervision of the actual operations of the power company. That was a task for which the trustees of a college or university might or might not be suited.

The close interweaving of a philanthropic trust and an investor-owned business was neither unusual nor frowned upon by governmental agencies in the 1920s. After World War II, however, the situation would change and finally reach a point where, for various reasons, the Endowment trustees would be forced to take legal action to modify J. B. Duke's plan.

J. B. Duke's obvious concern about and solicitude for the Duke Power Company also must be explained. The most important reason he wanted the best possible future for the company, aside from the fact that his perpetual philanthropic trust largely depended on it, was his profound belief that it was destined to play a major and crucial role in the industrial development of the Piedmont region of the Carolinas. In the first quarter of the twentieth century that development had already begun to happen, and J. B. Duke, while by no means the only actor in the drama, was indeed a major player. He believed, quite correctly as later decades would demonstrate, that the Carolinas' escape from near-bottom-of-the-list poverty would come primarily through industrialization. He meant for the Duke Power Company to play a large role in helping that to happen.

If J. B. Duke had given all of his stock in the power company, rather than just a substantial portion of such stock, to the Endowment, his motivation could hardly be questioned. He did not do that, however, and chose to place a significant amount of Duke Power stock in a trust for the benefit of his daughter Doris and other close relatives. He did this through the Doris Duke Trust, which he established at the same time he did The Duke Endowment. Two-thirds of the annual income of this private, family trust was to go to Doris Duke and one-third to J. B. Duke's nieces, nephews, and their descendants. Although Duke placed only $35,000 in cash and 2,000 shares of the Duke Power stock in the trust at the time of its creation, by his will he added 125,904 shares of the stock. Temporarily this meant that the Doris Duke Trust actually held more shares of the Duke Power stock than did the Endowment. That situation rapidly changed, however, and within a short span of time, by virtue of the restrictions on the Endowment's investments, its holdings dwarfed those of the Doris Duke Trust. By 1968 for example, the Endowment held 56.36 percent of Duke Power's common stock and the Doris Duke Trust held only 8.73 percent. Since all the trustees of The Duke Endowment (except for Doris Duke, who was to become a trustee upon reaching the age of twenty-one in 1933), also served as trustees of the Doris Duke Trust, it is clear that J. B. Duke had carefully made interlocking arrangements concerning the Duke Power Company, The Duke Endowment, and the Doris Duke Trust. One cannot argue, therefore, that J. B. Duke's concern about Duke Power arose from completely disinterested or unselfish motives. Yet the fact remains that he planned carefully for the Endowment to own a much larger share of the power company's stock than would the trust for his daughter and close relatives.[16]

In J. B. Duke's generosity toward his family, he was also following a tradition, one first established by Washington Duke and then practiced by Ben and J. B. Duke throughout their adult lives. Purists may well object, but the line between public and private (or family) beneficence was one that simply was not sharply drawn in the minds of this particular family.

In 1924 Ben Duke attempted to draw up a list of all the living descendants of his aunts and uncles, that is, lists of his cousins. Since the families had been large on both the paternal and maternal sides, Ben Duke ran into puzzling complications as he tried to distribute over $500,000. Because of that, when J. B. Duke decided to leave the sum of $2 million to be divided among the descendants of his aunts and uncles, he made no attempt in his will to specify the recipients by name. The executors of his will, therefore, faced a daunting task when all sorts of claimants, some of them fraudulent, came climbing out of the woodwork— or the family tree—from North Carolina to Georgia to Texas.[17]

Toward the end of his indenture, J. B. Duke summarized his intentions in creating the Endowment: he had, he declared, endeavored to make provisions in some measure for the needs of mankind along physical, mental and spiritual lines. Since his philanthropy was focused exclusively on the Carolinas, he admitted that he might have tried to extend aid to other causes and to other sections of the country. He asserted his own belief, however, that "so doing probably would be productive of less good by reason of attempting too much." He did not say, but certainly could have, that he had targeted two of the economically poorest states in the nation for his perpetual philanthropy.

The twelve persons whom J. B. Duke selected as the original trustees of the Endowment were, in the order of their signing the indenture, Nanaline H. (Mrs. J. B.) Duke, George G. Allen, William R. Perkins, William B. Bell, Anthony J. Drexel Biddle, Jr., Walter C. Parker, Alexander H. Sands, Jr., William S. Lee, Charles I. Burkholder, Normal A. Cocke, Edward C. Marshall, and Bennette E. Geer. While two of these, Mrs. Duke and Anthony Biddle, were family members, all of the remaining trustees were business associates of J. B. Duke. Allen, Perkins, and Sands had long been key figures in the New York office of J. B. Duke and were also principal officers or directors of the power company. William B. Bell, as a young lawyer in Perkins's office, became associated with the American Cyanamid Company in which J. B. Duke had a large interest, and in 1922 Duke picked Bell to become president of the company. Parker, Lee, Burkholder, Cocke, and Marshall were all leaders in the Duke Power Company; and Bennette Geer was an educator and textile manufacturer in South Carolina with whom J. B. Duke, as the major stockholder in one of the larger mills managed by Geer, became closely associated. (An alumnus of Furman University and then a teacher there for a number of years before becoming a textile manufacturer, Geer helped influence J. B. Duke's choice of Furman as a beneficiary of the Endowment.)

One of the first actions of the original trustees was to elect J. B. Duke and Dr. Watson Rankin as trustees, with the latter put in charge of planning and launching the work of the Endowment's Hospital and Orphan Section. So as 1925 began, J. B. Duke not only had the satisfaction of seeing his Endowment finally go into action, but he also could look forward to the unprecedentedly vast construction program to be undertaken at Duke University. For the rebuilding of the old Trinity College campus, for the building from scratch of the Tudor Gothic structures on new land west of the old campus, and for 5,000 acres of adjoining forest land, J. B. Duke would provide more than $19 million—not just the measly $6 million so unfortunately mentioned in the indenture. It promised to be an exciting time for the entrepreneur turned philanthropist.

12

DEATH CATCHES J. B. DUKE
BY SURPRISE

J. B. Duke certainly did not consider the establishment of the Endowment as a stopping point, for he was keenly interested in the vast construction work that lay ahead for Duke University. Vigorous and apparently in good health at age sixty-eight, he also still had many power plants to build in the Carolinas. In the spring of 1925 he and the other trustees of the Endowment met in Durham, in Ben Duke's home in fact, and made a number of important decisions concerning the physical lay-out of Duke University.

An essential preliminary for the building of the new university was the acquisition of additional land, for despite the fact that Trinity's campus was already spacious, it was not big enough for the new buildings that J. B. Duke had in mind. Land to the north of the campus, particularly in the general vicinity of Watts Hospital, would be needed for the possible medical school. By the spring of 1924 President Few's agents had been quietly securing options for land around the college for more than a year. When informed in May, 1924, that the price of various parcels of land under option totalled $161,000, J. B. Duke sent word to Few that "it would be all right to go that far but not to pay more than that, and be sure that you get all of it."[1]

Getting "all of it" at reasonable prices, however, proved to be increasingly difficult as rumors spread through Durham about Trinity's expansion, and land prices kept rising accordingly. With Few admitting that acquiring the desired land would "require some time" and J. B. Duke growing impatient, Few had a brainstorm. Walking with his

183

sons through a beautiful wooded area a mile or so to the west of the Trinity campus, where he had often ridden horseback as a younger man, Few hit upon the idea of expanding in that direction rather than north towards Watts Hospital. The ground rolled gently, there were mixed stands of pine and hardwoods, and no one, including the landowners, had ever dreamed of Trinity's going that far afield. "It was for me a thrilling moment when I stood on a hill," Few later wrote,"... and realized that here at last is the land we have been looking for."[2]

J. B. Duke gave his assent to an effort to acquire land in the new direction. Robert L. Flowers, operating with the utmost discretion, went to work acquiring land, not only for a new campus but also for an extensive new road (ultimately North Carolina highway number 751) that J. B. Duke wanted to give additional access to the campus. An old hand at acquiring extensive tracts of land for his various business ventures, J. B. Duke was responsible for Duke University's acquiring much more land than was immediately needed. Not until late March, 1925, however, did J. B. Duke make the final decision as to how the new land would be used.

With any luck at all, spring in the Carolina Piedmont, with its abundant wild dogwoods and redbud trees and other native flowers and shrubs, can be a splendid time. Such it was when J. B. Duke finally inspected the new land and, in consultation with Few and others, quickly decided: the Tudor Gothic buildings, with a soaring chapel at their center, would be built on the new land on a crest or plateau overlooking a deep ravine that J. B. Duke envisioned as a lake; there would be a large fountain in the center quadrangle, and water would cascade over falls that emptied into the lake. The long-desired coordinate college for women, instead of being crowded into a corner of the old campus, would occupy that entire campus (about 100 acres); and while several of the existing buildings on the old campus would be retained, some would have to go in order to make room for eleven new buildings to be constructed of red brick and white marble in the classical or Georgian style.

A prosaic work-diary or notebook of architect Horace Trumbauer's superintendent, B. M. Hall, is the best source — as well as one of the few documentary sources — for many of the important decisions concerning Duke University's physical plant that J. B. Duke, Few, and their associates made late in March 1925.

One of the Endowment trustees many years later vividly recalled two things about their meeting that spring in Durham. The first was that during one of the trustees' sessions in Ben Duke's home, young Doris Duke, then twelve, entered the room, climbed on to her father's lap, and remained there quietly for the remainder of the meeting.

The other memory was that J. B. Duke invited the trustees to inspect the new land with him. "We walked all over those grounds," Dr. Watson Rankin stated, "jumping ditches and crossing wagon roads and going through shrubbery and all that kind of thing, with Mr. Duke always in the lead. Again I was impressed with the man's vigor."[3]

Trumbauer's construction superintendent merely noted: "Met Mr. Duke today and went over the ground for the new University." Then the following day the superintendent recorded that he had met Trumbauer and another of the architects and "explained the new location of the layout on top of the hill[,] moving the chapel forward so it will come on the high ground." The superintendent noted also that the library was "to be moved over to a high spot to the right of where shown on plans, this being Mr. Duke's idea of how the layout should be." Further on, after mentioning various other activities, the superintendent wrote: "Went over to the new location and Mr. Duke approved of the general layout but wanted another fountain on the opposite hill to flow down into the lake that will be down in the ravine in front of the chapel."

On the third day of all the intense activity, Few, Flowers, and Professor Frank Brown (Few's close advisor in physical planning) attended a "full meeting" where, obviously for financial reasons, a reduction of over 900,000 cubic feet was worked out in the plans; at a subsequent session, however, "a portion of our saving was put back by Mr. Duke and Mr. Allen...." (Later, after J. B. Duke's death, some of those cuts had to be made anyhow.) Trumbauer and his associates headed back to Philadelphia with instructions to proceed with the working drawings, first for the eleven new buildings on the Trinity campus, soon to become known as the East Campus, and then for the Tudor Gothic structures to be erected on the new land, the West Campus. J. B. Duke had played a major role, therefore, in much of the planning for the two campuses of Duke University, all accomplished in three busy spring days in 1925.

Concurrently with the matter of the new land, J. B. Duke helped to decide another problem that keenly interested him: the kind of stone to be used in the projected Tudor Gothic buildings. He originally thought that the stone should come from one of the well-known quarries in the North, in Pennsylvania, New Jersey or Indiana. Accordingly, he arranged for car-loads of various stone samples to be shipped to Durham and for test walls to be built on the Trinity campus. Frank C. Brown, in the meantime, checked out the possibility of North Carolina stone and discovered that the state geologist had some specimens of stone from an abandoned quarry near Hillsborough, North Carolina, only a few miles from Durham. On the eve of J. B. Duke's inspection of the new land, Brown informed Trumbauer that a sample wall of local stone had been built. It was not only "much more attractive than the Princeton wall" and "much warmer and softer in coloring," but Brown estimated that it could be quarried and delivered on the ground at not more than $3.50 per ton, whereas he estimated that the Princeton stone would cost approximately $21.00 per ton. When Flowers informed Allen about the exciting possibilities of the local stone and how cheaply the "entire ridge" with "an almost unlimited supply" of stone could be purchased, J. B. Duke authorized the acquisition of the quarry and further testing of the stone.[4]

Pleased by the wide range of colors in the local stone — various shades of brown, yellow, black, blue, green, and gray — as well as reassured of its durability by tests conducted both in the state geologist's office and in the Bureau of Standards in Washington, J. B. Duke in late March, 1925, proudly led the trustees of the Endowment to the sample walls where balloting indicated an overwhelming preference for the native stone. J. B. Duke wanted additional walls built, however, with "less of the yellow and gold colors." Accordingly, Frank Brown suggested a wall showing "as predominating colors the dark blue, the light blue, the light green, the light gray, and the dark blue with face mottled with dark brown." All these colors, Brown avowed, could be obtained from the Hillsborough quarry "in unlimited quantities."[5] The buildings of Duke University's West Campus were inspired by a venerable style of English architecture, but, to J. B. Duke's immense satisfaction, the warmly colored stone would come from a neighboring hillside in Piedmont North Carolina.

J. B. Duke had long loved landscaping, and to lay out the grounds of the new campus as well as to redesign the old Trinity campus he selected one of the leading firms in the country, Olmsted Brothers of Boston, a firm founded by Frederick Law Olmsted, the creator of Central Park in New York and of many other famous parks. Even before J. B. Duke has seen the new land, he requested that contour maps of its central portion show all the large trees, for he clearly intended to build the new campus in such a fashion as to save as many of the significant trees as possible.

Apart from a few pioneers, the American public in the 1920s was not spending much time worrying about "the environment" or "ecology." J. B. Duke, however, was rather ahead of his times in his concern for the physical setting, the environment, in which educational activities were to proceed. Other than agreeing with President Few about the new university's pursuit of excellence rather than numbers and its national as well as regional service and orientation, J. B. Duke was content to leave the academic planning, the faculty recruitment, and similar problems in professional hands. He intended to provide the buildings, the grounds, and as much of the monetary means as he could and leave the rest to Few, Flowers, and Dean W. H. Wannamaker, and their associates on the faculty. Large problems, such as the location of the projected chapel, and small ones, such as the width of the hallways in the dormitories on East (J. B. Duke wanted, and got, wider ones) and the arrangements of the rooms within those buildings — all were of keen interest to the industrial entrepreneur who had turned philanthropist.[6]

As greatly interested as J. B. Duke was in the buildings and grounds of Duke University, he also had other large business concerns. In July 1925 he together with George Allen, W. S. Lee, and various officials of the Aluminum Company of America visited the Saguenay river in Quebec to inspect the power sites there, the undeveloped one of which Duke had earlier swapped for a one-ninth interest in the aluminum company. Duke and his party traveled on his private railway car, the "Doris," and Arthur Vining Davis, Secretary of the Treasury

Andrew Mellon, his brother R. B. Mellon, Roy A. Hunt, who later became president of Alcoa, and other officials of the aluminum company went on another private car.

There was much visiting back and forth between the private railway cars. On one occasion, when Andrew Mellon advocated investing money in works of art, J. B. Duke reportedly replied that such a practice was all right for others, but he was more interested in "putting it into Duke University and in the [other] schools and helping out the people there in North and South Carolina." At a much later date, Roy Hunt remembered Duke as quite alert and possessed of a sharp mind. Physically he kept up with the group in several days of fairly strenuous moving about in what was then a relatively undeveloped region. Hunt characterized J. B. Duke as a "soft-spoken" and "courteous Southern gentleman" who seemed "very friendly and very keen."[7]

While Duke's Canadian venture had turned out well, his power company in the Carolinas encountered serious problems in the summer of 1925. Prolonged drought in the Piedmont region caused many rivers and reservoirs to fall to perilously low levels, so low that the company's coal-burning steam plants, which had been built for auxiliary or standby use only, had to be operated around the clock, seven days a week. By August the company had to call for curtailment of power consumption, at first only for those customers in certain zones and then for all customers. This crisis for Duke Power had not come with the drastic speed of the devastating floods of 1916, but it was none the less acute.

J. B. Duke had grown increasingly aware of the need for additional steam plants even before the drought. His wife told a friend that for two years he had talked of nothing but steam plants, a subject that Mrs. Duke claimed not to understand. The drought in the summer of 1925 forced J. B. Duke to ponder steam plants more than ever.

Having visited Durham, Charlotte, and Canada in connection with his various projects, Duke joined his wife and daughter at his mansion in Newport, Rhode Island, in the later part of July 1925. There he became ill from unknown causes at the time, but he continued to confer regularly with Allen, Sands, Flowers and others who made the trip to Newport to see him. Mrs. Duke initially believed that he seemed to improve and would gradually regain his health. When his illness grew worse, however, he was carried by his private railway car to New York, and there his doctors discovered in September that he suffered from what they diagnosed as pernicious anemia, a disease for which there was no known cure at that time.

Despite his illness, Duke continued to make important decisions that vitally affected the power company, the Endowment, and Duke University. When his private nurse noticed his restlessness at one point and asked if he wanted something, he replied, "Please don't disturb me, I"m building a steam plant down South."[8] Sure enough, after studying blueprints and estimates, he authorized Norman Cocke and E. C. Marshall, who had come to New York to confer with him, to proceed with the construction of a large steam plant on the Yadkin river near Salisbury, North Carolina. With a projected capacity of 70,000 kilowatts, it would be the first large-scale central-station-type steam plant in the Duke Power system and one of the first power plants in the nation to utilize the new technology and equipment that allowed the burning of pulverized coal. J. B. Duke probably did not realize at the time that the large steam plant would also be a benchmark in the transition of the Duke Power system from water to steam (or coal) as its primary source of power.

In one sense, therefore, even before J. B. Duke died, one of the ideas that originally led him to structure the Endowment as he had began to lose some of its validity or, put another way, to be significantly diluted. As Duke explained in his indenture, in his long involvement with the development of water powers in the Piedmont Carolinas he had "observed how such utilization of a natural resource, which otherwise would run in a waste to the sea…, both gives impetus to industrial life and provides a safe and enduring investment for capital." His ambition, he continued, was "that the revenues of such developments shall administer to the social welfare, as the operation of such developments is administering to the economic welfare, of the communities which they serve." It was with these views in mind, he concluded, that he recommended the securities of the Duke Power Company as the prime investment for the Endowment. The power company's gradual shift after 1925 to an overwhelming dependence on steam plants, rather than a water power or hydro-stations, meant that the rivers of the Piedmont, the "natural resource" to which Duke had referred, were no longer the principal basis for either the power company or the perpetual philanthropic trust that was tied to it.

There was irony in the fact that J. B. Duke, up until the last days of his life, continued to display imaginative flexibility and the capacity to change directions in response to changed circumstances. Yet in his indenture, because of his great solicitude for the Duke Power Company, he mandated a highly restrictive, perpetual investment policy for the Endowment's trustees, a policy that actually denied the flexibility and the ability to adapt to changed conditions. Not until the early 1970s would the trustees succeed in gaining legal permission to modify the investment provisions of the indenture. Even then there remained a formidable obstacle to the program of investment diversification that the great majority of the Endowment trustees (but not including Doris Duke) wished to pursue.

The power company was not, however, the only thing on J. B. Duke's mind during his final days. In his will, which he signed in December 1924 when the indenture creating the Endowment was also signed, he provided that $10 million should be given to The Duke Endowment, $4 million of which was to be used to build and equip at Duke University a medical school, hospital, and nurses' home, with the income from the remaining $6 million to serve as an endowment for the university. His will further stipulated that the the remainder of his estate, after all other bequests had been made, should be added to The Duke Endowment. This would eventually turn out to be approximately $69 million, considerably more than the original $40 million given to the Endowment.

Despite these provisions in his original will, J. B. Duke continued to worry during his illness that he might not have provided enough money for the building program at the university. Accordingly, he summoned George Allen and added a codicil (Item XI) to his will. It provided (1) that an additional $7 million be placed in the building fund for Duke University; (2) that 10 percent of the annual income from his residuary estate (the above-mentioned $69 million) should go to Duke University; and that 90 percent of the annual income from the residuary estate should to to the Endowment to be used for "maintaining and securing hospitals."[9]

One should note that J. B. Duke was not just ill but a dying man as he made this last-mentioned provision for such lavish support of hospitals. If followed literally by the Endowment trustees, it would have made the hospital program of the Endowment by far the largest beneficiary. The indenture, however, gave the trustees "uncontrolled discretion" concerning annual allocations of income (except where Duke University was concerned), and the trustees would decide a few years after J. B. Duke's death that there was more income in this Item XI account for hospitals than could be properly and wisely used in the Carolinas and that they did not think it prudent or desirable to expand the hospital-building program into the states contiguous to the Carolinas. Accordingly, the trustees would proceed to make the four educational institutions, and especially Duke University, the prime beneficiaries of The Duke Endowment.

Soon after signing that last codicil to his will, J. B. Duke developed pneumonia, later lapsed into a coma, and died in his mansion on Fifth Avenue on October 10, 1925. He would have been sixty-nine years old on December 23. After a simple private service without eulogy or sermon in his New York residence, his body was carried by train to Durham. There, after services in Duke Memorial Methodist Church, he was buried beside his father in the family mausoleum in Maplewood Cemetery. Some years later, after the completion of the great chapel that he wanted on the high ground at the center of the Tudor Gothic buildings on the university's West Campus, the remains of Washington Duke, Benjamin Newton Duke (who died on January 8, 1929), and James Buchanan Duke were moved to three sarcophagi in a specially designed Memorial Chapel to the left of the chancel in the chapel of Duke University.

If J. B. Duke had lived longer, and death seemed to have taken him somewhat by surprise, he would, naturally, have exercised considerable power and influence in a variety of businesses and institutions but especially in the Duke Power Company, Duke University, and The Duke Endowment. As matters stood after his death, however, much of that power and influence were inherited by two men, George G. Allen and W. R. Perkins. Nanaline H. Duke, J. B. Duke's widow, had no strong or sustained interest in either business or philanthropy, and Doris Duke, not quite thirteen years old when her father died, was too young to become involved in such matters. Consequently, Allen and Perkins, more than anyone else, would play large roles in carrying on J. B. Duke's multiple enterprises. They depended heavily on Alexander Sands, for he too had worked closely with J. B. Duke for many years and was both tireless and impeccable in his attention to matters large and small related to J. B. Duke's various interests. In short, Duke's affairs were left in the trustworthy, competent hands of men who worked faithfully to carry on his work and fulfill his vision.

Back in 1914 President Few was first beginning to establish personal contact with J. B. Duke, who was himself just beginning to relate more directly with Trinity College. Few, a past master at the composition of graceful prose, concluded a letter to Duke in this fashion: "And speaking for myself I am particularly anxious that you shall get enduring personal satisfaction and happiness out of what you have done for Trinity College, because you are able to feel that through it you have done some permanent good upon the earth."[10]

Just what Duke thought of Few's highly idealistic concept is not known. Whether Duke ultimately succeeded in doing "some permanent good upon the earth" is perhaps best left to those who ponder his life to decide.

NOTES

Notes for the
PROLOGUE

1. John W. Winkler, *Tobacco Tycoon: The Story of James Buchanan Duke* (New York: Random House, 1942), p. 69.

2. John Wilber Jenkins, *James B. Duke: Master Builder* (New York: George H. Doran Company, 1927), p. 78.

3. Winkler, *Tobacco Tycoon*, p. 60.

4. Ibid., p.61.

Notes for Chapter 1
STARTING FROM SCRATCH

1. Washington Duke to John W. Wright and the Union Bethel African Methodist Episcopal Church, November 1, 1890, in Durham *Daily Globe*, November 5, 1890.

2. Jean B. Anderson, *Durham County* (Durham, N.C.: Duke University Press, 1990), p. 87.

3. Jenkins, *James B. Duke*, p. 27.

4. *Hillsborough Recorder*, June 4, 1840.

5. Nannie M. Tilley, *The Bright-Tobacco Industry, 1860–1929* (Chapel Hill: University of North Carolina Press, 1948), pp. 3–36.

6. *Durham Recorder*, April 16, 1900; Raleigh *News and Observer*, April 5, 1896.

7. Paul B. Barringer, *The Natural Bent: The Memoirs of Dr. Paul B. Barringer* (Chapel Hill: University of North Carolina Press, 1949), pp. 163–164.

8. *Durham Recorder*, April 16, 1900.

9. William K. Boyd, *The Story of Durham* (Durham: Duke University Press, 1925), p. 85.

10. Ledger, 1873–1877, Washington Duke MSS, Special Collections, Perkins Library, Duke University.

11. Jenkins, *Master Builder*, p. 58.

12. J. B. Duke to B. N. and Mrs. B. N. Duke, August 18, 1880, B. N. Duke MSS, Special Collections, Perkins Library, Duke University. Italics and misspellings in the original.

13. Biographical sketch of Wright in *History of North Carolina, IV: North Carolina Biography* (Chicago, 1919), pp. 198–199.

14. Boyd, *Story of Durham*, pp. 58–68. In the twentieth century the old Bull Durham factory became a part of the American Tobacco Company's large plant in Durham.

15. Ibid., p. 76.

16. Tilley, *Bright-Tobacco Industry*, pp. 504–510.

17. B. W. C. Roberts and Richard F. Knapp, "Paving the Way for the Tobacco Trust: From Hand Rolling to Mechanized Cigarette Production by W. Duke, Sons and Company," *North Carolina Historical Review*, LXIX (July, 1992), pp. 257–281, provides a more detailed account.

18. Tilley, *Bright-Tobacco Industry*, p. 510.

19. W. Duke, Sons and Company to Small, March 20, 1884, Edward Featherston Small MSS. Special Collections, Perkins Library, Duke University.

20. Ibid., April 11, 1884.

21. Ibid., May 8, 22, 1884.

22. Small's unpublished memoir, pp. 2–3, Small MSS.

23. W. Duke, Sons and Co., to Small, April 4, 1885, ibid.

24. Small's unpublished memoir, pp. 12–13, and undated newspaper clipping, Small MSS.

25. Patrick G. Porter, "Advertising in the Early Cigarette Industry: W. Duke, Sons & Company of Durham," *North Carolina Historical Review*, XLVIII (Winter, 1971), pp. 31–43, includes many illustrations.

26. *Nowitzky's Magazine*, as cited in Tilley, *Bright-Tobacco Industry*, pp. 557–558. Italics in original.

27. W. Duke, Sons and Co. to Small, February 6, 1885, Small MSS.

28. J. B. Duke to Small, January 27, 1886, Small MSS.

29. W. Duke, Sons and Co., to Small, May 23, July 7, 1884, Small MSS.

30. W. Duke, Sons and Co., to Small, October 4, 1884, Small MSS.

31. B. N. Duke to R. H. Wright, December 22, 1885, Richard H. Wright MSS, Special Collections, Perkins Library, Duke University.

Notes for Chapter 2
THE ORIGINS OF THE
AMERICAN TOBACCO COMPANY

1. Letterbooks of J. B. Duke, Special Collections, Perkins Library, Duke University. The manner in which these letterbooks became available is explained in a note on p. 26 of *The Dukes of Durham*.

2. Tilley, *Bright-Tobacco Industry*, pp. 568–576.

3. J. B. Duke to D. B. Strouse, June 18, 1886, in J. B. Duke letterbook no. 3.

4. Tilley, *Bright-Tobacco Industry*, p. 574.

5. Strouse to Duke, March 24, 1885, J. B. Duke letterbook.

6. Brief for defendants in *Richard H. Wright* against *J. B. Duke, B. L. Duke, B. N. Duke,* and *George W. Watts*, Supreme Court, City and County of New York [1891] p. 7, B. N. Duke MSS, 1966 addition. Hereinafter cited as Brief for defendants.

7. J. W. Hinsdale to Wright, January 13, 1885. R. H. Wright MSS.

8. Agreement and indenture of January 1, 1880, between R. H. Wright and Washington Duke, with endorsement of May 16, 1885, in R. H. Wright MSS, legal papers of the 1880s.

9. R. H. Wright to Wm. J. Curtis, May 10, 1893, R. H. Wright letterbook.

10. M. E. McDowell and Co. of Philadelphia, to Wright, June 29, 1885; Marburg Brothers of Baltimore, to Wright, July 6, 1885; W. S. Kimball and Co. of Rochester, to Wright, July 11, 1885. R. H. Wright MSS.

11. Brief for the defendants, p. 8, B. N. Duke MSS; Wright to W. J. Curtis, May 10, 1893, R. H. Wright letterbook.

12. Printed announcement of July 2, 1885, R. H. Wright MSS.

13. Brief for the defendants, pp. 3–4.

14. Brief for the defendants, p. 5

15. J. W. Hinsdale to Wright, June 15, 30, 1885, Wright MSS.

16. Brief for the defendants, pp. 5–6. Another legal action brought by Wright against the Dukes and George Watts went on from 1891 until it was settled out of court late in 1897. Readers wishing more details about the matter may find them in *The Dukes of Durham*, pp. 48–55.

17. Patrick G. Porter, "Origins of the American Tobacco Company," *Business History Review*, XLIII (Spring, 1969), p. 65.

18. Tilley, *Bright-Tobacco Industry*, pp. 574–576.

19. J. B. Duke to D. B. Strouse, November 26, 1885, J. B. Duke letterbook. Strouse claimed that the Allison machine in Kimball's plant infringed on certain Bonsack patents.

20. Watts to Strouse, November 21, 1885, sheaf in J. B. Duke letterbook no. 3.

21. Washington Duke as quoted in the Raleigh *News and Observer*, April 5, 1896; W. Duke, Sons and Company to Strouse, February 8, 1886, sheaf in J. B. Duke letterbook no. 3.

22. Watts to Strouse, April 2, 1886, sheaf in J. B. Duke letterbook no. 3.

23. Strouse to Wright, December 3, 1888, and April 2, 1889, R. H. Wright MSS.

24. Duke to Strouse, March 20, 1889, sheaf in J. B. Duke letterbook n. 1.

25. Duke to Strouse, March 27, 1889, ibid.

26. Strouse to Duke, July 8, 1887, ibid.

27. Duke to Strouse, July 19, 1887, sheaf in J. B. Duke letterbook no. 1.

28. Duke to Strouse, February, 2, 1888, ibid.

29. Strouse to W. Duke, Sons and Company, February 8, 1888, J. B. Duke letterbook.

30. Duke to Strouse, February 16, 1888, sheaf in J. B. Duke letterbook no. 1.

31. Strouse to Duke, February 20, March 7, 1888, J. B. Duke letterbook,

32. Duke to Strouse, March 16, 1888, sheaf in J. B. Duke letterbook no. 1.

33. Strouse to Duke, May 4, 1888, J. B. Duke letterbook.

34. Duke to Strouse, December 12, 1889, J. B. Duke MSS.

35. Strouse to Duke, March 23, 1889, and Duke to Strouse, March 27, 1889, J. B. Duke letterbook.

36. Strouse to Duke, April 8, 1889, J. B. Duke letterbook.

37. Porter, "Origins of the American Tobacco Company," p. 73.

38. U. S. Bureau of Corporations, *Report of the Commissioner of Corporations on the Tobacco Industry* (Washington, 1909) pt. 1, 65–66. Richard B. Tennant, *The American Cigarette Industry: A Study in Economic Analysis and Public Policy* (New Haven, 1950), also has a historical summary in the beginning portion of his book.

39. Duke to Strouse, November 19, 1889, sheaf in J. B. Duke letterbook n. 1.

Notes for Chapter 3
BUILDING AN INDUSTRIAL EMPIRE

1. David E. Shi, *Matthew Josephson, Bourgeois Bohemian* (New Haven, 1981), p. 157.

2. Ibid., pp. 143, 145, 156, 158.

3. Ibid., p. 187.

4. Alfred D. Chandler, Jr., *The Visible Hand: The Managerial Revolution in American Business* (Cambridge: Harvard University Press, 1977). p. 5.

5. Ibid., p. 1.

6. Ibid., p. 382.

7. Jenkins, *Master Builder*, p. 169.

8. Chandler, *Visible Hand*, p. 386.

9. Ibid., pp. 383–384.

10. Jenkins. *Master Builder*, pp. 168–169; Chandler, *Visible Hand*, pp. 385–386.

11. Chandler, *Visible Hand*, pp. 286–287.

12. Joseph C. Robert, *The Story of Tobacco in America* (Chapel Hill, 1949, 1967), p. 173.

13. Testimony of James B. Duke, in *United States* v. *American Tobacco Company*, U. S. Circuit Court, Southern District of New York, Equity Case Files, 1907–1911, Record Group 21, Files E1-216, vol. V, pp. 3295–3299, Washington National Records Center. Hereafter cited as Circuit Court MSS. A photocopy of the 238-page typescript of Duke's testimony is also available in J. B. Duke MSS.

14. J. B. Duke to B. N. Duke, December 24, 1892, B. N. Duke MSS.

15. Glenn Porter and Harold C. Livesay, *Merchants and Manufacturers: Studies in the Changing of Nineteenth-Century Marketing* (Baltimore, 1971) pp. 209–210.

16. J. B. Cobb to B. N. Duke, August 12, 1895, B. N. Duke MSS.

17. Cobb to B. N. Duke, August 26, 1895, ibid.

18. Bureau of Corporations, *Report on Tobacco*, pt. I, pp. 67, 97.

19. J. B. Duke to J. G. Butler, January 1, 1897, J. B. Duke letterbook.

20. Bureau of Corporations, *Report on Tobacco*, pt. I, pp. 97–98.

21. Porter, "Origins of the American Tobacco Company," p. 75.

22. Dominick and Dickerman [W. B. Dickerman?] to B. N. Duke, August 19, 1898, B. N. Duke MSS.

23. Circuit Court MSS, vol. V, p. 3325.

24. Bureau of Corporation, *Report on Tobacco*, pt. I, pp. 4–5, 73–74.

25. B. N. Duke to J. E. Stagg, February 10, 21, 1899, B. N. Duke MSS.

26. Circuit Court MSS, vol. V, pp. 3341, 3357.

27. Bureau of Corporations, *Report on Tobacco*, pt. I. pp. 3–5. The question of over-capitalization or "watered stock" is an old and thorny one—and a club often used against the likes of J. B. Duke and other such entrepreneurial capitalists. A recurring theme in the dry recital of economic data gathered by the Bureau of Corporations in its *Report on the Tobacco Industry* has to do with the alleged over-capitalization that resulted from the large sums charged up to goodwill, that is brand names and trademarks. A more modern economic historian, noting that in 1908 goodwill accounted for 55.5 percent of all assets in the American Tobacco Company's domestic tobacco manufacture, nevertheless concluded: "... From the point of view of investors, none of the goodwill, except in the case of the cigar group, represented 'water,' for adequate profits were earned on it." Tennant, *The American Cigarette Industry*, pp. 36–37.

28. Bureau of Corporation, *Report on Tobacco*, pt. I., pp. 103–104, 236.

29. Circuit Court MSS, vol. V, pp. 3375–3379.

30. Bureau of Corporations, *Report on Tobacco*, pt. I., pp. 141–145; Tennant, *The American Cigarette Industry*, p. 31.

31. Tennant, *The American Cigarette Industry*, pp. 32–33.

32. Ibid. The United Cigar Stores were careful to carry goods of independent manufacturers as well as those of the combination.

33. Bureau of Corporations, *Report on Tobacco*, pt. I., pp. 7–9, 114–127; Tennant, *The American Cigarette Industry*, pp. 34–36. The capital was subsequently raised to $40,000,000.

34. Bureau of Corporations, *Report on Tobacco*, pt. I., p. 9. J. B. Duke, Brady, Payne, Ryan, Widner, and Whitney each held 8.3 percent of the total issue of Consolidated stock, or approximately half. Ben Duke came next with 5 percent, and George Watts owned 2.5 percent. Moore and Schley held 23.5 percent of the stock for customers. Ibid., p. 119.

35. R. B. Arrington, executive secretary, to Prof, C. Trentanove, June 15, 1906, for the statue; J. B. Duke to H. M. Hanna, February 16, 1904, J. B. Duke letterbooks.

36. Tennant, *The American Cigarette Industry*, pp. 35–36; Bureau of Corporations, *Report on Tobacco*, pt. I., pp. 11–12.

Notes for Chapter 4
J. B. DUKE OFF DUTY

1. Harold U. Faulkner, *Politics, Reform and Expansion* (New York, 1959) p. 16.
2. Thomas C. Cochran and William Miller, *The Age of Enterprise: A Social History of Industrial America* (New York, 1942, 1961), p. 257.
3. Glenn Porter, *The Rise of Big Business, 1860–1910* (New York, 1973), p. 58.
4. Chandler, *The Visible Hand*, p. 384 and n. 9.
5. Watts to B. N. Duke, March 30, 1892, B. N. Duke MSS.
6. Jenkins, *Master Builder*, p. 194.
7. New York *American*, December 19, 22, 1905; Winkler, *Tobacco Tycoon*, pp. 89–90.
8. Washington Duke to J. B. Duke, October 17, 1894, B. N. Duke letterbook.
9. B. N. Duke to W. W, Fuller, June 16, 1896, B. N. Duke letterbook.
10. New York *Recorder*, April 20, 1895, as quoted in "National Register of Historic Places: Inventory—Nomination Form" —James B. Duke Estate...(n.d., 1984?). Hereafter cited as "National Register...Nomination Form." Pagination in this informative compilation is erratic; a copy of the document, kindly made available by Mr. Patrick Lerch of Duke Farms, is now in this author's possession but will be added to the J. B. Duke MSS.
11. Hibberd to B. N. Duke, April 24, 1895, B. N. Duke MSS.
12. "National Register...Nomination Form," p. 31.
13. Ibid., second section, pp. 3 ff.
14. *New York Times*, March 26, 1905, as quoted in ibid., p. 4.
15. Ibid.
16. Somerset (N.J.) *Messenger*, May 2, 1900, as cited in ibid., p. 2.
17. Ibid., p. 13.
18. Ibid., p. 6.
19. Ibid., p. 12.

Notes for Chapter 5
J. B. DUKE INVADES BRITAIN

1. J. B. Duke to D. B. Strouse, March 20, 1889, J. B. Duke letterbook no. 1.
2. B. W. E. Alford, *W. D. and H. O. Wills and the Development of the U. K. Tobacco Industry, 1786–1965* (London, 1973), p. 250. Hereinafter cited as Alford, *Wills*.
3. Bureau of Corporations, *Report on Tobacco*, pt. I, pp. 166–167.
4. Alford, *Wills*, p. 251.
5. Maurice Corina, *Trust in Tobacco: The Anglo-American Struggle for Power* (London, 1975), p. 26.
6. Ibid., p. 72.
7. Alford, *Wills*, p. 251.
8. Quoted in ibid, p. 259.
9. Ibid., p. 260.
10. Arnold J. Toynbee as quoted on the flyleaf of C. Vann Woodward, *The Origins of the New South 1877–1913* (Baton Rouge, Louisiana, 1951).
11. J. B. Duke to W. Duke, October 27, 1901, W. Duke MSS.
12. Corina, *Trust in Tobacco*, p. 89.
13. Bureau of Corporations, *Report on Tobacco*, pt. I, p. 169.
14. Parrish to W. R. Harris, March 28, 1902, E. J. Parrish letterbook.
15. Alford, *Wills*, p. 266.
16. Ibid., p. 167.
17. Ibid., p. 268.
18. Corina, *Trust in Tobacco*, p. 70.
19. Interview of Frank Rounds with Roy Hunt, 1963, Duke Endowment MSS, Perkins Library, Duke University.
20. Alford, *Wills*, p. 279.
21. Ibid., p. 269; Corina, *Trust in Tobacco*, p. 102.
22. Corina, *Trust in Tobacco*, p. 131.
23. Howard Cox, *The Global Cigarette: Origins and Evolution of British-American Tobacco 1880–1945* (Oxford and New York, 2000), pp. 332–333.
24. Ibid., p. 340.
25. Ibid.
26. Parrish to J. B. Cobb, first vice-president of the American Tobacco Company, April 23, 1900, E. J. Parrish letterbook.
27. Parrish to W. L. Walker, October 19, 1900, and Parrish to J. A. Thomas, June 20, 1901, E. J. Parrish letterbook.
28. Parrish to W. R. Harris, second vice-president of American Tobacco Company, February 20, 1902, E. J. Parrish letterbook; and K. Murai to Parrish, March 19, 1903, E. J. Parrish MSS, 1973 addition.
29. Parrish to K. Murai, April 25, 1903, E. J. Parrish MSS, 1973 addition.

30. James A. Thomas, *A Pioneer Tobacco Merchant in the Orient* (Durham, 1928), pp. 38–39.

31. Ibid., pp. 51, 54–55.

32. Ibid., p. 41.

33. J. B. Duke to W. Duke, September 27, 1902, W. Duke MSS; J. B. Duke to Wills, January 7, 1903, J. B. Duke letterbook.

34. Jenkins, *Master Builder*, p. 134.

35. Ibid., p. 133.

36. Cox, *Global Cigarette*, p. 343.

37. J. B. Duke to H. H. Wills, March 29, 1904, as quoted in Cox, *Global Cigarette*, pp. 97–98.

38. Cox, *Global Cigarette*, pp. 99–100.

39. Ibid., p. 115.

Notes for Chapter 6
KEEPING TIES TO CAROLINA—AND A MANSION ON 5TH AVE.

1. Charles P. Roland in his editor's preface to James C. Cobb, *Industrialization and Southern Society, 1877–1984* (Lexington, Kentucky, 1984), p. ix.

2. Paul K. Conkin, "Hot, Humid, and Sad," *Journal of Southern History*, LXIV (February, 1998), p. 11.

3. Durham *Tobacco Plant*, January 25, 1882.

4. September 14, 1888.

5. *Durham Recorder*, April 24, 1889.

6. J. M. Duke to W. Duke, December 25, 1894, W. Duke MSS.

7. E. N. M. of Franklinton, N.C. to B. N. Duke, March 1, 1899, B. N. Duke MSS.

8. J. T. Pinnix of Mullins, S.C., to B. N. Duke, March 17, 1900, B. N. Duke MSS.

9. F. L. Bailey to W. A. Erwin, January 28, 1914, B. N. Duke letterbook and MSS.

10. B. N. Duke to Brodie Duke, February 4, 1893, B.N. Duke letterbook.

11. B. N. Duke to W. G. McAdoo, July 6, 1918, B. N. Duke letterbook.

12. J. J. Spengler, "The New South: Exemplar of Hope Fulfilled," in A. R. Desai, ed., *Essays on Modernization of Undeveloped Societies* (Bombay, India, 1971), II, p. 385.

13. There are two valuable histories of Trinity College: Nora C. Chaffin, *Trinity College, 1839–1892: The Beginnings of Duke University* (Durham, 1950) and

Earl W. Porter, *Trinity and Duke, 1892–1924: Foundations of Duke University* (Durham, 1964).

14. Edwin Mims, "Trinity College: A General Sketch," *The Trinity Archive*, XV (November, 1901), p. 105.

15. J. C. Rowe to J. C. Kilgo, March 10, 1898, Kilgo MSS. Perkins Library, Duke University.

16. B N. Duke to S. Pool, October 10, 1894, and to Professor A. H. Meritt, May 2, 1895, B. N. Duke MSS.

17. W. Duke to J. C. Kilgo, December 5, 1896, B. N. Duke letterbook.

18. W. Duke to Kilgo, June 6, 1898, B. N. Duke letterbook.

19. Louis R. Wilson, *The University of North Carolina, 1900–1930: The Making of a Modern University* (Chapel Hill, 1957), pp. 31, 36.

20. Original manuscript of Page's address, Kilgo MSS.

21. J. E. Stagg to B. N. Duke, September 15, 1904, B. N. Duke letterbook.

22. *New York Times*, November 30, 1904.

23. Kilgo's memorial address, June 4, 1905, as quoted in Mason Crum, "The Life and Times of Washington Duke," unpublished manuscript in the Mason Crum Papers, Duke University Archives.

24. *New York Times*, September 1905–May, 1906; New York *American*, December 19, 22, 1905; April 24, 27, May 4, 1906. The quotation is from Winkler, *Tobacco Tycoon*, p. 177.

25. Jenkins, *Master Builder*, p. 199.

26. Tennant, *American Cigarette Industry*, p. 59.

27. Circuit Court MSS, vol. V, p. 3296.

28. Ibid., p. 3357.

29. Ibid., pp. 3392–3393.

30. Ibid., pp. 3397–3399, 3410.

31. A more detailed breakdown may be found in Bureau of Corporations, *Report on the Tobacco Industry*, pt. I, p. 28.

32. *United States v. American Tobacco Co.*, 164 F. 700, 704 (1908), as quoted in Tennant, *American Cigarette Industry*, p. 59.

33. *United States v. American Tobacco Co.*, 221 U. S. 186 (1911), as quoted in ibid.

34. Tennant, *American Cigarette Industry*, pp. 60–61.

35. Winkler, *Tobacco Tycoon*, pp. 208–209.

36. As quoted in Dixon Wecter, *The Saga of American Society* (New York, 1937), p. 375.

37. Allen Churchill, *The Upper Crust: An Informal History of New York's Highest Society* (Englewood Cliffs, N. J., 1970), pp. 141–143.

38. Soon after Duke's death in 1925, the house was assessed at $1,600,000 and the furnishings at $600,000. In 1957 Mrs. Duke and Miss Doris Duke gave the house to the Institute of Fine Arts of New York University. *New York Times*, April 4, 1962.

39. R. B. Arrington, executive secretary, to F. V. Dodd, October 28, 1909, J. B. Duke letterbook.

40. J. B. Duke to J. P. Morgan, June 22, 1908; J. B. Duke to J. D. Rockefeller, Jr., May l4, 1909, J. B. Duke letterbook.

41. R. B. Arrington to J. E. Stagg, May 18, 1909, J. B. Duke letterbook; B. N. Duke to J. A. Hogan, March 4, 1913, B. N. Duke letterbook.

42. R. B. Arrington to W. A. Taylor, March 28, 1908, B. N. Duke letterbook.

43. R. B. Arrington to J. C. Yager, September 26, 29, 1906, B. N. Duke letterbook.

44. Undated clipping in the "J. B. Duke" scrapbook, Southgate Jones MSS, Perkins Library, Duke University, for Mrs. Duke's dress; Rounds interview with Norman Cocke, p. 84, for the "brownie" story.

45. J. B. Duke, "Politics and Prosperity," *North American Review*, CCI (April 9, 1915), pp. 521–529.

46. Jenkins, *J. B. Duke*, pp. 220–230.

Notes for Chapter 7
ELECTRIFYING THE
PIEDMONT CAROLINAS
Part I

1. Richard B. DuBoff, "The Introduction of Electric Power in American Manufacturing," *Economic History Review*, 20 (December, 1967), p. 512.

2. W. A. Erwin to B. N. Duke, November 13, 1899, and W. A. Erwin to J. E. Stagg, August 1, 1901, B. N. Duke Papers.

3. W. A. Erwin to B. N. Duke, April 1, 1905, B. N. Duke Papers.

4. For more details about these matters, see Robert F. Durden, *Electrifying the Piedmont Carolinas: The Duke Power Company, 1904–1997* (Durham: Carolina Academic Press, 2001), Ch. I.

5. Photocopy of article containing text of a speech by W. Gill Wylie, [December 28], 1912, RG 34-01-01. 1123, Duke Energy Archives. This speech is also reprinted in Joe Maynor, *Duke Power: The First Seventy-five Years* (Albany, N.Y.: Delmar, 1980), pp. 11–13.

6. Photocopy of article on W. S. Lee by W. O. Sanders in *American Magazine* [early 1920s?] RG 34-01-01. 3298, Duke Energy Archives.

7. Jenkins, *J. B. Duke*, pp. 173–174. Jenkins obviously interviewed Lee to get this report.

8. Ibid., pp. 176–177.

9. R. B. Arrington to B. N. Duke, March 7, 1906, B. N. Duke Papers. The Duke brothers each loaned Dr. Gill Wylie a bit more than $118,000 so that he might purchase additional stock, and in October 1906 the capital stock was increased to $10,000,000.

10. Frank Rounds' interview with John Fox, June 1963, transcript, Oral History Project series, Duke Endowment Archives.

11. R. B. Arrington to J. W. Cannon, November 5, 10, 1908, J. B. Duke Letter Book.

12. Frank Rounds' interview with C. A. Cannon, transcript, Oral History Project series, Duke Endowment Archives.

13. DuBuff, "Electric Power in Manufacturing," pp. 510–518.

14. Quoted in James E. Brittain, ed., *Turning Points in American Electric History* (New York: Institute for Electrical and Electronic Engineers, 1977), p. 162.

15. "The Great Southern Transmission Network," *Electrical World*, May 30, 1914, reprinted in Brittain, *American Electric History*, p. 163.

16. Wade H. Wright, *History of the Georgia Power Company, 1855–1956* (Atlanta: Georgia Power Company, 1957), pp. 135–137.

17. Frank Rounds' interview with N. Cocke, 1963, transcript, Oral History Project series, Duke Endowment Archives.

18. B. N. Duke to J. B. Duke, July 2, 1913, B. N. Duke Letter Book, B. N. Duke papers.

19. Leonard S. Hyman, *American's Electric Utilities: Past, Present and Future*, 5th edition (Arlington, Va.: Public Utilities Reports, 1994), pp. 100–102.

20. Forrest McDonald, as quoted in James F. Crist, *They Electrified the South: The Story of the Southern Electric System* (n.p.: J. F. Crist, 1981), p. 68.

21. Jno. A. Law to J. B. Duke, October 21, 1912, and J. B. Duke to Jno. A. Law, October 23, 1912, RG 34-01-01. 2090, Duke Energy Archives.

Notes for Chapter 8
ELECTRIFYING THE
PIEDMONT CAROLINAS
Part II

1. Key 2767, Duke Energy Archives Chronology, Duke Energy Archives.

2. Frank Rounds' interview with C. E. Buchanan, August 1963, transcript, Oral History Project series, Duke Endowment Archives.

3. Quotation from Joe Maynor, *Duke Power: The First Seventy-five Years*, p. 41.

4. John Fox, outline history of Duke Power Company, p. 9, Duke Endowment Archives; Keys, 2774, 2767, Duke Energy Archives Chronology.

5. Ibid.

6. Frank Rounds' interview with Bertha (Mrs. E. C.) Marshall, October 1963, transcript, Oral History Project series, Duke Endowment Archives.

7. W. S. Lee and R. Pfaehler, "Reservoir and Plant for New Southern Water Power," *Engineering News-Record*, June 6, 1920, pp. 1088–1089; RG 34-01-01. 5470, Duke Energy Archives; Key, 391. Duke Energy Archives Chronology.

8. "Duke Power Electric Service in Piedmont North Carolina," memorandum of Norman Cocke, November 27, 1956, RG 34-01-01. 0490, Duke Energy Archives.

9. Key 2812 and 5329, Duke Energy Archives Chronology.

10. Frank Rounds' interview with Edward Williams, April 1963, transcript, Oral History Project series, Duke Endowment Archives.

11. Frank Rounds interview with A. C. Lee, April, July 1963, transcript, Oral History Project series, Duke Endowment Archives.

12. Frank Rounds interview with Norman Cocke, April 1963, transcript, Oral History Project series, Duke Endowment Archives.

13. Frank Rounds interview with Mrs. E. C. Marshall, October 1963, transcript, Oral History Project series, Duke Endowment Archives.

14. Ibid.

15. The Charlotte *News*, October 24, 1963, carried a story about the man who ran the store and remembered the Dukes coming there.

16. Frank Rounds interview with Norman Cocke, transcript, Oral History Project series, Duke Endowment Archives.

17. Frank Rounds interview with Mrs. Marshall, ibid.

18. Ibid.

19. Ibid.

20. W. R. Perkins, "An Address on the Duke Endowment: Its Origins, Nature, and Purposes," delivered to the Sphex Club at Lynchburg, Virginia, October 11, 1929. Printed pamphlet in Duke University Library.

21. Kilgo to Few, July 13, 1915, Few MSS.

22. J. B. Duke to Board of Church Extension and to Board of Trustees, Trinity College, April 22, 1920, J. B. Duke letterbook.

23. R. B. Arrington to B. N. Duke, March 25, 1911, B. N. Duke letterbook.

24. Alex Sands to B. N. Duke, April 2, 1917, and to Mrs. B. N. Duke, August 31, 1917, ibid.

25. David P. Massell, *Amassing Power: J. B. Duke and the Saguenay River, 1897–1927* (Montreat & Kingston: McGill-Queens University Press, 2000) is the most recent and comprehensive study of the subject. He explains (pp. 63–64) that from about 1899 forward, electrochemists on both sides of the Atlantic competed to develop the most effective process to fix nitrogen from the air by using electricity. As a chemical engineer of the era explained, when air was heated to

very high temperatures, it oxidized to form nitric acid and, on rapid cooling, remained in that form.

26. Ibid., p. 144.

Notes for Chapter 9
A MASSIVE ENTREPRENEURIAL GAMBLE IN CANADA

1. Massell, *Amassing Power*, pp. 66–67.
2. Jenkins, *J. B. Duke*, p. 188; Massell, *Amassing Power*, pp. 68–69.
3. Massell, *Amassing Power*, p. 44.
4. Ibid., p. 73.
5. Ibid., p. 84.
6. Ibid., p. 93.
7. Ibid., pp. 108–109.
8. Ibid., p. 162.
9. Ibid., p. 160.
10. Ibid., p, 161.
11. Ibid., pp. 384–385. After J. B. Duke's death, the aluminum company in 1926 acquired a controlling interest in the Duke-Price Power Company and its Isle Maligne plant.
12. Ibid., p. 197.

Notes for Chapter 10
CREATING CAROLINA PHILANTHROPY IN PERPETUITY
Part I

1. W. P. Few to J. B. Duke, February 1, 1919, Few Papers.
2. W. P. Few to J. B. Duke, February 27, 1919, Few Papers.
3. For a fuller discussion of "The Origins of the University Idea at Trinity" see chapter 1 of Robert F. Durden, *The Launching of Duke University, 1924–1929* (Durham: Duke University Press, 1993).
4. In Few's unpublished and unfinished history, "The Beginnings of an American University," Few Papers.

5. W. P. Few to J. H. Separk, May 28, 1921, and W. P. Few to C. W. Toms, July 23, 1921, Few Papers.

6. James F. Gifford Jr., *The Evolution of a Medical Center: A History of Medicine at Duke University* (Durham, N. C.: Duke University Press, 1972) pp. 11–34, has the most detailed study of this episode.

7. Raleigh *News and Observer*, December 28, 1922.

8. This suggestion of J. B. Duke's personal responsibility for the health-care area of the Endowment represents a modification of the thesis presented in the author's *The Dukes of Durham*, where only the family's long-standing pattern of giving is emphasized.

9. Raleigh *News and Observer*, November 23, 1920.

10. Raleigh *News and Observer*, February 25, 1921.

11. Raleigh *News and Observer*, February 25, 1921.

12. *Charlotte Observer*, February 26, 1921.

13. *Charlotte Observer*, March 9, 1921.

14. Raleigh *News and Observer*, April 14, 1921.

15. *Charlotte Observer*, October 12, 1923; Raleigh *News and Observer*, November 18, 1923.

16. Raleigh *News and Observer*, October 21, 23, November 11, 1923.

17. Raleigh *News and Observer*, October 25, 1923.

18. *Elizabeth City Independent* editorial, as reprinted in the Raleigh *News and Observer*, December 23, 1923.

19. *Charlotte Observer*, October 24, 1923.

20. *Natural Resources* editorial, reprinted in *Charlotte Observer*, November 5, 1923.

21. Raleigh *News and Observer*, November 23, 1923, January 13, 1924.

22. Raleigh *News and Observer*, January 13, 1924.

Notes for Chapter 11
CREATING CAROLINA PHILANTHROPY
IN PERPETUITY
Part II

1. Charles P. Roland in preface to James C. Cobb, *Industrialization and Southern Society, 1877–1984*(Lexington: University Press of Kentucky, 1984), p. ix.

2. Harold U. Faulkner, *The Decline of Laissez Faire, 1897–1917* (New York: Rinehart, 1951), p. 142.

3. Richard L. Wilson, "Cotton Spindles and Kilowatts: A Study of the Cotton Manufacturing Industry and the Southern Power Company" (master's thesis, University of North Carolina at Charlotte, 1980), p. 1.

4. Ibid.

5. George B. Tindall, *The Emergence of the New South, 1913–1945* (Baton Rouge: Louisiana State University Press, 1967), pp. 75–76.

6. C. Vann Woodward, *Origins of the New South, 1877–1913* (Baton Rouge: Louisiana State University Press, 1967), pp. 308–309.

7. Tindall, *The Emergence of the New South*, pp. 75–76.

8. There is more detail about these matters in both Durden, *The Dukes of Durham*, and Durden, *The Launching of Duke University*.

9. Allen to Few, September 18, 1924, Few Papers.

10. Flowers to Few, October 29 (two letters) and 30, 1924, Few Papers.

11. Flowers to Few, November 1, 1924, Few Papers.

12. A copy of the indenture is included as an appendix in both *The Dukes of Durham* and *Lasting Legacy to the Carolinas*.

13. Rounds's interview with Norman A. Cocke, Charlotte, N. C., 1963, pp. 106–107.

14. W. P. Few to J. H. Reynolds, December 29, 1924, Few Papers.

15. For more details about these matters, those interested are referred to the chapters on higher education in Durden, *Lasting Legacy to the Carolinas: The Duke Endowment, 1924–1994*.

16. The indenture establishing the Doris Duke Trust also stipulated that if Doris Duke should die without lineal descendants, the two-thirds share of the trust's holdings held for her benefit should go to The Duke Endowment. In 1988 when Doris Duke was seventy-five and had no living child, she adopted as her daughter an adult woman, Charlene Heffner (who was thirty-five). Following the death of Doris Duke in October 1993, Heffner, claiming to be a lineal descendant of Doris Duke, sought to obtain the two-thirds share (approximately $127 million) of the Doris Duke Trust. The trustees of The Duke Endowment, pointing out that the adoption of an adult was not legal in New Jersey when J. B. Duke established the Doris Duke Trust in 1924, argued, among other things, that Heffner could not be considered a lineal descendant. The New Jersey superior court agreed with the trustees in July 1995 and awarded the $127 million to the Endowment.

17. This matter is dealt with in Robert F. Durden, "Troubled Legacy: James B. Duke's Bequest to His Cousins," *North Carolina Historical Review* (October 1973), pp. 394–415.

Notes for Chapter 12
DEATH CATCHES J. B. DUKE BY SURPRISE

1. Alex Sands to Few, May 5, 1924, Few MSS.

2. Few's unfinished manuscript, "The Beginnings of an American University." pp. 6–7.

3. Rounds' interview with Rankin, pp. 57–58.

4. Brown to Trumbauer, March 20, 1925, F. C. Brown MSS, and Flowers to Allen, March 21, 1925, R. L. Flowers MSS.

5. Brown to B. M. Hall, April 18, 1925, F. C. Brown MSS.

6. J. B. Duke's involvement in the planning of what became the Woman's College buildings of Duke University may be traced in the Few, Flowers, and F. C. Brown MSS. Brown served as the liaison between Few and his associates in Durham, on the one hand, and Trumbauer and his staff in Philadelphia on the other. Relations were notably amicable, but various matters were referred to J. B. Duke for final decision.

7. Frank Rounds' interview with Roy A. Hunt in Pittsburgh, October and December, 1963. Duke Endowment Archives.

8. Jenkins, *J. B. Duke*, p. 259.

9. "Last Will and Testament of James B. Duke," J. B. Duke Papers; Jenkins, *J. B. Duke*, pp. 299–302.

10. Few to J. B. Duke, March 31, 1914, Few MSS.

Index

Abel, Julian: as pioneer African-American architect, 66, 98

African-Americans: are explicitly aided by The Duke Endowment, 176

Alamance County, 5

Allen, George G.: becomes close associate of J. B. Duke, 83–84; involved in planning for Duke University, 170–172; inherits much of J. B. Duke's power and influence, 191; mentioned, 94, 143, 175, 180, 187, 190

Allen, John F., 16

Allen and Ginter Company, 28, 36

Aluminum Company of America, 187

American Cigar Company, 52

American Cyanamid Company, 180

American Development Company, 120

American Home and Gardens, 65

American Mercury, 174

American Snuff Company, 51

American Tobacco Company: origins of its organization, 23–37; gains control of most of U. S. tobacco industry (except for cigars), 39–55; does not control price of leaf tobacco, 57–58; acquires overseas factories, invades Britain, and gains majority interest in new British-American Tobacco Company, 67–77; faces anti-trust action by the Federal government and is forced to dissolve, 94–97; continues in a much-shrunken form, 97; mentioned, 12, 162

Anglo-American tobacco war: is ended by establishment of British-American Tobacco Company, 73

Atlanta *Constitution*, 17

Atlantic Snuff Company, 51

Bank of Harnett (County), 88

"Battle Ax" chewing tobacco, 47

Bell, William B., 180

Biddle, Anthony, 171, 180

Biddle, Mary Duke, 172

Biltmore estate, 63, 66

Blackwell, William T., 15

Boer War, 67, 70

Parker, Walter C., 180
Parrish, E. J.: represents American Tobacco Company in Japan, 43; reports on tobacco war in Asia, 71–72; reports to J. B. Duke on the Japanese operation, 78–80
Payne, Oliver H.: allies with J. B. Duke, 48–50
Penobscot River, 121
People's (Populist) party, 57
Perkins, Thomas L.,175
Perkins, William R.: is involved in planning for Duke University and drafts indenture, 171–172; inherits some of J. B. Duke's power and influence, 191; mentioned, 94, 175, 180
Pfaehler, Richard, 135, 150
Piedmont and Northern electric railway, 127–128
Pierre Lorillard Company, 45
"Pin Head" cigarettes, 16
Pocantico Hills, 99
Price, Sir William, 149–151
Princeton University, 174
"Pro Bono Publico," 10
Progressive Era, 39, 101
Public Utility Holding Company law, 129
Pullman Company, 100

Queen Mary, 101
Queen Victoria, 69, 70

Raleigh *News and Observer*: leads Democratic attack on the "tobacco trust," 58; attacks J. B. Duke and opposes rate increase, 160–166
Rankin, Dr. Watson S.: proposes community hospitals and greatly influences J. B. Duke, 158–159; heads Hospital Section and is named Endowment trustee, 181; mentioned, 176
Recorder (Durham), 86
Reid, Whitelaw, 63
R. J. Reynolds Tobacco Company, 51
Republican party: appears in North Carolina, 3
The Robber Barons, 39–40
Robinson, W. S. O'B., 161
Rockefeller, John D., 36, 39, 40
Rockefeller, John D., Jr., 99
Rocky Creek hydrostation, 125
Roney, Ann, 5
Roney, Artelia: marries Washington Duke, 5
Roney, Elizabeth, 5
Roosevelt, Theodore, 54, 76, 102
"Rough Point" mansion in Newport, 140
Russell, Lillian, 58
Ryan, Thomas Fortune, 49, 50, 72–73

Saguenay River, 146 and *passim*